G000123255

An
ISLAMIC
RENASCENCE

A rational perspective for the 21st century

Sheikh Mohammed Jakir Ahmed Jabbar

Mereo Books

1A The Wool Market Dyer Street Cirencester Gloucestershire GL7 2PR
An imprint of Memoirs Publishing www.mereobooks.com

AN ISLAMIC RENASCENCE

First published in Great Britain in 2018
by Mereo Books, an imprint of Memoirs Publishing

The address for Memoirs Publishing Group Limited can be
found at www.memoirspublishing.com

The Memoirs Publishing Group Ltd Reg. No. 7834348

Typeset in 9/12pt Bembo

by Wiltshire Associates Publisher Services Ltd.
Printed and bound in Great Britain by Biddles Books

My Lord! Increase me in Knowledge

Chapter 20, Ta Ha, Verse 114, Holy Qur'an

This book is dedicated to the
dissemination of rational thought and
to the revolutionaries who have given
their lives in the struggle against oppression.

Not to forget my son and inspiration,
Sheikh Muhammad Jawad Alexander Jakir

'Let us give up the hate, let us begin to talk.
Let's give up our prejudices, let's begin to understand each other.'

The Author

CONTENTS

CHAPTER 3
Muhammad – 'the Seal of the Prophets'

CHAPTER 4
Succession and the Seeds of War and Division

CHAPTER 5
The End of Time – the Islamic Narrative

PART II

CHAPTER 6
Contemporary Islam and the Rise of Militancy

CHAPTER 7
The Muslim Ummah: Out of the Abyss

CHAPTER 8
One Ummah: Renewal of the Islamic Caliphate

CONCLUSION
Thoughts to Ponder Upon

APPENDICES

Appendix 1

Appendix 2

Appendix 3

Appendix 4

AUTHOR'S PREFACE

I firmly believe that an Islamic renascence should encompass two interrelated and overlapping themes. Firstly, as examined in Part 1 of this book, it involves a rational study and understanding of the Islamic Faith, challenging any extremist interpretation or irrational narrative (including a rational exposition of the life and deeds of the Prophet Muhammad and the schism that followed His death). Secondly, it comprises a rational defiance against authoritarian rule in the Muslim Ummah with emphasis on political pluralism based on a liberal political discourse, as explored in Part II of this work. While there is a substantial amount of published material out there on Islam, perhaps too much, there are relatively few publications providing a critical analysis that challenges the radical interpretation of Islam within the context of an Islamic renascence, as this study has endeavoured to do. To put it another way, an Islamic renascence should be about

1

a renewal based on a rational debate and not a revival based on rigid orthodoxy underpinned by a narrow/extremist narrative.

It is worth noting that in the contemporary world Islam is taking centre stage, not least in its appeal as a global religion with followers throughout Europe and the United States, as well as in its traditional heartlands, but also in the backdrop of the tragedy of 9/11, the United States led 'War on Terror' and the continued detention in Guantanamo Bay of suspected Al-Qaeda operatives in conditions defying the Geneva Convention. Furthermore, the continued threat of so-called Islamic Terrorists/Jihadists, more recently in the form of ISIL/Da'esh with its rampageous legacy across Iraq and Syria and terrorist attacks in Europe, not to forget the contentious 'Peace Process' between Israel and the Palestinians, are just some of the reasons that have brought about a renewed focus on Islam, both by the younger generation of Muslims and non-Muslims alike.

The failed Arab Spring, the rise of ISIL and the increasing tensions in the Middle East along sectarian lines resulting in proxy wars being played out in that region are giving rise to a seismic shift in the geopolitics of the Arab World. We must not underestimate the inspiration and rationale behind the Arab Revolt of 2011 and its potential revival that could change the political landscape in the Middle East, as well as having profound implications for international politics, regional security and global economic infrastructure.

I have seriously endeavoured through this book to bring to the reader a rational approach to the study of Islam, presenting the fundamental features of Islam into focus, stressing factual analysis and rational deduction. Numerous materials have been extensively sourced, meticulously studied and critically evaluated. I take this opportunity to apologize for any errors. I sincerely desire that this work will provide a platform that will inspire readers, especially, young Muslims and non-Muslims alike, to engage in further faith-based research of their own and hopefully find answers to questions that trouble those young inquisitive minds.

This book should also be useful to anyone who wishes to gain a first-hand, lucid and brief introduction to a Faith of otherwise vast magnitude at different academic levels. Knowledge of Islam is not and should not be the exclusive domain of so-called 'Islamic scholars'. Rather every Muslim must make a conscientious effort to understand the core message of Islam so that they may not be led astray. The quotations from the Holy Qur'an and numerous Ahadith collections are not always exhaustive in relation to the subject matter being dealt with. Here I have exercised discretion in the selection of relevant verses. I strongly believe that this treatise on Islam will challenge many misconceptions of the Islamic Faith often drummed up by vested interests in achieving their political agenda.

This discourse seeks to address the contentious issue of whether Islam or its so-called radical interpretation presents the most significant challenge to the worldwide predominance of Western Democracy and Capitalism since the end of the Cold War. The ISIL phenomenon is examined in particular detail, along with the geopolitics that surround it.

The relentless pace with which events are unfolding both in the Middle East and on the global political scene, makes it difficult to draw any definitive conclusions. Nevertheless, I have tried to shed a new perspective on current and future global political strategies.

The views expressed in this study are solely my own and no adverse inference should be made about either my family, my employer or my voluntary roles in the community.

This book, which is the second of five anticipated publications in the same genre, is an attempt to provide a counter-narrative to so-called 'radical Islam' that has manifested itself into unprecedented acts of violence against innocent civilians, both Muslims and non-Muslims alike. Building on this, the third book will seek to provide a counter-narrative to the extremist interpretation of the Holy Qur'an and is expected to be completed sometime in the near future.

I would like to strongly reiterate that in the course of this work no deliberate attempt has been made to overtly criticise any individual dead or alive, nor to belittle, discredit or bring into disrepute any religion, belief or practice. Neither is this work intended to prejudice the reputation, interests or security of any country or nationality but rather to promote intellectual dialogue and a healthy exchange of ideas. This book is not intended to be a platform for inciting or condoning violence and should not be treated as such.

Sheikh Mohammed Jakir Ahmed Jabbar

Cert.HE (Cardiff); LL.B (Hons) (Wolverhampton); LL.M (Northumbria); ACILEx
September 2018/Muharram 1440 (Al-Hijrah)

INTRODUCTION

CHALLENGING MISCONCEPTIONS

From the appearance of *Homo sapiens* to the present day and beyond, the miracle of birth, the life we live and the certainty of death and their place in the cosmos, have been, and will continue to be, the driving force behind faith. Faith in a supreme Deity above and beyond material comprehension provides order amid chaos. Man takes back a modicum of control through surrender to God via prayers, sacrifices, piety and charity – core characteristics emphasized by all major religions. Faith has played a pivotal role in sustaining humanity. All the major religions began their journey as rebellions against oppression, ignorance and indulgence. Essentially, faith has been Man's redemption from himself. Religion has only provided shape and form to his faith.

Islam is one of the success stories of the world religions. From the deserts of an inconspicuous corner of Arabia a mere fourteen centuries ago re-emerged a monotheistic faith that now professes more than one and a half billion followers (one-fourth of mankind) spread across several continents. Islam, which means acceptance and surrender, commitment and submission to the one true God, is the dominant faith in the countries of the Middle East, North Africa, much of East Africa down to Kenya, Soviet Central Asia, Iran, Afghanistan eastwards to include the South Asian countries of Pakistan, Bangladesh and Maldives to Malaysia and Indonesia. Even though they are a minority in India, Muslims there number more than 177 million. And while the official Chinese figure puts the number of Muslims at 17 million, around 23 million plus is closer to the truth. Of the three major monotheistic religions, Islam embraces and embodies the fastest growing body of religious believers in the contemporary world and after Christianity is the world's second largest religion.

Unlike Christianity, which is divided between Eastern Orthodoxy, Catholicism and Protestantism, Islam is far from being a private religion of personal conscience and ethics. Rather it is a complete way of life governing every aspect of human interaction laid down by ALLAH through his Messenger, Muhammad.

Islam belongs to the same family of religions as Judaism and Christianity. The Patriarch of the three is the Prophet Ibrahim (Abraham), a descendant of Nuh's (Noah's) son Shem as illustrated in **Chapter 57, Al–Hadid, Verse 26** of the Holy Qur'an: '*And we sent Noah And Abraham, and established In their line Prophethood And Revelation.*' The three monotheistic religions are rays from the same lamp and, barring some (albeit fundamental) differences (discussed later), they have strikingly common grounds. All emphasize the unseen, eternal, omnipotent Creator, the most compassionate and merciful imposing his structured will on earth. Yet the seeds of enmity and distrust between Islam and Christianity planted many centuries ago between 1095, marking the seeds of the first Christian Crusade at the behest of the Papacy;

'Dues vult' (God wills it), and the penultimate medieval Crusade of 1248, the tolerance preached by the Prophets, Isa (Jesus) and Muhammad has been manipulated for vested political interests.

The medieval Christian Crusades achieved nothing substantial in terms of real power and influence; in fact the second Crusade ended in defeat, while the third Crusade was inconclusive. What the Crusades did achieve was the savage deaths of tens of thousands, violation of married women and widows and the sacking of wealth. The battle cry was more driven or inspired by an irrational craving for land and power dictated by the political realities of the day rather than for spiritual advancement or the appeasement of God. The so-called 'Holy War' was sustained by barbarism and aggression in the name of glorifying God in the perceived defence of Christendom against the expanding and encroaching Islamic Empire. In fact, on 15 July 1099, following a siege of Jerusalem, the first crusading army stormed into the Holy City, slaughtering the Muslim and Jewish inhabitants there without mercy. So bloody was the massacre that women and children were savagely raped and murdered, with some chroniclers describing it as a 'mad frenzy' of mayhem, while others have described it as 'targeted ethnic cleansing'. In fact, one may argue that ISIL (Islamic State of Iraq and the Levant, also referred to as Da'esh) is the 21st century Islamic version of the Medieval Christian Crusades. ISIL too orchestrated mayhem across the Middle East but in what they perceived to be in the defence of (Sunni) Islam against Western imperial influence and Shi'ite dominance in the region. Their tactics, like the Crusades, were marked by brutal savagery and the annexation of vast expanses of land. Indeed, history teaches us that the greatest atrocities committed by man have been for the love of God. (Today, with thousands of civilians dead and billions of dollars spent, ISIL has been routed out of much of Syria and Iraq only three and half years after it declared its so-called Caliphate with Abu Bakr al-Baghdadi as its leader).

It must be emphasized, however, like different strands of thread interwoven to make a fine tapestry the affinity and heritage of the monotheistic religions is clearly narrated in **Chapter 2, Al Baqarah, Verse 136** of the Holy Qur'an' where it states: ' *Say (O Muslims): We believe in Allah and that which has been sent down* *to us and that which has been sent down to Ibrahim (Abraham), Isma'il (Ishmael), Ishaq (Isaac), Ya'qub (Jacob), and to Al-Asbat [the offspring of the twelve sons of Ya'qub (Jacob)], and that which has been given to Musa (Moses) and Isa (Jesus), and that which has been given to the Prophets from their Lord. We make no distinction between any of them, and to Him we have submitted (in Islam).'*

With a common monotheistic lineage, Islam requires Muslims to believe in all the revealed books mentioned in the Holy Qur'an. They are the Tawrat (Torah) revealed to Prophet Musa (Moses); the Zabur (Psalms) revealed to Prophet Dawud (David); the Injil (the original Gospel) revealed to Prophet Isa (Jesus) and the Qur'an, revealed to the final Prophet and Messenger Muhammad. The Qur'an also mentions the Suhuf–i-Ibrahim (Scrolls of Abraham). By no measure or form therefore is Islam an advancement or continuation of Arab paganism. In fact, the theme underlying the core message of Islam is its unrestrained rebellion against paganism, idolatry and religious bigotry repeatedly expressed in verses of the Holy Qur'an.

It was only when preceding revelation(s) became corrupted following distortions in the Divine texts as mentioned in **Chapter 3, Al-Imran, Verse 78** of the Holy Qur'an, where it states: *'And Lo! there is a party of them who distort the Scripture with their tongues, that ye may think that what they say is from the Scripture, when it is not from the Scripture. And they say: it is from ALLAH, when it is not from ALLAH; and they speak a lie concerning ALLAH knowingly,'* that a subsequent revelation followed with Islam being the last religion/revelation as illustrated in **Chapter 5, Al-Ma'idah, Verse 3** of the Holy Qur'an where ALLAH proclaims: *'This day I have perfected your religion for you, completed my favour upon you, and have chosen for you Islam as your religion.'*

Nothing comes between man and ALLAH in Islam. There is no requirement for so-called spiritual intermediaries. The concept of priesthood is alien to classical Islamic tradition but is now prevalent in many Muslim countries inspired by Christian missionaries of the last few centuries. The influence exercised by some so-called 'pirs' (spiritual preachers), who are prevalent in poorer Muslim countries and have amassed considerable wealth and power exploiting ignorant and naive Muslims, is contrary to the spirit of true Islam. Too often does one notice the influence these so-called 'spiritual intermediaries' exercise over large swathes of people purporting to be divested with Divine Authority. With many Muslim countries making a rapid transition from an agrarian economy to fast urbanisation, compounded with competing interests and ambitions, devotees flock towards these pirs in the misplaced belief that they will provide them with answers and solutions to their frustrations, hopes and aspirations. Many also look to these pirs for miracle cures for even severe illnesses, putting their trust in so-called 'faith healing'. While some successful and well-established pirs involve themselves in 'corporate social responsibility', investing in community projects, nevertheless, many of these pirs and their families also happen to be successful entrepreneurs running business empires and amassing considerable personal wealth.

These pirs will continue to exercise power and influence over vast swathes of the population so long as the general Muslim population in those countries fails to exercise a rational understanding of the religion of Islam themselves and rather relies on spiritual preachers to fulfil their spiritual void. In Islam the path to attaining salvation in this life and in the hereafter is attainable through observance of the 'Five Pillars of Islam' and firm belief in the 'Seven Articles of Faith' (discussed in Chapter Two). Observance of the Five Pillars by devout Muslims does not require the intercession of so-called spiritual intermediaries. In fact, intervention by these so-called pirs is unnecessary and undesirable, especially when these numerous pirs have their own different interpretations of the religion of Islam. In fact, during the rule of the 'Khulafa Ur Rashidin' (the rightly-guided Caliphs), pirs did not exist.

Every human being will be made to account for his/her own deeds on earth. This is clearly narrated in **Chapter 35, Al-Fatir, Verse 18** of the Holy Qur'an, which states, *'No bearer of burdens shall bear another's burden. And if a heavy laden soul calls another to carry some of its load, nothing of it will be carried, even if he should be near of kin. You (O Muhammad) can only warn those who fear their*

Lord unseen and have established prayer. And whoever purifies himself (of sin) only purifies himself (for the benefit) of his own soul. And to ALLAH is the (final) return.'

Indeed, ALLAH has a close bond with humanity, for the first human, Adam, was fashioned by ALLAH, who gave Adam life. Humanity is Adam's progeny. Between ALLAH and man's soul there is a covenant which has been re-affirmed throughout human history in the form of successive prophets and the four true Divine Books. There is no hierarchy of authority to clutter the Islamic Faith. There is nothing comparable to an organised church. Any personal financial contribution in the way of Islam, though encouraged, is nevertheless entirely voluntary and free from any kind of undue influence. Though there are scholars on Islamic law (Ulama) there is nothing equivalent to the bishops, archbishops or popes that can be found in the Christian Church. Surely, there is nothing further from the truth than to compare the institution of the Vatican to the true status of the holy sites of Mecca or for that matter, Medina. When leading prayers in the mosque, the Imam is only the first among equals. Religious authority in Islam resides in the Holy Qur'an and according to Sunni Islam the Hadith as well, to which every Muslim has ready access. The Holy Qur'an is available in its unaltered Arabic version (the standardized text commencing from the reign of Caliph Uthman [644-656]), though it has been subsequently translated into numerous languages. Of the six authoritative collections of Hadith, the most authentic Ahadith (plural for Hadith) are widely received as the Sahih Al-Bukhari and Sahih Muslim.

While reverence towards the departed is expected, the excesses that often surround the 'Mazaars' (burial places of Prophets, saints and so-called pirs) are not in conformity with Islamic Shari'ah. These Mazaars that are found in plenty in the Indian sub-continent are often a magnet for song, dance and addiction, not least profiteering by some of the committees which manage these sites. All such actions are frowned upon by authentic Islamic texts. Too often do we find so-called 'devotees' prostrating themselves before such burial sites. Such fanatical worship is contrary to core Islamic tenets. All worship is for the unseen one true God. The

Prophet Muhammad is recorded as saying, *'Beware of those who preceded you and used to take the graves of their prophets and righteous men as places of worship, but you must not take graves as mosques: I forbid you to do that'* **(Sahih Al-Bukhari)**. At the same time, however, it must also be emphasised that the sanctity of burial sites must be preserved and not subject to desecration in the name of 'puritanical Islam'. The Islamic Faith does not cater for extremism in any manner, shape or form.

In September 2014, it was reported by some Western media outlets that following a consultation exercise by a leading Saudi cleric, controversial 'proposals' were being circulated among the supervisors of the al-Masjid an-Nabawi in Medina to remove the Prophet Muhammad's body to the nearby Al-Baqi Cemetery to be anonymously interned, out of concern that the current burial site was leading to veneration by pilgrims amounting to shirk or idolatry. Whichever way you look at this contentious issue though, to physically remove the Prophet Muhammad's body from its current burial site would amount to nothing less than sacrilege. No rational discourse can provide justification for such a callous and reckless move. If the Saudi political and religious elite do go ahead with such a violation of the Prophet's burial site it will almost certainly cause outrage and consternation across the Muslim Ummah, including Muslims of the Middle East. So much so, that Wahabi Islam will find itself on a serious back footer, setting in motion a trajectory that will mark the collapse of the Saudi Monarchy.

Subsequent to the publication of the story in the Western media, however, the General Presidency of the Two Holy Mosques denied any reports of plans to remove the Prophet Muhammad's body. It would be pertinent to point out here that the greatest threat to the survival of the Saudi Monarchy is its close association with the ideology of militant Wahabi Islam.

Islam does not cater for tribes or races between Muslims. Unfortunately, however, today's global Muslims are divided not only on geopolitical lines but also on their interpretation of the Faith, as well as on their standing in society. Prior to the discovery of oil in 1938, Arabs living in the Hijaz (western side of the Arab Peninsula) who were largely nomads, lived mainly off revenue generated from pilgrims making the Holy Pilgrimage to Mecca from across the Muslim Ummah. It was discovery of oil in Dhahran that subsequently changed the political geography of Saudi Arabia enabling it to export its brand of Wahabi Islam while increasingly finding itself at odds in embracing modernity.

Followers of the Islamic Faith possess a collective morality. Though the nation-states comprising the 'Muslim Ummah' (world-wide community of Islam) may at times be immersed in bitter geopolitical rivalry amongst themselves, in faith, nevertheless, the vast majority of Muslims across the globe (irrespective of national identity) are passionately united in their observance of the Five Pillars of Islam, if not in anything else, particularly in their declaration of the Shahadah (Oneness of God and the Prophethood of Muhammad), as well as in their vehement acceptance of the Divine truth of the Holy Qur'an. It is this passionate affirmation that underlines the strength and mysticism that characterizes the rationale behind the resurgence of Islam as a global phenomenon, especially in the face of perceived persecution of Muslims, particularly in Palestine, Iraq, Afghanistan and not too long ago in Chechnya, Bosnia, and Lebanon but more recently in Myanmar.

Western societies and governments fail to understand this and therefore fail to comprehend the 'Muslim psyche'. Capitalising on this, radical groups manifest themselves into expressions of extremism. This only underlines the importance of understanding and advocating the correct interpretation of the Holy Qur'an and not its dissection to single verses or even phrases from verses that serve extremist agenda deliberately contorting the true meaning of the Holy Qur'an. While some will argue that the majority of Qur'anic verses are stand-alone verses imparting a separate call to the Divine, the caveat is that such verses must not be read out of context. But instead the Qur'anic verses be read and understood within the Spirit of the Divine Call and Guidance.

From an inconspicuous corner of the Arabian Peninsula, within two centuries of the Prophet Muhammad's death, the Islamic Empire, under its successive Caliphs, spanned three continents from Spain to the gates of China, absorbing the then formidable Sassanid Empire and two-thirds of the Byzantine Empire, ranking the emerging Islamic Empire larger than the self-destroying Roman Empire. This is not to say that Islam advocates aggression or war for the sole purpose of sacking lands, power or wealth, or to forcibly convert unbelievers. In fact this is flatly prohibited in **Chapter 2, Al-Baqarah, Verse 256**, of the Holy Qur'an, where Allah says: *'Let there be no compulsion in religion: Truth stands out Clear from Error: whosoever Rejects Tagut (anything worshipped other than Allah) and believes in Allah hath grasped the most trustworthy Handhold that never breaks. And Allah heareth and knoweth all.'*

There is however, a clear obligation of self-defence upon Muslims. This is expressed in **Chapter 2, Al-Baqarah, Verses 190–193** of the Holy Qur'an: *'Fight in the cause of Allah Those who fight you But do not transgress limits; For Allah loveth not transgressors. And slay them Wherever ye catch them, And turn them out From where they have Turned you out; For persecution Is worse than slaughter; But fight them not At the Sacred Mosque, unless they (first) Fight you there; But if they fight you, Slay them. Such is the reward Of those who reject faith. But if they cease, Allah is Oft-Forgiving, Most Merciful. And fight them on Until there is no more persecution And the religion becomes Allah's. But if they cease, Let there be no hostility Except to those Who practice oppression.'*

Unfortunately, in reality the distinction between aggression and self-defence has often been blurred, giving rise to misconceptions about the Islamic duty of Jihad. While this will be analysed in some detail later, simply put, acts of 'terror' resulting in the death of innocent civilians clearly transgresses limits. Muslims are required to provide a measured but effective response to persecution, and it must be appropriately directed. Consequently, innocent civilians can never be legitimate targets of war or jihad. In fact, such a course of conduct is prohibited in Islam.

Regrettably, however, in recent military campaigns where Muslims have been on the receiving end, Muslim civilians and non-combatants have been legitimate game, often dismissed in military terminology as 'collateral damage'. Here are some contemporary examples. The Soviet invasion and occupation of

Afghanistan between December 1979 and February 1989 resulted in more than 1 million fatalities, with more than five million Afghans fleeing to Pakistan and Iran. It is reported that in the 1980s half of the world's refugees were Afghan nationals. It is also estimated that another two million Afghans were displaced within the country, while three million Afghans, mostly non-combatants, were maimed or wounded. In July 2006, Israeli military incursions into Lebanon, in what is referred to as the second Lebanon War, resulted in 1200 people being killed, mostly Lebanese citizens, with UNICEF estimating 30% of them to be children. The Israeli authorities have persistently denied such claims, while the Israeli Government-appointed Winograd Commission found that Israeli Defence Forces did not target civilians and that evidence of war crimes was biased and without basis. On the contrary, Human Rights Watch and Amnesty International alleged the use of 'indiscriminate air strikes' by Israel that resulted in civilian deaths.

The Bosnian War between April 1992 and December 1995 bears testimony to targeted ethnic cleansing of the civilian Muslim population of Bosnia and Herzegovina. With UN Security Council Resolution 713 (1991) enforcing an arms embargo in the former Yugoslavia, the Bosnian Muslim civilian population (Muslim Bosniaks) were effectively denied their inalienable right to defend themselves against the subsequent Bosnian Serb onslaught that was supported by the Serbian government of Slobodan Milošević and the Yugoslav People's Army (JNA). The 'genocide' of Muslim Bosniaks will forever be remembered by the Srebrenica Massacre and the systematic and targeted rape of Muslim women and girls, particularly in Eastern Bosnia during the Foća massacres. Many Bosniak women and girls were gang-raped repeatedly by Bosnian Serb forces and sold as sex slaves. Estimates of the numbers raped are above 20,000. (How many children were born as a result of sexual violence is unknown, but many of them were abandoned.) This was the most potent way Serbs could assert superiority and victory over the Muslim Bosniaks. The Srebrenica Massacre is Europe's worst massacre since the holocaust directed against Jews during World War II, and it witnessed the execution of 8,000 unarmed men and boys, with the United Nations proving impotent to stop the massacre. The hurt and anguish is still very much imbedded in the psyche of the Bosnian people, as was evidenced by the reaction of the crowd who threw bottles and stones at the Serbian Prime Minister, Aleksandar Vucic, chasing him and forcing him to flee a ceremony to commemorate the 20th anniversary of the Srebrenica Massacre. The continued stubborn refusal of the Government in Belgrade to accept the Srebrenica Massacre as genocide stokes anger and serves as a potent stumbling block in the way of reconciliation.

As a consequence of the Second Gulf War of 2003 and its aftermath, Iraqi civilians have also suffered enormously, not only in terms of fatalities but also in terms of the millions of Iraqi civilians who have lost their homes, rendering many of them refugees. The United States-led invasion of March 2003, ironically termed Operation Iraqi Freedom, resulted in the occupation of Iraq. More than 500,000 Iraqis died (Lancet Survey), 150,000 according to the Chilcot Report and not less than 100,000 according to the Iraqi Body Count (IBC). The invasion was perpetrated on the pretext of preventing Saddam Hussein's regime from deploying weapons of mass destruction (WMD) against the West and its allies within the Middle East, when in fact what actually transpired was regime change.

As to Iraq's 2003 potential to deploy WMDs against the Western coalition and their Middle Eastern regional allies, some within 45 minutes, this assertion subsequently transpired to be a myth. In fact, following the invasion, the US-led Iraq Survey Group (ISG) Report authored by Charles Duelfer concluded in 2004 that Iraq had neither stockpiles nor an active nuclear, chemical or biological weapons programme at the time of the war. As to the financial cost in waging this conflict it has reportedly been in the region of 1 trillion dollars.

As to the Western leaders who advocated the case in favour of invasion, they have always insisted that they acted on the intelligence advice that was available to them at the time, believing what they did was right. Little solace is that to the tens of thousands of innocent civilian families who have lost loved ones due to violent deaths.

The findings of the much-anticipated Chilcot Inquiry make interesting reading in the context of the United Kingdom's involvement in the Iraq war. If one recalls, the United Kingdom was the United States key ally during the Second Gulf War. Let us examine some of the Inquiry's key findings. The Iraq Inquiry highlights the fact that war against Iraq was 'not the last resort'. In effect, the United Kingdom had decided to join military action before all diplomatic efforts for disarmament had been exhausted. In fact, France, Germany and Russia in February 2003 in a joint memo called for a programme of continued and reinforced inspections with a clear timeline alongside a military build-up to exert maximum pressure on Iraq to disarm. As he sought to make the case for military action to MPs in the House of Commons and the public in the build up to the invasion in March 2003, the then Prime Minister was found to have deliberately exaggerated the threat posed by the Iraqi regime while disregarding warnings of the potential aftermath following military action. There was an ingrained belief that Saddam Hussein's regime had retained chemical and biological warfare capabilities since the end of the first Gulf War of 1991 and the regime was determined to preserve and possibly enhance these capabilities including at some point to attain nuclear capability. The Chilcot Report, however, found that 'these judgements about Iraq's capabilities… were presented with a certainty that was not justified'.

While the Inquiry Report did not reach a view on the legality of the war it did however find that the circumstances and processes by which it was ultimately decided that there was a legal basis for the United Kingdom to participate in the war was 'far from satisfactory', in fact, 'perfunctory' while 'no formal record was made of the decision, and the precise grounds on which it was made remains unclear'. In response to the letter of 14 March 2003 from the then Attorney General's office to No. 10, it was the then Prime Minister who decided that, so far as the United Kingdom was concerned, Iraq was and remained in breach of UN Security Council Resolution 1441 (2002). The Report further found, however, that the United Kingdom undermined the authority of the UN Security Council by not seeking a second UN resolution explicitly authorising war on the basis that Saddam Hussein was in breach of UN resolution 1441 (2002) after being aware that there was no majority consensus in the Security Council for war in March 2003.

The Chilcot Report rejected the then Prime Minister's claim that the subsequent sectarian strife could not have been predicted. Rather the Report found that there was no credible post-war plan or strategy on the part of the government. In fact, the United Kingdom had no influence on Iraq's post-war US-run administration. In particular, the UK had little influence over the day-to-day policy decisions taken by the coalition provisional authority in Baghdad headed by US-appointed Paul Bremner. The United Kingdom 'failed to meet its strategic objectives' in Iraq by the time it withdrew its forces in 2009.

The Chilcot Inquiry found that British forces were seriously ill-equipped and there was 'wholly inadequate' planning and preparation for the post-conflict phase of operations. It also found that the Ministry of Defence (MoD) rushed to plan the invasion but was slow to react to the security threats on the ground, particularly from the use of improvised explosive devices (IEDs) that killed scores of troops. What caught the media's attention was the then Prime Minister's apparently unqualified support to the US President months before the invasion that 'he would be there whatever'.

With regard to the plight of refugees, in 2008, the UNHCR reported an estimated 4.7 million Iraqi refugees. Of them around 2 million fled to neighbouring countries and beyond, while 2.7 million people were internally displaced.

Following publication of the Iraq Inquiry Report on 06 July 2016, understandably the former Prime Minister expressed regret and apologised both for the loss of life to UK servicemen and women and the victims of the sectarian violence that followed the invasion. But what consolation does that provide the grieving families of the 150,000-plus Iraqi civilians who have died as a result of the war and its consequential aftermath? Not to mention the many babies being born post-invasion with congenital birth defects allegedly as a consequence of the use of depleted uranium

(DU) munitions by Allied forces and in a country that even today is far from stable. Will the Western conscience take responsibility for this? Indeed, the elected Governments of the US, the UK and the 'coalition of the willing' truly believed that they held the moral high ground. Never again should military intervention be perpetrated on a sovereign nation unless it has the clear backing of the UN Security Council based upon a thorough process of intelligence gathering underpinned with post-conflict strategies. Similar sentiments were expressed in the Chilcot Inquiry Report. That is not to say Western powers should be complaisant to credible threats that threaten their national security such as those posed by Al-Qaeda and ISIL, as well as, taking action against genocides being committed overseas, for example by the regime of Bashar al-Assad against citizens of Syria by deploying chemical weapons and by the Myanmar military against Rohingya Muslims by committing murder, plunder and rape, forcing 700,000 to flee the slaughter and seek refuge in squalid camps in neighbouring Bangladesh.

Interestingly, Labour MPs turned out in force on 30 November 2016 to help defeat a Parliamentary motion tabled by the SNP calling for Tony Blair to be held to account for allegedly misleading Parliament over the Iraq war by 439 votes to 70. No doubt, any such investigation would have brought up unpleasant truths that might very well have exposed the Labour party, opening up further wounds to the cold war within the party. There appeared to be a convenient consensus in the House that personalising the Chilcot Report risked undermining the important issue of ensuring that such a 'catastrophic foreign policy decision' is not repeated, as against (as put forward by Alex Salmond of the SNP) creating a precedent whereby any future Prime Minister would be made personally accountable for his/her actions to the House of Commons on such a military policy decision in the way it was perceived to have been taken.

It would not be out of place to suggest that there is an undeniable causal link between the invasion of Iraq and its catastrophic aftermath and the rise of a 'radical Islamic narrative' that lends support to the debate of a 'clash of civilisations'. ISIL, to sustain itself feeds on an extremist narrative stirred up by an internal *fitna* (civil war) in the Middle East between Sunni and Shi'ite Islam underpinned by a firebrand Wahabi ideology.

Indeed, the Arab world, particularly from the perspective of existing despotic regimes in the region, is no doubt a better place without Saddam Hussein than if he had been in power today, given his unpredictability and military ambition to become a regional superpower. The people of Iraq, post-Saddam, have made some progress in building their government by approving a new constitution, as well as holding successive elections for Parliament and provincial governments. But then, given the rampant corruption in the political machinery of government, previous high levels of sectarian violence and the violent spread of ISIL coupled with endemic poverty, for most Iraqi's, it would appear that one tyrant has been replaced by many tyrants ruling in the guise of a sham democracy. In fact, it was former Shi'ite Prime Minister Nouri al-Maliki who was increasingly accused by his opponents of exercising authoritative rule that failed to bridge tensions with the Sunni and Kurdish populations that resulted in sectarian violence on a daily basis.

And here lies the challenge. If democratic reforms sweep the Middle East, does the region risk supplanting one dictator with an elected dictatorship of many? The mind-set of the people in the region must change and fundamental democratic principles such as limited government, the rule of law, an independent judiciary and free media must be promoted and embraced.

While there will always be politicised debate of who can be considered combatants or victims of war crimes, sadly, the worst affected are invariably always going to be women and children. As a consequence of some of these long-term military conflicts many Muslim women and children have been displaced from their homes, forced to flee to neighbouring countries, often falling victim to sex trafficking and prostitution. Tragically, many children have also been rendered orphans and left traumatised, with little support from their governments.

Fundamental to the understanding of Islam, both from a religious and political perspective, is the appreciation of Tawhid (Faith in the Unity/Oneness of ALLAH). It has three facets, namely faith in the Oneness of the Lordship of ALLAH (Tawhid-ar-Rububiyyah), the Oneness of the worship of ALLAH (Tawhid-al-Uluhiyyah) and Oneness of the names and qualities of ALLAH (Tawhid-al-Asma was-Sifat).

The first facet declares the Sovereignty of ALLAH over all creation. In **Chapter 2, Al-Baqarah, Verse 107** of the Holy Qur'an it states: *'knowest thou not that it is ALLAH unto Whom belongeth the sovereignty of the Heavens and the earth; and ye have not, besides ALLAH, any friend or helper?'*

Another verse of the Holy Qur'an making a similar pronouncement is **Chapter 5, Al-Ma'idah, Verse 120**: *'Unto ALLAH belongeth the Sovereignty of the heavens and the earth and whatever is therein, and He is able to do all things.'*

ALLAH is the sustainer of all that was, is and shall be and there is no intercessor with Him save with His permission. ALLAH has no beginning and no end. He is the eternal absolute, the one and only Creator. His structured will transcend the Universe – all that is seen and unseen.

The second facet requires that none has the right to be worshipped but ALLAH alone, and in Him alone do believing men seek refuge, shelter and protection. They neither worship nor seek sustenance from the angels, messengers, prophets, saints, pirs, idols or celestial bodies and their proximity or orbit in relation to the planet Earth. This is narrated in **Chapter 1, Al-Fatihah, Verse 5** of the Holy Qur'an. Needless to say, all Muslims make this declaration every day in their daily prayers: *'Thee (alone) do we worship, and Thine aid (alone) we seek.'*

And ALLAH mentions in **Chapter 67, Al-Mulk, Verse 29** of the Holy Qur'an: *'Say: He is the Beneficent. In Him we believe and in Him we put our trust. And ye will soon know who it is that is in error manifest.'*

Again in **Chapter 40, Al-Ghafir, Verse 60** of the Holy Qur'an, ALLAH states: *'And your Lord hath said: Pray unto me and I will hear your prayer. Lo! those who scorn My service, they will enter hell, disgraced.'*

While in **Chapter 3, Al-Imran, Verse 160** of the Holy Qur'an it mentions: *'If ALLAH helps you, none can overcome you: and if He forsakes you, who is there after Him that can help you? And in ALLAH (alone) let believers put their trust.'*

Furthermore, **Chapter 9, At-Taubah, Verses 34-35** of the Holy Qur'an mentioned below, gives a dire warning of so-called holy men who manipulate people's belief, giving the impression that the only way to ALLAH's favour is through them, often reaping financial reward for themselves. We can certainly extend the rationale behind the verses below to some of the so-called pirs and celebrity preachers that can be found in the Indian subcontinent, including my ancestral home of Bangladesh. '*O you who believe! Verily, there are many of the rabbis and monks who devour the wealth of mankind in falsehood, and hinder them from the Way of ALLAH.* '

The same verses provide a similar warning to Muslims who dedicate their lives in the accumulation of wealth and do not spend it according to the Shari'ah: '*And those who hoard up gold and silver, and spend it not in the Way of ALLAH, announce unto them a painful torment. On the Day (Day of Judgement) that (money, gold and silver) will be heated in the Fire Of Hell and with it will be branded their foreheads, their flanks, and their backs, (and it will be said unto them)*', '*this is the treasure which you hoarded for yourselves. Now taste of what you used to hoard.*'

The third facet refers to Divine attributes being vested in ALLAH alone. This is narrated in **Chapter 7, Al-A'raf, Verse 180,** of the Holy Qur'an: '*ALLAH's are the fairest names. Invoke Him by them. And leave the company of those who blaspheme His names. They will be requited what they do.*' A similar narrative can be found in **Deuteronomy 5-6**, namely, '*You shall not make wrongful use of the name of the Lord your God, for the Lord will not acquit anyone who misuses His name*'.

It is commonly accepted that the Holy Qur'an and Hadith refer to 99 names/attributes. Some of those attributes/names are mentioned in **Chapter 59, Al-Hashr, Verse 23** of the Holy Qur'an: '*He is ALLAH, besides Whom there is no other god;- the Sovereign, the Holy, the Source of Peace (and Perfection), the Guardian of Faith, the Preserver of Safety, the Exalted in Might, the Irresistible, the Supreme: Glory to Allah! (High is He) above the partners they attribute to Him.*'

Again in **Chapter 59, Al–Hashr, Verse 24**, the Holy Qur'an states: '*He is Allah, the Creator, the Evolver, the Bestower of Forms. To Him belong the Most Beautiful Names: whatever is in the heavens and on earth, doth declare His Praises and Glory: and He is the Exalted in Might, the Wise.*'

In order to begin to understand the nature of ALLAH it is useful to recognise and understand the attributes of ALLAH. Appendix 1 of this book gives a fuller description of the 99 attributes of ALLAH.

Widely accepted as representing one third of the Message contained in the Holy Qur'an, as recorded in Sahih Al-Bukhari, the doctrine of Tawhid is exemplified in **Chapter 112, Al-Ikhlas, Verses 1–4:** '*Say: He is ALLAH, The One; ALLAH, the Eternal, Absolute; He begetteth not, Nor is He begotten; And there is none comparable unto Him.*'

There must be conscious acceptance of Tawhid and complete adherence to it in our everyday lives. Belief without practice has no place in Islam.

Physical representations (images) of God are forbidden in Islam just as they have been forbidden in the Ten Commandments and the book of Leviticus in the Old Testament. Worshipping preconceived images of God is not a mark of faith encouraged by either of the monotheist religious texts. Islam, however, goes a step further. Physical representations of the Prophet Muhammad in any form, including statues and pictures, are also forbidden. Though Muslims are often provoked into reacting angrily when the Prophet Muhammad is depicted with libellous connotations in different media streams, Muslims, it must be remembered, do not worship Muhammad.

It would be too simplistic to label the Holy Qur'an as merely a book. Muslims believe it is the last of the Divine Revelations. It is the principal source of Islamic Law/Shari'ah. It is the word of ALLAH, a recital of the dialogue between the Creator and humanity through the Prophet Muhammad. From a human perspective the Holy Qur'an has been remarked as a miraculous achievement of sublime artistry. For a one-time shepherd, and later a trader who could neither read nor write to produce such magnificent artistry is inconceivable in the backdrop of sixth century pagan Arabia. This will be further explored in the next chapter.

The followers of the Islamic Faith are an inspired people. This is reflected in their history. A major achievement of classical Islamic civilization was the preservation, study and dissemination of Greek, Indian and Chinese scientific tradition of late antiquity that later formed the basis of Western science and philosophy. It laid the foundation for the 'Age of Reason', igniting the flame of the European Renaissance. It must be remembered that Renaissance European civilization took shape in the shadow of powerful and already progressive Islamic empires, such as the Ottoman and Moghul empires. Further back, when much of medieval Europe was reeling under plague and religious bigotry, Islamic culture was flourishing expressed in its architecture and academic pursuits in the sciences. The cities of Cordoba, Seville and Toledo bear testimony to these advances under the rule of the Moors in Al-Andalus (in present day Spain and Portugal).

While the Middle East is often considered to be the traditional heartland of Islam, by no means is it today representative of the Muslim Ummah. More than two thirds of all Muslims now reside not in the Middle East but in the Asia-Pacific region, North and sub-Saharan Africa, with a sizeable number living in Europe. There are around 500 million Muslims living in the Indian subcontinent alone, representing almost a third of the Muslim Ummah. As a country, Indonesia has the world's largest Muslim population of 209 million. Around 44 million Muslims now live in Europe, which is about 6% of Europe's population. Many of them have the right to vote. In the United Kingdom, Muslims represent around 4.8% of the population and are second or third generation migrants. There are more Muslims in Germany than there are in either Oman or Bahrain. Interestingly enough, Saudi Arabia (the birthplace of Islam) has around 25 million Muslims, which constitutes only 1.6% of the Muslim Ummah, yet commands one of the strongest Gross National Product per capita incomes in the Muslim Ummah alongside the United Arab Emirates and Kuwait. A report by the Pew Research Center's Forum on

Religion & Public Life titled 'The Future of the Global Muslim Population, projections for 2010-2030', published in January 2011, predicted that the world's Muslim population is expected to increase by 35% in the next 20 years. In that case, there will be around 2.2 billion Muslims by 2030, representing 26.4% of the world's population of 8.3 billion.

In its demographic study titled, 'The Future of World Religions: Population Growth Projections, 2010-2050' published in April 2015, the Pew Research Center further found that between 2010 and 2050, global Muslims are projected to increase at 73%, which is faster than the increase in the world's population as a whole (expected to be at 35%) and any other major religious group. Various reasons have been cited for this predicted change in the global religious profile, including the size of Muslim youth populations and their high fertility rates, as well as people switching faiths. In which case, there will be a near parity between the 2.8 billion Muslims (30% of the world's population) and the 2.9 billion Christians (31% of the global population) respectively in 2050. Interestingly, the study observes that using the same projection models beyond 2050, Muslims will outnumber any other major religious group by 2100, making up 35% of the global population. Other studies have also forecasted that in fact, Islam will indeed be the predominant religion between 2050 and 2100 should China, Russia or Africa embrace an Islamic renewal with vast sways of people converting to Islam. Maybe this explains why apparently every effort is being made by vested corporate media streams to malign the religion of Islam, associating it with terrorism at every opportunity and in every manner, shape or form. Nevertheless, with global Muslims dominating the religious landscape at the turn of the next century important questions must be asked at this point. In what direction is the Muslim Ummah heading? What socio-political and economic ramifications will this increased growth in population sizes have on the Muslim Ummah?

If current political and economic trends continue to endure the Muslim Ummah will implode upon itself highlighting the urgent need for an Islamic renascence that will culminate in a renewed political and economic alliance in the form of an Islamic Caliphate under the banner/slogan of 'One Ummah'. At the same time a serious intellectual re-think based on 'ilm' of the current trends of Islamic study and research is vital. A rational examination of the tenets of Islam that will act as an effective counter-narrative to the so-called 'radical interpretation of Islam' is essential. In fact, it is the ignorance of Islam that feeds into a narrow and extremist narrative. Furthermore, with the lack of established democratic institutions in many Muslim majority countries, including the lack of civil liberties and an independent judiciary together with a volatile Middle East ruled by military dictators and Royal dynasties with millions of Muslims living in abject poverty and in war-ravaged countries without access to education and basic necessities, the situation will only become more and more desperate. The rise of extremist groups such as Al-Qaeda and recently ISIL, which have adopted an extremist interpretation of the religious tenets of Islam, is particularly worrying in terms of their global influence in attracting Muslims to their misguided ideology, as well as, the atrocities carried out by them. The continuous rise and proliferation of such extremist groups in the future, which are no more than a spin-off from the proxy wars being played out between Sunni dictators in the Middle East and predominantly Shi'ite Iran and its affiliates, will only weaken the Muslim Ummah, making it more fractious. With major Muslim population increases predicted to take place in India, Indonesia, Pakistan and Bangladesh and regions of Africa accounting for a sizeable percentage of the total global Muslim population by around 2050, a lot also hinges upon the progress made by these countries in terms of consolidating and strengthening their democratic institutions and processes, as well as the economic empowerment of young Muslim men and women.

Currently, more than three quarters of the Muslim Ummah are adherents of Sunni Islam and comprise developing countries. Many are heavily resigned to elected dynastic rule, such as Bangladesh and (until August 2018 with the swearing in of Imran

Khan as Prime Minister) Pakistan, while a sizeable majority of those populations live in dire poverty. We witnessed with both hope and apprehension the wave of protests in the Arab World (Bahrain and Syria amongst them) against dictatorships and a move in favour of political pluralism. What became crucial for Western policy makers was what form of government these new representative democracies would produce, particularly in the backdrop of Arab perceptions of Western interference in the region both past and present. It was feared by vested interests that subsequent democratic elections would produce non-secular governments with the MENA (Middle Eastern and North African) countries ending up embracing fundamentalism through the front door. With the apparent failure of the 'Arab Spring', what these countries have ended up with are pro-Western puppet governments backed by corporate stakeholders such as has been observed in Egypt with many more countries becoming 'failed states' such as Syria and Libya. We will explore this area in more depth in Chapter Six.

The principal theological split between Islam and Judaism arises over which of the two sons the prophet Ibrahim (Abraham) was prepared to sacrifice at ALLAH's command to show his obedience. Followers of the Jewish Faith believe that it was Ishaq (Isaac), the younger of the two sons. The Holy Qur'an directly contradicts this, rendering a different account. Ibrahim (Abraham) had only Isma'il (Ishmael) at the time of the proposed sacrifice and Ishaq (Isaac) was born subsequently as a bounty to Ibrahim (Abraham) for his obedience. This is narrated in **Chapter 37, As-Saffat, Verses 101–113**: *'So we gave him, Ibrahim tidings of a gentle son. And when (the son) was old enough to walk with him, Ibrahim said: 'O my dear son! I have seen in a dream that I must sacrifice thee. So look what thinkest thou?' He said: 'O my father! Do that which thou art commanded. Allah willing, thou shall find me of the steadfast.' So when they had both submitted to ALLAH, and he (Ibrahim) had laid him (Isma'il) prostrate on his forehead (for sacrifice), We called out to him, 'O, Ibrahim! 'Thou hast already fulfilled the dream!' Lo! thus do we reward the good. Lo! that verily was a clear test. And we ransomed him with a momentous sacrifice. And we left for him among generations (To come)* *in later times: 'Peace and salutations To Ibrahim!' Thus do we award the good. For he was one of our believing Servants. And we gave him tidings of the birth of Ishaq, a prophet of the righteous. And we blessed him and Ishaq. And of their seed are some who do good, and some who plainly wrong themselves.'*

The Holy Qur'an makes it clear however, that ALLAH is the God of all creation with the Prophet Muhammad as His last messenger sent to all mankind, not limited to any race or region and includes the Arabs and Israelites. This is made clear in **Chapter 7, Al-A'raf, Verse 158** where it states: *'Say (O Muhammad): O Mankind! Lo! I am sent unto you all, as the messenger of ALLAH, to whom belongeth the sovereignty of the heavens and the earth. There is no God but He: it is He that giveth both life and death. So believe in ALLAH and His Messenger, the prophet who can neither read nor write, who believeth in ALLAH and in His words and follow him that happily ye may be led aright.'*

With Christianity the theological split essentially lies with the concept of Trinity, Islam brandishing it as a form of polytheism and denying outright the divinity of Isa (Jesus) as expressed in no uncertain terms in **Chapter 112, Al-Ikhlas, Verses 1-4** of the Holy Qur'an where it states: *'Say: He is ALLAH, The One; ALLAH, the Eternal, Absolute; He begetteth not, Nor is He begotten; And there is none comparable unto him.'*

Again in **Chapter 5, Al-Ma'idah, Verses 72-75**, the Holy Qur'an says: *'Surely, they have disbelieved who say: ALLAH is the Messiah, son of Maryam (Mary).' But the Messiah (Isa himself) said: 'O Children of Israel! Worship ALLAH, my Lord and your Lord.' Verily, whosoever sets up partners (in worship) with ALLAH, then ALLAH has forbidden Paradise to him, and the Fire will be his abode. And for the Zalimun (polytheists and evildoers) there are no helpers. Surely, disbelievers are those who say: 'ALLAH is the third of the three (in the Trinity).' But there is no God but the one God. And if they cease not from what they say, verily, a painful torment will befall on the disbelievers among them. Will they not turn with repentance to ALLAH and ask His forgiveness? For ALLAH is Oft-Forgiving, Most Merciful. The Messiah (Isa), son of Maryam, was no more than a Messenger; many were the Messengers that passed away before him. His mother Maryam* *was a saintly woman. They both used to eat earthly food. See how We make the revelations clear to them; yet see how they are deluded away (from the truth).'*

Furthermore, it is stated in **Chapter 19, Maryam, Verses 88–93**: *'And they say: the Beneficent hath taken unto him a son. Assuredly ye utter a disastrous thing. Whereby almost the heavens are torn, and the earth is split asunder and the mountains fall in ruins. That ye ascribe unto the Beneficent a son. For it is not consonant With the majesty of the Beneficent that He should choose a son. There is none in the heavens and the earth but cometh unto the Beneficent as a slave.'*

The Holy Qur'an does however confirm the birth of Isa (Jesus) of a Virgin – Maryam (Mary), but only as a sign unto mankind. This is clearly narrated in **Chapter 19, Maryam, Verses 16–21**: *'Relate in the Book (The story of) Mary, when she withdrew from her family to a place in the East. She placed a screen (to screen herself) from them: Then We sent to her Our angel, and he appeared before her as a man in all respects. She said: 'I seek refuge from thee to (Allah) Most Gracious: (come not near) if thou dost fear Allah.' He said: 'Nay, I am only a messenger from thy Lord (To announce) to thee the gift of a pure son.' She said: 'How shall I have a son, seeing that no man has touched me, And I am not unchaste?' He said: 'So (it will be): Thy Lord saith, 'That is Easy for Me: and (We Wish) to appoint him as a Sign unto men and a Mercy from Us': It is a matter (So) decreed.'*

The circumstances surrounding the birth of the prophet Isa (Jesus) is no doubt an affirmation unto mankind of ALLAH's omnipotence, compassion, mercy, and sovereignty over all creation.

Another crucial issue on which Islam and Christianity differ theologically is the crucifixion. In the Islamic narrative, Isa (Jesus) was not crucified on the cross. He was taken unto ALLAH. **Chapter 4, An-Nisa, Verses 157–8** of the Holy Qur'an states: *'And because of their saying: We slew the Messiah Jesus son of Mary, ALLAH's messenger – they slew him not nor crucified, but it appeared so unto them; and Lo those who disagree concerning it are in doubt thereof; they have no knowledge thereof save pursuit of conjecture; they slew him not for certain. Nay, ALLAH raised him up unto Himself; and ALLAH is exalted in power, Wise.'*

To suggest the separation of Islam from the state overlooks the inescapable convergence of religion and politics. Islam, like Judaism and Christianity, is inherently political. If we turn back the pages of history the three major monotheistic religions essentially began as rebellions against persecution perpetrated by the political establishment of the time. It culminated in the successful defiance and in some cases the uprooting of the existing political order. Briefly, with Judaism it was the defiance of the Jewish people against the slavery of Pharaoh that brought them out of Egypt and ultimately into 'Israel'. With Christianity it was defiance against the Roman Empire and the misguided practices carried out by the religious establishment in the so-called Temple of God in Jerusalem. With Islam it was defiance against the oppression of the leaders of Mecca who thrived on the trade generated from idol worship that subsequently led to the victory of Mecca by Muslim forces, the destruction of the idols housed in the Ka'bah and the banishment of idol worship in Arabia with Mecca becoming the centre-point/spiritual capital of Islam. The very essence of the three monotheist faiths is revolution against tyranny, whether such oppression is religious, social, and economic or a combination of the three.

The three monotheist religions were conceived from wars, but only in response to persecution. The Book of Exodus narrates how Moses and Joshua had to fight many battles in their search of the 'Promised Land', including the battle against the Amalekites. Christianity only saw the light of day when Roman Emperor Constantine had a vision of a figure of the Cross prior to his battle with Maxentius in 312 AD, which he subsequently won and in return declared that all religions including Christianity would be tolerated throughout his empire. Emperor Constantine later converted to Christianity but to consolidate his power-base he needed to unify his empire under a single religion. To do this he had to find common ground on contentious aspects of the Christian doctrine. He did this by summoning the Council of Nicaea in 325 AD. This in turn laid the platform for the spread of Christianity in the West. The turning point for Islam was the (bloodless) conquest of Mecca by the Prophet Muhammad.

The triumph over Mecca was the springboard from which the message of Islam spread across Arabia and beyond. Prior to that however, the Muslims had to fight several battles perpetrated upon them, mostly by the rulers of Mecca. Of these, the Battle of Badr proved most decisive, for defeat in this Battle would have had catastrophic consequences for the early Muslims.

Muslims believe the Ka'bah in Mecca is the spiritual beacon of the soul. Islamic tradition has it that it marks the site of the first altar dedicated to the worship of the one true God built by the Prophet Adam. Prophet Ibrahim (Abraham) later rebuilt the foundations of the Ka'bah with his son Isma'il (Ishmael) as stated in **Chapter 2, Al-Baqarah, Verse 127** of the Holy Qur'an: *'And remember when Ibrahim (Abraham) and his son Isma'il (Ishmael) were raising the foundations of the House (With this prayer): 'Our Lord! Accept (this service) from us: Verily you are the All-Hearing, the All-Knowing.'*

The Ka'bah marks the qibla (direction of salat/prayer) for global Muslims. Most mosques will have a mihrab (wall niche) indicating the direction of salat. Though the Ka'bah is often termed the House of ALLAH, pilgrims do not worship the Ka'bah or the black stone encased in its eastern corner wall. From that perspective the Ka'bah is a brick structure. In Islam all worship is for ALLAH alone – the unseen one true God. The first qibla for the early Muslims was the Noble Sanctuary in the Old City of Jerusalem. The change in direction of prayer followed a revelation the Prophet Muhammad received after His hijrah to Medina. This is illustrated in **Chapter 2, Al-Baqarah, Verse 150: '***And from wheresoever you start forth (for prayers), turn your face in the direction of the sacred mosque (at Mecca), and wheresover you are, turn your faces towards it (when your pray) so that men may have no argument against you except those of them that are the wrongdoers, so fear them not, but fear Me! – And so that I may complete My Blessings on you and you may be guided.'*

The Ka'bah itself has undergone several renovations since the time of Prophet Muhammad. Today the sacred mosque is dwarfed by the Abraj Al Bait Towers Complex including the Royal Mecca Clock Tower boasting a myriad of shopping malls, five-star hotels and luxury apartments. Dozens of key sites dating back to the birth of Islam and linked to events associated with the Prophet Muhammad have already been lost. This is in line with the Wahabi puritanical version of Islam as hardline clerics oppose the preservation of historical sites linked to the Prophet as they believe it encourages shirk (in this case, the idolization of the Prophet Muhammad). The spirituality of the Hajj nevertheless, is gradually becoming side tracked by the overwhelming consumerism that is recently taking hold.

The tragic events surrounding the Hajj in 2015 witnessed the death of almost 1000 Muslim pilgrims in two separate incidents followed by the political ramblings between Saudi Arabia and Iran, with the Saudi authorities blatantly refusing to accept sole responsibility backed by its religious establishment which caused plenty of consternation across the Muslim Ummah.

Islam, as a code of life, professes liberation from the evil indulgences that tempt the soul, not least the 'seven deadly sins'. Far from being a restraint on one's personal freedom, faith in Islam is an expression of one's spiritual liberation and intellectual enlightenment.

In the 7th Century, when women were treated as chattels with little or no rights guaranteed by the societies in which they lived, be it Europe, Africa or Asia, including the Arab peninsula, Islam gave women rights that had Divine sanction. For example, women were given rights of inheritance, the right to choose their husbands, the right to divorce, the right to learn and the right to carry on in business. The right most often misunderstood by some Feminist groups and the Western media is the right of women to command respect from their male counterparts through the concept of the 'veil'. This is narrated in **Chapter 24, An-Nur, Verses 30-31** of the Holy Qur'an: *'Say to the believing men to lower their gaze and guard their modesty. That is purer for them. Lo! ALLAH is aware of what they do. And say to the believing women that they should lower their gaze, and guard their modesty; that they should display of their adornment only that which is (ordinarily) apparent, that they should draw their veils over their bosoms, and not reveal their beauty except to their husbands, their fathers, their husbands' fathers, their sons,* *their husbands' sons, their brothers or their brothers' sons, or their sisters' sons, or their women, or their slaves, or male attendants who lack vigour, or children who know naught of women's nakedness. And they should not strike their feet so as to reveal what they hide of their adornment. And O ye Believers! Turn unto ALLAH together, in order that ye may be successful.'*

The Holy Qur'an requires that Muslim men and women be modest in their appearance as well as in their attitude towards each other. For Muslim women the veil forms part of their modesty. In fact, for many Muslim women the veil also marks their religious and sometimes cultural identity, particularly those living in the West. It is a subtle political statement of their individuality. And it is this expression of their individuality that has fallen foul of right-wing politicians, often being seen as a barrier to inclusion of ethnic and religious minorities in western society forming part of a wider debate about multiculturalism in Europe. The veil has over time taken different forms often defined by cultural interpretation. Predominantly, there is the hijab (head scarf), niqab (veil for the face that leaves the eyes clear) and the burka (most concealing of all veils that covers the body and the face, often leaving only a mesh screen to see through).

France became the first European country on 11 April 2011 to ban the full-face veil in public places. The European Court of Human Rights upheld the ban on 2 July 2014 after a case was brought by a French woman who argued that the ban violated her freedom of religion and expression. In Belgium the full-face veil was banned in July 2011. In December 2012, the Belgium Constitutional Court ruled that it did not violate human rights with the European Court of Human Rights upholding the Belgium ban in 2017. In the Netherlands, in November 2016, Dutch legislators backed a ban on the full veil (niqab and burka) in public places such as schools, hospitals and public transport. Most recently, in Denmark a ban on wearing face veils in public came into force on 1 August 2018. In the United Kingdom there is currently no ban on the veil, but schools are allowed to decide their own dress code. However, a public stir was caused when former Foreign Secretary Boris Johnson, in an article published in the *Daily Telegraph* in early August 2018, said though full-faced veils should not be banned, it was 'absolutely ridiculous' that women chose to 'go around looking like letter boxes' and said they looked like 'bank robbers'. These views drew a chorus of criticism from within his own party and beyond, demanding that he apologise for the comments. The Conservative party faced criticism for not addressing anti-Muslim prejudice in its own ranks. Though there is nothing to suggest that his views will give rise to incidents of Islamophobia nevertheless, prior to making these comments Britain had already seen a rise in Islamophobic hate crimes with reports that Muslim women have had their burkas pulled off by thugs on the streets. This is essentially due to ignorance and misconceptions of the religious tenets of Islam, which this book seeks to redress and challenge by enlightening the reader. Though in countries like Saudi Arabia and Iran women are forced to wear the full veil in public, often enforced by the so-called 'morality police' and being therefore arguably under compulsion to do so, there is no such duress in the United Kingdom. (It would be pertinent to mention here that given the notoriety associated with these so-called morality police, a renewed Caliphate in the Muslim Ummah must do away with it.) The comparatively small number of Muslim women who choose to wear the veil in the United Kingdom do so willingly and without pressure. In Britain at least, in this context, the veil does not symbolise oppression.

Though polygamy is permitted in Islam, it requires that each wife be treated equally. **Chapter 4, An–Nisa, Verse 3** states: '... *Marry women of your choice, two or three or four; and if ye fear that ye cannot do justice (to so many) than one (only) or that which your right hands possess. Thus it is more likely that ye will not do injustice.*'

Debate surrounds the concept of justice in the above verse. Some view it in materialistic terms, ie financial equality. Others enjoin the requirement of emotional equality, ie to treat each of their wives with equal emotional devotion. Too often do men take on further wives for the sole purpose of satisfying their sexual desires, often at the cost of emotional turmoil with the existing family. Though sexual relationships outside marriage are forbidden in Islam that is not to say that polygamy in Islam is a licence for debauchery.

Nikah (marriage) is a legal contract, and the parties are free to agree upon its terms. This is particularly so when it comes to the Mehr (free gift) that is payable by the groom at the time of marriage, though there is provision for all or part of the Mehr to be deferred. In which case, if the husband dies or the spouses get divorced before full payment, the Mehr debt becomes payable immediately. In Western matrimonial law it is very much akin to a pre-nuptial agreement. The Mehr provides the wife financial security and independence for it is hers to save or spend as she pleases. The Mehr becomes her exclusive property. In many countries however, it is the bride's father or guardian who establishes the marriage contract in her name. It should be emphasized here that the Mehr is not akin to a 'bridal-price' or dowry.

The practice of forced marriage is alien to Islam. In those Muslim societies where dowry is common place and where Muslim girls are encouraged to agree to arranged marriages, it is more of a cultural practice and has nothing to do with Islam. Furthermore, the nikah must not be viewed as a contract for the sale of goods (here the prospective wife) with the Mehr forming the consideration or price. As far as the treatment of the wife goes, the Prophet Muhammad reminded the Ummah in His Last Sermon that a wife should be treated fairly and that both husband and wife have reciprocal rights over each other.

The Holy Qur'an forbids Muslims to marry idol worshippers until they worship the one true God, i.e., ALLAH alone. This is narrated in **Chapter 2, Al-Baqarah, Verse 221** where it states, *'And marry not the idolatresses till they believe;'*... *'And do not give your daughters in marriage to idolaters till they believe …'* This is not to say that Muslims who have or are likely to marry idol worshippers should be subjected to violence or have their marriages annulled. Transgression of this sort is not the way of Islam. Then again, the marriage of Muslims to people of the Scriptures, ie Christians and Jews, is permitted. This is stated in **Chapter 5, Al-Ma'idah, Verse 5** of the Holy Qur'an where it states, *'This day are (all)* *good things made lawful for you.'... 'And (lawful in marriage are) chaste women who are believers and chaste women of those who received the Scripture before you when ye give them their marriage portions and live with them in honour, not in fornication, nor taking them as secret concubines. Whoso denieth the faith, his work is vain and he will be among the losers in the Hereafter.'*

Divorce is frowned upon and is viewed only as an unavoidable recourse of last resort where all efforts at reconciliation have failed. **Chapter 2, Al-Baqarah** and **Chapter 65, At-Talaq** of the Holy Qur'an deals extensively with the issue of divorce. Though the husband may divorce his wife unilaterally by pronouncing 'talaq' three times, the first two pronouncements must be followed by a waiting period to ascertain whether or not the wife is pregnant. If she is with child, reconciliation is preferred but if the divorce does nevertheless go ahead then the mother will have custody of a male child until he is the age of 7 or until puberty in case of a female child. Financial allowances are to be made by the husband during the term of the pregnancy and for nursing the child, in which case, care of the mother rests with the father. The spouses may also divorce by mutual consent that takes the form of legal renunciation of the marriage contract. Under Shari'ah, the wife may also initiate a divorce to release herself from the contract of marriage where the marriage has broken down subject to a waiting period and attempts to effect reconciliation have failed. This form of divorce is referred to as faskh. Consequently, talaq pronounced three times in the heat of an argument does not constitute an annulment of the marriage contract. Waiting periods are prescribed between the pronouncements and efforts at reconciliation is encouraged.

There is a considerable degree of confusion surrounding **Chapter 2, Al-Baqarah, Verse 230** of the Holy Qur'an where it states; *'So if a husband divorces his wife (for a third time after having pronounced the divorce twice previously), he cannot, after that remarry her until after she has married another husband and he has divorced her. In that case, there is no blame on either of them if they re-unite, provided they can keep the limits ordained by ALLAH. Such are the limits ordained by ALLAH which He makes plain to those who have knowledge (of* *the consequences of violating those limits).'* Entering such a 'Halala' marriage (as it is known) after a heated argument where the husband pronounces talaq thrice constitutes a misconception of this verse. Furthermore, those unscrupulous men and agencies who offer to step in to contract a second marriage and consummating it with a view of subsequently divorcing the women so as to allow her to go back to her first husband are not only making a complete mockery of the Quranic verse but sexually exploiting these women. This is a particularly concerning problem in some Muslim communities in western societies. One would expect the Imams of mosques of these communities to come out and condemn this vice outright, denouncing debauchery in the name of Islam. It is understood from the traditions of the Prophet Muhammad that He cursed those who arranged and entered into such fictitious marriages.

Both men and women are accountable for their own actions before ALLAH. Islam applies equally to both genders in the spiritual context of the Hereafter and Judgement Day.

The derogatory image often portrayed by vested right-wing elements against Islam in the context of gender inequality lies not with the Faith but more with the different interpretations of the Divine Texts practised in different parts of the Muslim Ummah as the Ulama find it increasingly difficult to reconcile with modernity. Consequently, the applications of Shari'ah with regard to women's rights vary between Muslim countries. However, as some developing Muslim countries do embrace modernity as an inevitable consequence of mass urban migration, birth control and the changing face of global consumerism, this has meant an increasing emphasis by families on educating their female children. Consequently, as these countries prosper economically women are playing an increasing role in their countries' socio-economic and political future.

The term 'jihad' is often misunderstood by Muslims and non-Muslims alike, with the Western media often associating it with Islamic extremism. In fact, jihad essentially lends itself to the idea of 'struggle', namely an individual's inner struggle to lead one's life according to Shari'ah, overcoming temptation to evil impulses and vices which is also often referred to as the greater jihad. The idea of a lesser jihad refers to an outward expression of one's 'taqwa' (fear) of ALLAH to bring society in conformity with Islam through 'da'wa' (invitation) and not violence. There is therefore, no credible link between the term jihad and terrorism. (In fact, those who seek to either profess or link terrorism to jihad have surely misunderstood its true meaning.) However, both historical and contemporary writings of many Ulamas have sought to associate the term jihad with armed struggle or a Holy War, particularly against colonial rule and foreign invasion or occupation of Islamic lands. Consequently, a body of Islamic jurisprudence, otherwise referred to as 'fiqh al-jihad', has evolved surrounding the concept of Holy War. With many Muslim nations seeking to wrestle themselves from colonial rule during the last century the term jihad became the perfect scapegoat for a more radical interpretation of the term. Such a restrictive application of the term jihad has also set the platform for many so-called contemporary armed jihadist movements such as Al-Qaeda and ISIL.

Contrary to the understanding of jihad employed by these radical groups, 'armed jihad' is defensive in nature and only to be employed when Muslim countries come under attack. However, any force used should be proportionate and not directed against civilian targets. Moreover, women, children and old people are not to be killed or tortured, while Muslims must desist from fighting should the enemy seek terms for peace. Rape and sexual exploitation of women and children cannot be used as a weapon of war. Reports of rape of Yazidis and Catholic women by ISIL can never be justified as an act of jihad. The phenomenon of 'jihadi brides', many of whom are below the age of consent and were in fact being used by ISIL fighters for sexual exploitation, also has no place within the meaning of jihad. The jurisprudence of military jihad is very much akin to the concepts of 'jus ad bellum' (justification of and limits to the use of force) and 'jus in bello' (body of legal norms governing rules of battle), otherwise commonly understood in Western military terminology by the phrase 'Just War', but defined by the moral parameters of Islamic Shari'ah.

On the other hand, the Arab Revolt of 2011 can be aptly described as an act of lesser jihad. Islam does not justify or sanction despotic or tyrannical rule. There is no conflict between (liberal) political Islam and political pluralism in its broad sense. Mass peaceful demonstrations against autocratic regimes to bring about democratic reform is in line with true Islam. It is interesting to note Russian President Vladimir Putin's remarks in his speech at the 70th United Nations General Assembly on 28 September 2015 accusing those who support democratic revolutions in the Middle East of being responsible for bringing about violence, poverty and social disaster to the region. It must be remembered however, that the dire and perilous situation in Syria is the consequence of President Bashar al-Assad's overwhelming armed response to the mass demonstrations which then spiralled out of control, taking the form of a civil war that allowed ISIL to subsequently intervene in the conflict, taking advantage of the protracted nature of the war. ISIL emerged essentially as a military machine to counter Shi'ite dominance in the Middle East. Any critical investigation of the sources of financial funding to ISIL will reveal patronage by private Sunni donors in the region, often condoned by their respective states. The failure of the Arab Spring is primarily linked to the spontaneous outburst of the people in the region demanding democratic rights and freedoms in defiance of autocratic regimes in the absence of an effective strategy to implement credible reforms to oversee a peaceful transition to democratic processes following the fall of the dictator. Consequently, any attempt to spark a second Arab uprising must be well thought-out with a prescriptive stratagem to ensure a smooth transition to democratic processes. A possible approach is discussed in Chapter Eight.

While it can be argued that the dynamics required to qualify as a revolution usually necessitate violence, given the magnitude of changes brought to the political, social and economic order of the state, nevertheless, major socio-political changes can occur without large-scale political violence. For example, the collapse of communism in Eastern Europe in 1989 that also led to the collapse of the USSR in 1991 was indeed a revolution initiated by peaceful means supported by mass demonstrations.

We often find the term 'Islamic Shari'ah' being bandied about in different media streams, often being associated with religious extremism. Let us take this opportunity to briefly examine what Shari'ah actually refers to. Essentially, it is the moral code of religious law in Islam. On translation Shari'ah means a 'clear straight path', i.e., the enlightened path that leads to ALLAH. It encompasses rules for every aspect of spiritual, social and physical life. Among other things, it governs the rules relating to worship, ritual, conduct as well as legal matters. There are two primary sources of Shari'ah Law. They are the Holy Qur'an and then the numerous Ahadith, the later embodying the Sunnah (examples and traditions) of the Prophet Muhammad. It is the Holy Qur'an that forms the main basis of Shari'ah Law. It states the principles, while the numerous Ahadith provide the details for their application. For instance, while the Holy Qur'an requires Muslims to establish salat (prayer) and pay zakat it does not describe the complete details how to do so. The numerous Ahadith provide those details.

Both the Holy Qur'an and Ahadith may be interpreted by secondary sources of Shari'ah Law often referred to as Fiqh. They are Ijma (consensus), Qiyas (decision by analogy or reasoning based on similar circumstances choosing the best solution) and Ijtihad (independent reasoning). The secondary sources of Shari'ah, however, only apply when a definitive answer cannot be found in the Holy Qur'an and then the Sunnah of the Prophet. Where a definitive answer is available in the Holy Qur'an then neither the Ahadith nor the secondary sources can override this. But religious interpretation is never that black and white. Evidently there are shades of grey.

Fiqh is the science of Islamic jurisprudence. It refers to the 'understanding' of Islamic laws based on the Holy Qur'an and the Sunnah. There are multitudes of scholarly views within this science. However, within Sunni Islam four established madhahib (plural for schools of legal thought) have developed, with each madh'hab named after its founder. They are the Hanafi, named after Abu Hanifah Nu'man bin Thabit; the Maliki, named after

Malik bin Anas; the Shafi'i, named after Muhammad bin Idris Al-Shafi'i; and the Hanbali, named after Ahmad bin Hanbal. Among the four schools of legal thought, the Hanafi School is the oldest and most diverse, being the official school of Islamic thought under the Ottoman and Moghul Empires. Rooted in history, the four schools have geographical delineations. Consequently, the Hanafi School is now predominant among the Sunnis of Central Asia, Afghanistan, Bangladesh, Pakistan, India, China, Iraq, Syria, Turkey, Albania, Bosnia, Kosovo, Macedonia in the Balkans and the Caucasus. Of the four schools, Hanafi is considered to be the more liberal putting greater emphasis than the other three on Ijma and Qiyas. It would be safe to say that the different approaches of the four schools reflect their geopolitical history.

Within Sunni Islam all four schools of legal thought are respected as valid, promoting exchange of ideas and views between them. Nevertheless, stark differences appear in the way adherents of the four madhahib offer Salat (their daily prayers). This can often cause confusion among the young generation of Muslims living in Europe and America, where adherents of all the four schools practise their faith in the same smelting pot.

Often when verses of the Holy Qur'an are taken out of context and deliberately contorted to fit into an extremist narrative an irrational reaction is conjured against the Shari'ah by people who lack proper understanding of the meaning of the Holy Qur'an.

Halal (that which is permitted) and Haram (that which is prohibited) feature strongly in the day-to-day lives of devout Muslims. Their everyday application can particularly be seen with respect to dietary rules. Muslims are allowed to eat meat, with the exception of pork, provided of course, the animal was killed pronouncing the name of ALLAH by a clean and sharp knife severing the blood vessels. Muslims are not permitted to eat the meat of any carnivorous animal or dead carcass. There are however, exceptions, and that is when Muslims find themselves faced with a choice between starvation and eating haram, or prohibited food. It could be agreed or reasoned that such instances would obviously include survivors of natural calamities and victims of war and conflict where halal food is in scarce supply. This is clearly stated in **Chapter 2, Al-Baqarah, verses 172–173**: *'O ye who believe! Eat of the good things that We have provided for you, and be grateful to ALLAH, if it is (indeed) He whom ye worship. He hath only forbidden you carrion, and blood, and the flesh of swine, and that on which any other name hath been invoked besides that of ALLAH. But he who is driven by necessity, neither craving nor transgressing, then it is no sin for him. Lo! ALLAH is Oft-Forgiving, Most Merciful.'*

The consumption of alcohol is expressly forbidden and so is the sale of it by Muslims. This is evident from **Sahih Al-Bukhari, Volume 5, Book 59, Hadith Number 590:** *Narrated by Jabir bin Abdullah: That he heard ALLAH's Apostle saying in the year of the conquest (of Mecca) while he was in Mecca, 'ALLAH and His Apostle have made the selling of wine (ie alcoholic drinks) unlawful.'*

Certainly, profiteering from the selling of alcohol falls squarely within the parameters of the above Hadith. There is nothing in the Holy Qur'an to contradict this analysis. In fact, **Chapter 2, Al-Baqarah, verse 219** supports this: *'They question thee (Muhammad) concerning strong drink and game of chance. Say: In both is great sin. And some utility for men; but the sin of them is greater than their usefulness. And they ask thee what they ought to spend. Say: That which is superfluous. Thus ALLAH maketh plain to you (His) revelations that happily ye may reflect.'*

The prohibition in the dealing of alcohol is therefore binding upon Muslims under Shari'ah. Interestingly, we do not find many Ulamas in the West being vocal in their respective communities discouraging the sale of alcohol by Muslim businessmen. This is particularly the case in the United Kingdom, where the catering trade forms the backbone of many businesses owned by Muslims. Many of these businesses contribute to the local mosques and madrassahs. Consequently, some Ulamas often cite financial necessity. On the other hand, some Muslim scholars rebut this argument as farcical, exclaiming that a refusal to sell alcohol would only mean a reduction in profits. They also argue that these catering establishments can retain their non-Muslim customers by allowing them to bring their own wine rather than selling it to them. Unfortunately, contained in this debate is a wide divergence of opinion.

It is regrettable that today the Muslim Ummah is in a state of decline, primarily because the Ummah has lost faith in its own potential. This is essentially because the majority of Muslim States suffer from endemic corruption in all spheres of socio-economic life. We see a divergence from the teachings of the Holy Qur'an, underlined by an unrelenting pursuit of consumerism and selfish personal financial gain across the Ummah. Furthermore, Muslim States have lost faith in their ability to achieve economic emancipation attainable through the advancement of scientific learning based on an increased manufacturing platform. To add to its woes the Muslim Ummah has failed to effectively respond to modernity. Muslim states have either reacted irrationally to it or embraced it at the cost of their cultural and political identity as Muslims.

Other reasons for the decline include the lack of political pluralism and the overwhelming concentration/hoarding of economic wealth and political power in the hands of the ruling elite. Such economic wealth is often derived from the natural resources of their respective countries (oil in particular), as is the situation in North Africa and the Middle East. It was hoped the Arab Spring would benefit the populations of those countries rather than amount to a change in the political 'Old Guard' only as was seen with Egypt. Meanwhile, there has been an increasing trend of the ruling elite in some of those countries to invest their nation's oil-generated wealth outside their own countries for fear of potential renewed political turmoil. Saudi Arabia's move, as part of its 'Vision 2030' economic transformation plan that involves creating a sovereign wealth fund into the world's largest, by selling a 5 percent stake in the oil giant Saudi Aramco, is arguably another way of investing its wealth outside the Kingdom. The Arab Spring of 2011 had shown an increasing willingness of citizens to defy the autocratic rule of their national leaders in favour of political pluralism. Then again, the tragic acceptance of elected dynastic rule in the name of democracy is often marred by feuding party political violence, as is the situation in both Pakistan and Bangladesh, which also happen to be the second and third most populous Muslim majority states in the Muslim Ummah after Indonesia, and restricts the Ummah's capacity for unity and growth. This will be picked up again in Chapter Seven. Importantly, global Muslims must resort to the promotion and dissemination of ilm (rational knowledge of Islam) if they are to be successful.

The opportune time is now for the Muslim Ummah to undergo a renascence. In which case, a clear, effective and well thought out stratagem is required that will usher in political pluralism doing away with dynastic rule, as well as, ushering economic emancipation for all its citizens, irrespective of gender, religious affiliation or ethnicity. It is the mismanagement of resources, lack of social mobility and gender inequality that is creating an increasing and alarming disparity of wealth. Left unchecked, it will give rise to resentment and contempt leaving a fractious Ummah to pick up the pieces from the inevitable fallout from social strife. At the centre of any renascence is required a rational intellectual debate. With adherents of the religion of Islam projected to be the dominant Faith from 2050 onwards, it is all the more imperative that an effective counter narrative to so-called radical Islam is adopted otherwise the Ummah will implode upon itself.

A critical interpretation of the first revelation of the Holy Qur'an to the Prophet Muhammad (cited at the beginning of Chapter One) highlights the importance of the accumulation of knowledge through the understanding of the sciences and its dissemination. The Muslim Ummah today should have been at the forefront of scientific breakthroughs that would have in turn benefitted not only the Ummah but the rest of humanity. Unfortunately, the Muslim Ummah has been experiencing a crisis of faith through its failure to rationalize its understanding of the Holy Qur'an with some exhorting an extremist narrative hijacking the true essence of the religion of Islam. These themes are explored in some detail in the following chapters.

PART I

'All truth passes through three stages. First, it is ridiculed. Second, it is violently opposed. Third, it is accepted as being self-evident.'

Arthur Schopenhauer
German philosopher

CHAPTER ONE

The Holy Qur'an – The Word of ALLAH (The Recital)

THE FIRST REVELATION

'*Read! In the Name of your Lord Who has createth, Createth Man from a clot. Read: and thy Lord is Most Bounteous, Who teacheth by the pen, Teacheth man that which he knew not.*' **Chapter 96, Al-Alaq, Verses 1–5**.

Both from a physical and a psychological perspective, the experience of the first revelation for the Prophet Muhammad was both overwhelming and intense. It is beyond the comprehension of our ordinary day-to-day life experiences to truly fathom what the Prophet went through. It came upon Him unsought, launching Him into a spiritual realm He could never have imagined.

In the month of Ramadan, in the year 610 AD while immersed in one of His frequent solitary meditations in a cave known as Hira at the top of Jabal al-Nur (Mount of Light), near Mecca, the archangel Jibrail (Gabriel) came to Muhammad, ordering Him to recite. Muhammad replied He could not recite. Then when ordered a third time and overwhelmed in Jibrail's embrace, the Prophet Muhammad recited verses 1–5 of Chapter 96 of the Holy Qur'an as mentioned above. The Prophet would later recall when on the mountainside that wherever He looked there stood before Him on the horizon Jibrail in the form of a man, saying: *'O Muhammad! Thou art the apostle of GOD and I am Jibrail.'* Following what can only be described a tremendous experience, the Prophet hurriedly rushed to His home, trembling under a blanket in the comfort of his wife Khadija. She later consulted her cousin Waraqa ibn Nawfal, who was learned in the Scriptures (Torah and the Gospel). On hearing from Khadija the experience of Muhammad, Waraqa said he had no doubt that what Muhammad experienced was Divine Revelation and that surely He was the Prophet as foretold in the Scriptures. In **Chapter 61, As-Saff, Verse 6** of the Holy Qur'an it states: *'And (remember) when Isa (Jesus), son of Maryam (Mary), said: 'O Children of Israel! I am the Messenger of ALLAH unto you, confirming the Taurat [(Torah) which came] before me, and giving glad tidings of a Messenger to come after me, whose name shall be Ahmed.' But when he (Ahmed, ie Muhammad) came to them with clear Signs, they said: 'This is plain magic.'*

The first revelation marks the commencement of Muhammad's Prophetic Mission. So momentous was this event that it would change the course of the future of mankind. The rest of the Holy Qur'an would be revealed in stages, piecemeal, over the 23-year period of His Prophetic Mission. This is mentioned in **Chapter 17, Al-Isra, Verse 106** of the Holy Qur'an: *'And (it is) a Qur'an which We have divided (into parts), in order that you might recite it to men at intervals. And We have revealed it by stages.'* The criticism that the Prophet Muhammad was delusional at the time of the first revelation holds no weight therefore, given the continuity in the revelation.

Within the first revelation is the key to unravelling the depth of knowledge and dominion of the Holy Qur'an. It is akin to the Rosetta Stone, for it translates the numerous facets/dimensions of the Divine message. All knowledge comes from ALLAH, the creator of all that is seen and unseen, for unto ALLAH alone belongs the dominion of heavens and the earth. Like any major work the opening lines/thoughts sets the stage for the rest of the text. An expediential study of Human DNA, may very well answer the question that has for centuries baffled philosophers and scientist alike, namely the purpose of our existence as human beings.

The Holy Qur'an is an expression of ALLAH's Divinity to mankind. Being the Divine word of God, it is the spirit that lies within the meaning of ALLAH's speech that is eternal. ALLAH speaks to mankind through the Holy Qur'an and it is therefore 'light and guidance'. Indeed, the Holy Qur'an imparts spiritual knowledge apparent only to those who possess resolute faith in and deep understanding of the tenets of Islam. The word Qur'an means 'to recite'. Parts of the Holy Qur'an are a recital of the dialogue between ALLAH and the Prophet Muhammad directed to all humanity. The Holy Qur'an is a universal scripture addressed to all mankind and not limited to any chosen people.

FORM AND STRUCTURE OF THE HOLY QUR'AN

The Holy Qur'an is divided into 30 equal Divisions and has 114 Surahs (Chapters) of varying length. The longest Chapter, Al-Baqarah, consists of 286 ayats (verses), while the shortest Chapters, namely Al-Kawthar, Al-Asr and An-Nasr, consist of three verses each. The entire Holy Qur'an has 6236 verses. The Surahs have two principal categories. Those Chapters revealed to the Prophet Muhammad in Mecca both prior to and after his migration to Medina are referred to as Meccan, while those Chapters revealed to Him in Medina are referred to as Medinan. Of the 114 Chapters, 86 are classified as Meccan while 28 are classified as Medinan.

The Meccan Chapters deals mainly with the doctrine of Tawhid (Unity and Oneness of ALLAH), Risallah (Prophethood of Muhammad) and Akhirah (the final accountability of mankind in the presence of ALLAH). The Medinan Surahs, on the other hand, deal with the Faith's ritualistic and legal aspects such as Zakat, Sawm and the Hajj, as well as rules relating to social, economic and state policies, rules for declaring war and dealing with war captives, rules for accepting converts, divorce proceedings as well as, rules of punishment for various crimes. The Medinan Chapters also emphasise the unified message of the past prophets, condemns the hypocrites and draws upon the finality of the Divine Revelation with the Prophet Muhammad as the Last Prophet. The longer Medinan Chapters appear towards the front of the Holy Qur'an, while the shorter and in most cases earlier Meccan Chapters appear at the back. This arrangement can be traced back to the original Uthmanic Codex. Sunni Muslims, in particular, believe that the order and sequence of the Holy Qur'an was Divinely inspired.

It may be noted that the Holy Qur'an puts emphasis on the way it is to be recited, placing importance on patience and understanding. **Chapter 73, Al-Muzzammil, Verses 4** states: *'And recite the Qur'an (aloud) in a slow, (pleasant tone and) style.'*

THE COLLECTION AND COMPILATION
OF THE HOLY QUR'AN

The collection and compilation of the Holy Qur'an relates to three distinct but overlapping (interconnected) periods of time. They are the time of the Prophet Muhammad, the time of the Rashidun Caliphs, Abu Bakr and Umar, and finally the time period of Uthman. Given this, the standardised copy of the Holy Qur'an was completed and dispatched to different parts of the then Islamic Ummah in the year 650 AD, merely 18 years after the Prophet's death. Of them, the Topkapi (Turkey) and Samarkand (Uzbekistan) codices are claimed to be the original copies sent out by the Rashidun Caliph Uthman.

It is universally accepted by Muslims that the Prophet Muhammad could neither read nor write, with the Holy Qur'an referring to the Prophet as 'al-nabiyy al-ummiy', which has been interpreted as the 'unlettered Prophet'. There is no historical evidence to suggest that the Prophet actually wrote parts of the Holy Qur'an Himself. The Prophet Muhammad would proclaim the revelations as they came to Him to His Companions, who would in turn memorise them. Often scribes, on the Prophet's instructions, would record the revelations using whatever writing materials were at hand. Chief among the scribes was Zayd Bin Thabit. It would be worthwhile realising that during the time of the Prophet Muhammad oral transmission based on memory was the preferred norm of communication, given that writing materials were in short supply. A guarantee of accuracy and authenticity was usually accepted where the exact same text was known by memory by a number of people.

What was not available during the Prophet's lifetime was a single material collection encompassing all the revelations in one place. This was not possible given the continuity of revelation that went on up until the time of the Prophet Muhammad's death. Furthermore, the need for a single codex was not urgently felt or considered necessary, primarily because many of the Prophet's Companions were Hafiz, i.e., had memorised vast portions of the revelations marking the tradition of hifz (entrusted to memory). More importantly, Prophet Muhammad was alive Himself. The Islamic community had the Prophet to refer to on matters of Faith. This last point is narrated in **Chapter 16, An-Nahl, Verse 44** of the Holy Qur'an: *'(We sent them) with Clear Signs and Scriptures. And we have sent down unto thee (also) the Message; That thou (Muhammad) mayest explain clearly to men what is sent for them, and that they may give thought.'*

Perhaps if the Holy Qur'an had been recorded into a single codex during the Prophet Muhammad's lifetime, the Shi'ite critique that verses were dropped in the Uthmanic Codex would not have arisen. It must be stressed that the principal divergence between Shi'ite and Sunni Islam is not solely based on religious doctrine but more on politics over issues of succession and leadership following the death of the Prophet Muhammad.

Shortly after the death of the Prophet, Abu Bakr (the first Rashidun Caliph), at the insistence of Umar (the second Rashidun Caliph), commenced the task of bringing together all the revelations, both written and oral, into one volume. Abu Bakr entrusted this task to Zayd Bin Thabit. Sunni scholars believe that the principal reason behind the initiative to collect the Holy Qur'an was the death of numerous Qurra (those who could recite the Qur'an from memory) at the Battle of Yamamah and the fear that large parts of the Holy Qur'an would be lost unless collected together, as many more Quranic reciters may die on other battlefields. This is narrated in **Sahih Al-Bukhari, Volume 6, Book 61, Hadith Number 509.** With an expanding Ummah founded on religious doctrine, it became all the more imperative to compile the Holy Qur'an to prevent inconsistencies in the Divine Text that could fracture the emerging Ummah on religious-political lines.

Heading the Committee of Compilers, Zayd Bin Thabit insisted on a number of conditions being satisfied before accepting any text as suitable for inclusion. They include the requirement that at least two reliable witnesses should testify that they had heard the same recital directly from the Prophet and the revelation was originally written down in His presence. Umar is known to have kept a complete copy of the revelations with his daughter Hafsah, who also happened to be one of the wives and then the widow of the Prophet Muhammad.

It is understood that the collected revelations with Hafsah were not the official codex in terms of arrangement and dialect or public circulation. Rather it was during the rule of Uthman (the third Rashidun Caliph) that a major drive started to compile a standardised copy. Again the task fell upon Zayd Bin Thabit. The traditional view is that along with Abdullah ibn Zubayr, Sa'd ibn al-As and Abdur Rahman bin al-Harith, the official codex was prepared from the copy kept with Hafsah bint Umar but in the dialect of the Prophet's tribe of Quraysh. Copies of this official codex were then sent to different corners of the expanding Islamic Ummah. Any other variant copies were ordered to be destroyed.

Given the increasingly turbulent rule of Uthman, one may ponder as to the extent to which all different versions were destroyed. It must be remembered that the collection and compilation of the Holy Qur'an was taking place in the backdrop of the numerous external wars the Rashidun Caliphs were engaged in, as well as, the growing internal tensions between Ali and his predecessors to the Caliphate and their supporters. What the internal schism boils down to is a struggle for power between the Prophet's blood family and His families through marriage. As explained to some depth in Chapter Four, the Islamic Ummah was expanding, rapidly bursting out of the confines of Mecca and Medina engulfing the entire Arab Peninsula and beyond. Consequently, those who supported Ali's claim to the Caliphate over Abu Bakr, Umar and Uthman allege that the mus-haf (collected revelations) not only differed in arrangement to Ali's own collection but also that the standardised copy produced by Ali's predecessors excluded all revelations with explicit references to the virtues of the Prophet's family. However, there is no evidence to suggest that when Ali became the fourth and final Rashidun Caliph, he took steps to impose his collection of the Holy Qur'an (if any).

The Holy Qur'an itself makes representations that Divine Providence will secure its authenticity. This is narrated in **Chapter 15, Al-Hijr, Verse 9**: *'Verily, We have sent down the Message and surely, We will guard it (from corruption).'*

In this context, the Holy Books of the Taurat (Torah) and the Injil (original Gospel) have subsequently been corrupted in the form of additions, subtractions and alternations to the original Text. The Uthmanic Codex has remained unaltered for the last fourteen hundred years.

MUHAMMAD AND REVELATION

While there are sensitivities and controversies surrounding Prophet Muhammad's role in relation to the revelations He received, nevertheless, the Holy Qur'an is a miracle attributed to Muhammad and the sign of His Prophethood. The nature and scope of this miracle is illustrated in **Chapter 29, Al-Ankabut, Verses 50-51** of the Holy Qur'an where it states: *'They say: 'Why have no Signs been sent down to him by his Lord?' Say, 'The Signs are indeed with ALLAH, and I am indeed a plain warner.' Do they not think it is enough that We have sent down to you the Scripture that is recited to them? Verily in it there is mercy and a Reminder to those who believe.'*

It goes without saying that the power of the written word is permanent and overcomes the constraints of time and place.

The Prophet Muhammad is understood to have said: '*Never once did I receive a revelation without thinking that my soul had been torn away from me.*' The process of revelation was an intensely exhaustive experience for the Prophet, both physically and mentally. Occasionally a great heaviness would fall upon Him, His face covered with sweat while His body would feel wrapped by convulsions. The revelations did not come easy to the Prophet. There are two competing views on the nature and modes of revelation.

The traditional view that is taught in most madrassahs (religious schools), particularly in the poorer developing countries, is that the Prophet Muhammad recited verbatim the verses as they were revealed to Him by the Angel Jibrail (Gabriel). The revelations would come to Him in a clear verbal form. The revelations were the words of ALLAH transmitted through the mouth of the Prophet Muhammad. This is supported by the fact that there is a clear distinction between the Prophet's own speech and the linguistic narrative in the Holy Qur'an. The Qur'anic revelations are eloquent par excellence, while it is inconceivable how the Prophet, who could neither read nor write, could produce such exquisite literary perfection. Its literary genre did not resemble any of the known poetic styles at the time or rhythmic prose for Arabic literature. Furthermore, matters dealt with by the Holy Qur'an in terms of science are revolutionary by the standards of prevailing scientific knowledge in 7th century Pagan Arabia. For instance, in **Chapter 21, Al-Anbiya, Verse 30,** the Holy Qur'an states: '*Do not the disbelievers see that the heavens and the earth were a closed-up mass, then We opened them out? And We made from water every living thing. Will they not then believe?*' That it is ALLAH and not the Prophet Muhammad who speaks through the Holy Qur'an is evidenced by the way many of the revelations are addressed to Muhammad often by name, some prefixed by the word 'Say!' with ALLAH addressing the Prophet Muhammad in the first person singular and plural.

The non-traditional view is that like the other three Rasuls, the Prophet Muhammad too had to struggle to make sense of the revelations, particularly so when they came upon Him not as dictated words but rather as visions or emotions. The Prophet described them as sometimes coming unto Him like the reverberations of a bell, and that was the hardest upon Him, the reverberations abating when He was aware of their meaning. Both these views are encased, nevertheless, in **Sahih Al-Bukhari, Volume 1, Book 1, Hadith Number 2:** *'Narrated by Aisha: Al-Hartih bin Hisham asked ALLAH's Messenger, 'O ALLAH's Messenger! How is the Divine Inspiration revealed to you?' ALLAH's Messenger replied, 'Sometimes it is (revealed) like the ringing of a bell, this form of inspiration is the hardest of all and then this state passes off after I have grasped what is inspired. Sometimes the Angel comes in the form of a man and talks to me and I grasp whatever he says.'*

It is worth noting that both views refer to a Divine Source of revelation. The revelations were therefore, not of the Prophet's own making, fabrication or forgery. This becomes clear from **Chapter 52, At-Tur, Verses 33–34** of the Holy Qur'an, where it states: *Or do they say: 'He (Muhammad) has forged it (this Qur'an)?' Nay! they have no faith! Let them then produce a recitation like unto it (the Qur'an) if they speak the truth!'*

And again in **Chapter 11, Hud, Verse 13** of the Holy Qur'an it mentions: *Or they say: 'He (Muhammad) forged it (the Qur'an).' Say: 'Bring you then ten forged Surah like unto it, and call (to your aid) whomsoever you can, other than ALLAH, if you speak the truth!'*

While in **Chapter 10, Yunus, Verses 37–38** the Holy Qur'an states: *'And this Qur'an is not such as could ever be produced in despite of ALLAH; but it is a confirmation of (the Revelations) which went before it, and an exposition of that which is decreed for mankind – wherein there is no doubt – from the Lord of the Worlds.' Or do they say: 'He Muhammad has forged it?' Say: Bring then a Surah like unto it, and call upon whomsoever you can besides ALLAH, if you are truthful.'*

In what can only be described as a compelling revelation, the Holy Qur'an, **Chapter 69, Al-Haqqah, Verses 41–52** clearly states: *'It is not the word of a poet, little it is ye believe! Nor is it the word of a soothsayer (or a foreteller), little it is ye remember! This is the Revelation sent down from the Lord of the Worlds. And if he (Muhammad) had forged a false saying concerning Us (ALLAH), We surely would have seized him by his right hand, And then We certainly would have cut* *off the artery of his heart, And none of you could have withheld Us from (punishing) him. But verily, this (Qur'an) is a Reminder for the God-fearing. And verily we know that there are some among you that belie (this Qur'an). And indeed this Qur'an will be a source of bitter regret for the disbelievers. And verily, this Qur'an is an absolute Truth with assured certainty. So glorify the name of they Lord, the Most Almighty.'*

That the Prophet Muhammad was Divinely inspired is further demonstrated in **Chapter 42, Ash-Shura, Verses 51–53** of the Holy Qur'an, which illustrates the modes of revelation: *'It is not granted to any human being that ALLAH should speak to him unless (it be) by inspiration, or from behind a veil, or that (He) sends a Messenger to reveal what He wills by His Leave. Verily, He is Most High, Most Wise. And thus We have sent to you (O Muhammad) Ruh (a revelation, and a mercy) of Our Command. You knew neither the Book nor the Faith? But we have made it (this Qur'an) a light, guiding with it whoever We will of Our servants. And verily, you (O Muhammad) are indeed guiding (mankind) to the Straight Path, the path of ALLAH, to whom belongs all that is in the heavens and all that is in the earth. Verily everything will return to ALLAH (for decision).'*

Divine inspiration is again evidenced from appreciating the processes of memorising, transmission and transcription of the Holy Qur'an as narrated in **Chapter 75, Al-Qiyamah, Verses 16–19**: *'Move not your tongue concerning (the Qur'an, O Muhammad) to make haste therewith (memorisation of the revelation). It is for Us to gather it (in your heart) and to give you (O Muhammad) the ability to recite it (the Qur'an). And when We have recited it to you (O Muhammad through Jibrail), then follow its (the Qur'an's) recitation. Then it is for Us (ALLAH) to make it clear (to you).*

Further explanation of the above verses is provided in **Sahih Al-Bukhari, Volume 1, Book 1, Hadith Number 5.** While in **Chapter 20, Ta Ha, Verse 114** it states: *'Exalted be ALLAH, the one who is truly in control. And be not in haste (O Muhammad) with the Qur'an before its revelation is completed to you, and say, 'My Lord! Cause me to grow in Knowledge.'*

THE HOLY QUR'AN AS A LIVING REVELATION

The Holy Qur'an occupies an unparalleled position to its reciters in comparison to other Divine Books. Madrassahs across the Muslim Ummah and beyond are churning out Hafize Qur'an (people who have committed to memory the entire Holy Qur'an) in their tens of thousands every year. Across several continents, more than a billion and half practising Muslims recite verses of the Holy Qur'an in their compulsory daily prayers. The Holy Qur'an is therefore, a living revelation, not restricted to the confines of a book kept in the mosques, madrassahs or homes of Muslims. Rather, it is the heart of the Ummah that beats life into the souls of all Muslims every time it is recited. All attempts, therefore, to undermine the Holy Qur'an are futile. They amount to no more than bigoted steps adopted by ignorant people with the malicious intent of provoking a violent response by deliberately attacking the sentiments of passionate young Muslims. The 'International Judge the Qur'an Day' was a travesty beyond any rational comprehension. It amounted to no more than bigoted theatrical rhetoric based on misinformation that had no meaningful substance. This followed the 'International Burn a Qur'an Day' sought to mark the ninth 9/11 anniversary. The 'accidental burning' of the Holy Qur'an at a US military base by US Forces stationed in Afghanistan as reported in February 2012 by various media platforms is regrettable. Previously, claims of the Holy Qur'an being desecrated by soldiers at Guantanamo Bay Prison as reported by different media streams in response to an inquiry that was sparked by a *Newsweek* magazine report (later retracted) that a Holy Qur'an was flushed down the toilet is equally deeply disturbing.

An inquiry led by the commander of the US detention centre at Guantanamo Bay, Brigadier General Jay Hood, reported back in 2005, finding five instances of intentional and unintentional mishandling of the Holy Qur'an by US guards at Guantanamo. For the ignorant, the Holy Qur'an is alleged to be a book of war, with Islam posing a political and military threat to free people throughout the world, particularly in the United States and Europe. Taking this forward, it is worrying to hear of reports that United States military officers were being taught a course at a staff training college in North Virginia to prepare for a 'total war' against Islam and using 'Hiroshima-style tactics' on Mecca and Medina. It is understood that the Pentagon suspended the above-mentioned course in April 2012 following an-uproar. We invite the sceptics to read the Divine Revelation setting aside their prejudices and try to comprehend its core message. Verses of the Holy Qur'an must be understood within the context of the Holy Qur'an as a whole and not in isolation in order to fit into a narrow or an extremist narrative.

As many European countries prepared to go to the polls in 2017, far-right candidates reportedly went on record saying that they would put a prohibition on the Holy Qur'an if voted into power. The Dutch Freedom Party (PVV) leader, Geert Wilders, for instance, vowed to ban the Qur'an if elected, comparing it to Hitler's *Mein Kampf*, as well as closing all mosques and putting an end to immigration from Islamic countries. His call for total 'de-islamification', one may argue, constitutes paranoia and amounts to 'islamophobia on steroids'. Such extremist narratives thrive on perpetuating division, mistrust and hatred.

CHAPTER TWO

The Five Pillars of Islam and the Seven Articles of Faith

The conception that there are five basic principles of the Islamic Faith was first conveyed in the Sahih Hadith Collections by Al-Bukhari. Narrated by Ibn Umar: *'ALLAH's Messenger said, 'Islam is based upon (the following) five (principles): They are the declaration of faith (Shahadah) to testify that none has the right to be worshipped but ALLAH and Muhammad is the Messenger of ALLAH; offering of the (compulsory) prayer (Salat) dutifully and perfectly; paying wealth tax (Zakat); performing the pilgrimage (Hajj), and fasting during the month of Ramadan (Sawm).* **(Sahih Al-Bukhari, Volume 1, Book 2, Hadith Number 7).**

These had come to be called the Five Pillars (Arkans) of Islam by the tenth century.

SHAHADAH

'La ilaha illal lahu muhammadur rasulul lah'
'There is no God but ALLAH, Muhammad is the messenger of ALLAH'

The Shahadah, otherwise referred to as the Declaration of Faith, has two aspects to it but one core theme. The first aspect requires Muslims to confirm their faith in the Unity and Oneness of ALLAH (Tawhid) (which has been discussed at some length in the Introduction). It declares the Monotheist doctrine of One God. Taking it from the Arabic: La means no; ilaha meaning God; illa meaning but; Lah meaning ALLAH. Importantly, the very basis of the Faith of Islam is expressed with a negative in defiance of Shirk (associating partners to ALLAH). All the Messengers of ALLAH have conveyed the message of Tawhid. The Holy Qur'an states this in **Chapter 21, Al-Anbiya, Verse 25:** *'And We did not send any Messenger before you (O Muhammad) without revealing to him: None has the right to be worshiped but I ALLAH, so worship Me (alone and none else).'*

Shirk is an unforgivable sin. This is narrated in **Chapter 4, An-Nisa, Verse 48** of the Holy Qur'an: *'Verily, ALLAH forgives not that partners should be set up with Him (in worship), anything less than that He forgives to whoever He will, but whoever sets up partners with ALLAH in worship, he has indeed invented a tremendous sin.'*

The second aspect relates to Risalah and confirms Muhammad's Prophetic mission as the Messenger of ALLAH to whom was revealed the last of the Divine Revelations in the form of the Holy Qur'an. The Prophet Muhammad was not sent to any particular nation or community but to all mankind and for all time. In **Chapter 34, Sabah, Verse 28** of the Holy Qur'an it states: *'And We have not sent you (O Muhammad) except as a giver of glad tidings and a warner to all mankind, but most men know not.'*

The Prophet Muhammad is proclaimed by ALLAH as 'Khatam-an-Nabiyyin' (the last of the chain of the true Prophets). With Him, Prophethood came to an end. No other Prophet will come after Him. This is narrated in the Holy Qur'an in **Chapter 33, Al-Ahzab, Verse 40:** *'Muhammad is not the father of any one of you men; but he is the Messenger of ALLAH and the last (end) of the prophets. And ALLAH is Ever All-Aware of everything.'*

One simple sentence, yet the Shahadah stirs the soul of every believing Muslim. So tremendous is its effect when truly understood and appreciated that the early Muslims accepted martyrdom in face of persecution from the rulers of Mecca yet still would not renounce the Shahadah. Pronunciation of the Shahadah in Arabic with intent (with knowledge of its meaning), before two qualified witnesses, is all that is formally required to become a Muslim. A qualified witness does not involve going to some Imam, Ulama (religious scholar) or so-called pir (spiritual preacher) for that matter. Any Muslim who has taken the oath him/herself can stand as witness for another who wishes to enter the fold of Islam. The religion of Islam, like the true tenets of Judaism and Christianity, does not cater for pomp or ceremony. Islam is a practical down to earth religion that invites humanity through 'da'wah' (invitation) to embrace the religion of Islam. Every day during the Adhan (Call to Prayer), the Shahadah rings out across the Muslim Ummah to which Muslims respond by offering their Salat thereby reaffirming their Declaration of the Faith. The central theme of the Shahadah is therefore Unity of Faith in the religion of Islam.

SALAT

Central to the Faith of Islam is the Salat, ie the observance of the compulsory five daily prayers with due care and attention. It is the second pillar of Islam. There is no necessity to take the assistance of spiritual intermediaries to offer the Salat. It can be offered alone in the confines of the home. All religions, monotheist or not, have a pattern of ritual prayer. In Islam it takes the form of Salat.

Having said this, the prime importance of Salat is that it brings the community together when offered in congregation (Salat al-Jama'ah), be it at the local mosque or other religious meeting/gathering place. When offering Salat; irrespective of race, class or wealth, all stand shoulder to shoulder, united in their worship of ALLAH. The Imam (one who leads the congregational prayers at the mosque) is only the first among equals. Prayers held in congregation provide unity and strength to Muslims. The daily prayers are preceded by the Adhan (Call to Prayer). Facing towards

Mecca, the Muazzin (nominated person in the mosque who makes the call to prayer) calls out to the locality that it is time to offer Salat at the mosque. In Muslim majority countries 5 times a day the call for Salat (Adhan) rings out across the cities, towns and villages inviting Muslims to offer their prayers. The structure of the Adhan is in the following chronological order: 'ALLAH is the Greatest' (4 times); 'I bear true witness that there is no God but ALLAH (2 times); 'I bear true witness that Muhammad is the Messenger of ALLAH' (2 times); 'Come for Prayer' (2 times); 'Come for Salvation' (2 times); 'ALLAH is the Greatest' (2 times); 'There is no God but ALLAH (1 time). During the early morning/ Fajr prayers, 'Prayer is better than sleep' is narrated twice before 'ALLAH is the Greatest' towards the end of the Adhan. The five daily prayers have prescribed times that should be adhered to. To this effect the Holy Qur'an states in **Chapter 4, An-Nisa, Verse 103:** *'After performing the ritual prayer, continue to remember ALLAH, standing, sitting and reclining. And when ye are in safety, observe proper prayer. Prayer is obligatory for the believers at fixed hours.'*

The names and times of the five daily prayers are as follows. The first is the Fajr (early morning) prayers, which commences after the break of dawn and ends before sunrise. The prayer is made up of 2 raka'ats pre-farz sunnat and 2 raka'ats farz prayers. Then comes the Zuhr (early afternoon) prayers. This prayer must be offered after midday until afternoon. This Salat is made up of 4 raka'ats pre-farz sunnat, 4 raka'ats farz, 2 raka'at post-farz sunnat and 2 raka'at nafl prayers. Following on, then comes Asr (late afternoon) prayers. It commences after the end of the time for Zuhr prayers until before sunset. The prayer is made up of 4 raka'ats pre-farz sunnat and 4 raka'at farz prayers. After that come the Maghrib (evening) prayers. The time for this prayer starts immediately after sunset and ends on the fading of twilight. Relative to the other Salat the time duration to offer the Maghrib prayers is short. The prayer consists of 3 raka'at farz prayers, 2 raka'at post-farz sunnat and 2 raka'at nafl prayers. The last prayer of the day is the Isha (early night) prayer. This commences after the fading of twilight and ends before the following dawn but is preferred to be offered before midnight. This prayer consists of 4 raka'ats pre-farz sunnat, 4 raka'ats farz, 2 raka'ats post-farz sunnat, 2 raka'at nafl and 3 raka'at witr prayers.

The raka'at refers to a unit of prayer. The farz raka'ats are compulsory to the performance of the Salat. The sunnat raka'ats are optional but are preferred, though some religious schools differ on the question of offering sunnat prayers. Though strong emphasis is placed on Jama'ah Prayers; Muslims can, nevertheless, perform the five daily prayers on their own on a clean surface, but similar to congregational prayers always facing in the direction of the Ka'bah in Mecca. Muslims must approach the five daily prayers in a state of physical cleanliness. This is achieved through the performance of ablution. In addition to the compulsory five daily prayers there is Salatul Jum'ah or 'Friday Prayers' that are held in congregation.

ZAKAT

Like Salat, the Zakat too is an act of worship and obedience – a form of 'Ibadah'. The Zakat can more aptly be described as an annual wealth tax rather than charity. It is the rightful claim of the poor against the rich. It is obligatory upon all Muslims to pay the Zakat who fall within the parameters of wealth specified in various Hadith. The importance of Zakat can be grasped from the following Hadith. Narrated by Abu Ma'bad in **Sahih Bukhari, Volume 2, Book 24, Hadith 573**: *ALLAH'S Apostle said to Muadh when he sent him to Yemen, 'You will go to the people of the Scripture. So, when you reach there, invite them to testify that none has the right to be worshipped but ALLAH, and that Muhammad is His Apostle. And if they obey you in that, tell them that ALLAH has enjoined on them five prayers in each day and night. And if they obey you in that tell them ALLAH has made it obligatory on them to pay the Zakat which will be taken from the rich among them and given to the poor among them. If they obey you in that, then avoid taking the best of their possessions, and be afraid of the curse of an oppressed person because there is no screen between his invocation and ALLAH.'*

The concentration and hoarding of wealth in the hands of a few where the majority live in abject poverty is not representative of an Islamic society. Dire consequences lie in wait for those who do so. This is emphasised in **Chapter 3, Al-Imran, Verse 180** of the Holy Qur'an: *'And not let those who hoard up that which ALLAH has bestowed upon them of His bounty think that it is good for them. Nay, it is worse for them. That which they hoard will be hung around their necks on the Day of Resurrection. ALLAH's is the heritage of the heavens and the earth: ALLAH is well aware of everything you do.'*

The frantic pursuit and hoarding of wealth is forbidden in Islam. This is emphasised in **Chapter 9, At-Taubah, Verse 34** of the Holy Qur'an: *'They who hoard up gold and silver and spend it not in the way of ALLAH, unto them give tidings (O Muhammad) of a painful doom.'*

In the modern context, gold and silver logically it refers to cash in all its manifestations and to land and property, amongst other things.

The Zakat in reality operates as a welfare tax, whereby the well-to-do are encouraged to voluntarily give to the poor. For the most part Zakat is distributed in the month of Ramadan. It is also obligatory on all Muslims on whom Zakat is compulsory to pay Zakat-ul-fitr on the completion of Ramadan but definitely before the Eid-ul-Fitr prayers. This is narrated by Ibn Umar in **Sahih Bukhari, Volume 2, Book 25, Hadith 585**: *'The Prophet ordered the people to pay Zakat-ul-Fitr before going to the Eid Prayer.'*

In addition to Zakat, Muslims who can afford to should also give charity, called 'Sadaqa'. Furthermore, any personal financial contribution in the way of Islam through the establishments of mosques or madrassahs for instance, though encouraged, is nevertheless, entirely voluntary.

HAJJ

Every Muslim of every nationality yearns to make the pilgrimage to Mecca (perform the Hajj) at least once in their lifetime in spiritual fulfilment of their duty to ALLAH and in observance of one of the Five Pillars of Islam. This is narrated in **Chapter 3, Al-Imran, Verses 96-97** of the Holy Qur'an: *'Verily, the first House* *(of worship) appointed for mankind was that at Mecca, full of blessing, and a guidance for all mankind. In it are manifest signs of ALLAH's guidance; the place where Ibrahim stood up to pray; And whosoever enters it, he attains security. Pilgrimage to the House is a duty mankind owes to ALLAH, -those who can afford the journey. Whosoever disbelieves, (let him know) Lo! ALLAH stands not in need of any of His creatures.'*

The Hajj is performed in the twelfth lunar month of the Islamic Calendar between the eight and thirteenth Dhu'l Hijjah. The climax of the Hajj is offering prayers on the plains of Arafat. Muslims believe that it is on this plain that Adam and Eve were reunited and Adam made his covenant with ALLAH. Again the Prophet Muhammad delivered His Farewell Sermon prior to his death from a hillock on the plains of Arafat. It is also where the Prophet Muhammad received the final revelation. The tenth Dhu'l Hijjah marks Eid-ul-Adhar, which is observed across the Globe by Muslims in remembrance of Prophet Ibrahim (Abraham) who was prepared to sacrifice his first and at the time only son – Isma'il (Ishmael) on the command of ALLAH in a trial of faith.

Through the Hajj all Muslims reaffirm their support in the unity and indivisibility of the Ummah. Irrespective of race, sex or class all pilgrims (between 2-3 million of them) clothed in white assemble for one sole purpose: the worship of the one true God. Among the main Hajj rituals it involves the Tawaf (circumbulation) of the Ka'bah. The Ka'bah, situated in the al-Masjid al-Haram (the sacred mosque) serves as the spiritual focal point of Islam. It was through the destruction of the idols housed in the Ka'bah when Muslim forces conquered Mecca under the leadership of the Prophet Muhammad in the month of Ramadan, 8 Al-Hijri (630 AD) that Islam really took hold in Arabia paving the way for the spread of Islam. The triumph over Mecca is referred to as Fateh-e-Mubeen, 'The Glorious Victory'.

SAWM

The Holy Qur'an prescribes for all Muslims, irrespective of race, colour or social standing, fasting in the month of Ramadan, which is the ninth lunar month of the Islamic Calendar. Subject to the sighting of the Crescent Moon, Ramadan may last for 29 or 30 calendar days. From dawn till dusk able Muslim men and women abstain from food, drink and conjugal relations. The Fast is intended to act as a 'spiritual cleansing' of the physical body and mind. During this month Muslims resign themselves to contemplating in the Divine in submission to ALLAH. Sawm helps to develop taqwa (fear of ALLAH), ie self-restraint to overcome worldly desires and evil indulgences drawing oneself nearer to ALLAH. This is narrated in **Chapter 2, Al Baqarah, Verse 183** of the Holy Qur'an: *'O ye who believe. Fasting is prescribed for you, as it was prescribed before you, so that you may ward off evil.'*

Observing Sawm in the month of Ramadan was specifically mentioned by the Prophet Muhammad in his Farewell Sermon.

The sick are explicitly exempt from fasting during Ramadan. So are travellers making a journey in that month, but they must make up for it later in the year. Infants are not required to fast. This is mentioned in **Chapter 2, Al Baqarah, Verse 185** of the Holy Qur'an: *'The month of Ramadan in which was revealed the Quran, a guidance for mankind, and clear proofs of the guidance, and the Criterion (of right and wrong). And whosoever of you is present, let him fast the month, and whosoever of you is sick or on a journey, (let him fast the same) number from other days. ALLAH desireth of you ease; He desireth not hardship for you; and (He desireth) that you should complete the prescribed period, and that ye should magnify ALLAH for having guided you, so that ye may be thankful.'*

The breaking of the daily fast after sunset with family and friends followed by the offering of Maghrib prayers is an important highlight of Ramadan. Devotees also perform Tarawih prayers, in addition to the Isha prayers where very often chapters of the Holy Qur'an are recited. These prayers are usually held in congregations at local mosques, so Ramadan serves to unite Muslims in a common enterprise, achieving a renewed sense of brotherhood and community spirit. The prominence Muslims attach to the Fast is exemplified in the following prayer that is commonly recited when breaking the Fast: *'O ALLAH! I fasted for Thee and I believe in Thee and I put my trust in Thee and with the sustenance Thou hast given me, I now break the fast.'*

The month of Ramadan concludes with the celebration of Eid-ul-Fitr. The significance of this day is the Eid-ul-Fitr prayers being offered at mosques across the Muslim Ummah that are usually held in the mornings and in congregation. All Heads of State and Heads of Government of every Muslim majority state will also offer these prayers in congregation. Muslims will exchange Eid greetings with one another and visit family and friends putting aside differences. The Eid therefore, serves to cement bonds of brotherhood and friendship.

The month of Ramadan is of immense significance in the hearts and minds of Muslims. It was during this month on the night termed 'Lailatul Qadr' (Night of Power) that the Holy Qur'an was first revealed to the Prophet Muhammad marking the beginning of His Prophetic mission. It was also during Ramadan that Mecca was conquered under the leadership of the Prophet Muhammad whereby the Ka'bah was cleansed of idols. Consequently, idol worship was banished and Arabia liberated itself from pagan worship.

It is clear that the Five Pillars of Islam have one underlying theme at their core, namely unity of the Muslim Ummah in submission to the worship of the one true GOD. While the First Pillar relates to Shahadah, ie declaration of faith in Tawhid and the Risalah of Muhammad the remaining Four Pillars relate to Ibadah, ie actions performed to gain ALLAH's favour.

SEVEN ARTICLES OF FAITH

Complementing the Five Pillars of Islam are the Seven Articles of Faith. In expressing their faith in the Shahadah (Declaration of Faith) it is imperative for Muslims to profess their belief in the Seven Articles of Faith. This Declaration of Faith is narrated in **Al-Imanul Mufassal** as follows: *'I believe in Allah, in His angels, in His books, in His messengers, in the Last Day [Day of Judgement] and in the fact that everything good or bad is decided by Allah the Almighty, and* *in the life-after-death.'* Its importance is illustrated in **Chapter 5, Al–Ma'idah, Verse 5** where it states, *'…And whosoever disbelieves in the Oneness of ALLAH and in the other Articles of Faith, then fruitless is his work, and in the Hereafter he will be among the losers.'*

BELIEF IN THE ONENESS OF ALLAH

Belief in the oneness and unity of ALLAH invokes the doctrine of Tawhid, which has been discussed at some length earlier in the introduction. Muslims believe that there is no God but ALLAH and all worship is due to ALLAH alone. Muslims do not associate partners with ALLAH for that is shirk (an unpardonable sin).

BELIEF IN THE ANGELS OF ALLAH

Muslims are required to believe in the angels of ALLAH. They are created from Nur (Divine Light) for the purpose of serving ALLAH, with the vast majority of them being tasked with specific functions. Man, on the other hand, is created from clay and has been given free will unlike the angels. The Jinn are created from smokeless fire, including Iblis (the Devil). It is commonly misunderstood that Iblis was an angel himself and their leader. On the contrary, Iblis was the most prominent among the Jinn who fell from ALLAH's Grace after failing to prostrate before Adam on ALLAH's command and therefore, banished from Heaven. This is narrated in **Chapter 18, Al–Kahf, Verse 50**: *'Behold! We said to the angels, 'Prostrate To Adam': they prostrated except Iblis, He was one of the Jinns, and he broke the Command Of his Lord. Will ye then take him and his progeny as protectors Rather than Me? And they are enemies to you! Evil would be the exchange for the wrong-doers!'*

Again in **Chapter 7, Al–A'raf Verses 12–18** it states: *'(ALLAH) said: 'What prevented thee (Iblis) from prostrating when I commanded thee?' He said: 'I am better than he: Thou didst create me from fire, and him from clay'. ALLAH said: 'Get thee down hence, it is not for thee to be arrogant here: get out, for thou art of the meanest (of creatures).' He (Iblis) said: 'Give me respite till the day they are raised up.' ALLAH said: 'Be thou among those who have respite.' He (Iblis) said:*

'Because thou hast thrown me out, lo I will lie in wait for them on Thy Straight Way: 'Then will I assault them from before them and behind them, from their right and their left: Nor wilt Thou find, in most of them, Gratitude (for Thy mercies).' ALLAH said: 'Get out from this, despised and expelled. If any of them follow thee,- Hell will I fill with you all.'

Prominent among the angels is Jibra'il (Gabriel) who is the Archangel and brought the revelation from ALLAH to Muhammad and the other Rasuls (Messengers). Another important angel is Azra'il, also known as Malakul Mawt (angel of death) and is responsible for ending our life on earth by removing our souls from our physical bodies. Again there is the angel Israfil, who is tasked with the job of blowing the trumpet at the end of time that will herald in the Day of Judgement. Having no free will, angels are incapable of committing sin. Jinn similar to Man, on the other hand, are capable of free will to choose between good and evil. They are tempted to commit sin through the evil whispers of Iblis and his minions. Both Man and Jinn therefore, seek refuge with ALLAH to overcome these evil temptations. This is narrated in **Chapter 114** of the Holy Qur'an: *'Say I seek refuge in the Lord of Mankind, The King of mankind, The God of mankind, From the evil of the sneaking whispherer, who whisphereth in the hearts of mankind, of the jinn and of mankind.'*

BELIEF IN THE DIVINE REVELATIONS

This Article of Faith requires Muslims to believe in all the Divine revelations, ie the Tawrat (Torah) revealed to the Prophet Musa (Moses); the Zabur (Psalms) revealed to the Prophet Dawud (David); the Injil (the original Gospel) revealed to the Prophet Isa (Jesus); and the Qur'an, revealed to the final Prophet and Messenger Muhammad. However, the Divine revelations preceding the Holy Qur'an are believed by Muslims to have been lost, corrupted, forgotten, neglected and even concealed by vested interests, whether it was for the furtherance of political ambition or religious orthodoxy. The Uthmanic Codex, on the other hand, has remained unaltered for the last fourteen hundred years, being compiled within only 20 years of the Prophet Muhammad's death. In Islam the Holy Qur'an therefore, takes precedence over the preceding Divine Texts to the extent of any inconsistencies between them.

BELIEF IN THE MESSENGERS OF ALLAH

As a part of their Faith, Muslims must believe in all the Prophets and Messengers of ALLAH. The Holy Qur'an mentions 25 of the most prominent Prophets by name. ALLAH has sent Prophets and Messengers to all nations at different times. This is narrated in **Chapter 10, Yunus, Verse 47** of the Holy Qur'an where it states: *'To every nation (was sent) a Messenger: when their Messenger comes (before them), the matter will be judged between them with Justice, and they will not be wronged.'*

It must be reiterated that the Prophet Muhammad was sent to all mankind and is the last prophet and messenger till the end of time. Muhammad is proclaimed by ALLAH as the last of the chain of the true Prophets, 'Khatam-an-Nabiyyin'. All the Prophets preached worship and submission to the one true God. Four of the prophets mentioned in the Holy Qur'an were sent with books of guidance. As mentioned above they are the Prophet Musa (Moses); the Prophet Dawud (David); the Prophet Isa (Jesus) and the final Prophet and Messenger Muhammad. It must be emphasised that from the point of view that Jews, Christians and Muslims believe in true monotheism they are brothers in Faith.

BELIEF IN THE DAY OF JUDGEMENT

Muslims are required to believe in the Day of Judgment. It is when all mankind will stand before their Lord in judgement for their actions on earth. This is stated in **Chapter 83, Al-Mutaffifinn, Verse 6**: *'The day when (all) mankind stand before the Lord of the Worlds.'*

Everyone will be judged on their each and every action as narrated in Chapter **99, Az-Zalzalah, Verses 7-8**: *'And whoso doeth good an atom's weight will see it then, and whoso doeth ill an atom's weight will see it then.'*

ALLAH warns mankind in **Chapter 82, Al-Infitar, Verse 19** that the Day of Judgment will belong to ALLAH alone. Mankind will be helpless that Day: *'A day on which no soul hath power at all for any (other) soul. The (absolute) command on that day is ALLAH's.'*

A study of Chapters 83 and 84 of the Holy Qur'an also gives further insight into the Day of Reckoning. Everything we do in this worldly life, every intention we have, every thought we entertain, and every word we say, are all recorded. On the Day of Judgment they will be revealed. People with good records will be generously rewarded and warmly welcomed to the Heaven of God, and those with bad records will be punished and cast into Hellfire.

BELIEF IN LIFE AFTER DEATH

The belief that there is life after death forms the cornerstone of all the three monotheist religions, for upon this belief hinges the concept of Heaven and Hell, ie reward and punishment for one's actions on earth. Throughout the ages, Prophets and Messengers have been sent inviting people to Paradise and warning them against giving in to evil indulgences that lead to Hellfire. Closely intertwined with the Islamic belief of life after death is the fact that all mankind will stand in judgement before ALLAH. Belief in an afterlife gives respite to those who fear ALLAH and observe the religious tenets of Islam, especially those who are oppressed and persecuted. For the Godfearing, the belief that life on earth is temporary and life after death is eternal provides solace to the soul. It should not, however, form the basis of satisfying oneself with a sense of revenge against the evildoers. As Muslims it is our duty to invite the wrongdoers to the path of Islam rather than be complaisant to their actions, eager that they will end up in Hellfire.

BELIEF IN PREDESTINATION

Referred to as Al-Qadr, predestination requires all Muslims to believe that events take place according to the exact Knowledge of ALLAH. They include the creation of our known Universe with the single command: 'Be!' as well as the destiny of mankind. Everything that has resulted from that 'Act of Creation' is within the realm of Divine Knowledge and control. In the Holy Qur'an in **Chapter 5, Al-Ma'idah, Verse 120** it clearly states, '*Unto ALLAH belongeth the Sovereignty of the Heavens and the Earth and whatever lies therein and He is able to do all things*'. ALLAH has also given mankind free will to make choices and decisions, but these are limited to our finite nature. Some view this article of predestination as defeatist, implying that the poor in society must accept their station in life as fate. But this is a misinterpretation. ALLAH has given humanity vast opportunities to realise its full potential, but it is our mismanagement of resources that has led to disparity of wealth

According to a report published by Oxfam in January 2016 titled, 'An Economy for the 1%', ahead of the annual World Economic Forum meeting at Davos in Switzerland, the accumulated wealth of the richest 1% will soon equal the rest of the 99% of the global population. While the richest 62 billionaires have the same wealth as the poorest 50% of the world population (more than 3.6 billion people), and 700 million people still live on less than two dollars a day. Add to this the concentration and hoarding of wealth by oppressive despots and dynastic rulers and we need to re-evaluate the causes of global poverty. A proper living wage for all workers was one of the points raised by the Oxfam report, as well as ending the global network of offshore tax heavens used by wealthy individuals and companies, allowing them to hide an estimated 7.6 trillion dollars. It is argued that this global system of tax avoidance through lost tax revenues denies poorer countries the resources they need to tackle poverty. If we take Africa for example, the report highlighted that almost a third of rich Africans' wealth, a total of 500 billion dollars, is held offshore in tax heavens which costs African countries 14 billion dollars a year in uncollected tax revenues. Though the report findings have been criticised we cannot escape the fact that the rising tide of inequality has been breathtaking. The increasing use of foodbanks across the EU for instance, with children going to school hungry and pensioners making the painful choice of whether to purchase food or put the heating on during winter months, is a matter of grave concern. The desperate poverty in rural China, Pakistan, Bangladesh and India, which by 2050 will command a third of the global population, is surely eye opening. War-torn and drought-stricken countries in Africa and failed states of the Middle East add to the desperate plight of humanity. With the world population projected to reach around 8.3 billion by 2030, the impact of climate change on weather patterns, which is likely to affect harvests, will impact heavily on people living in rural communities who rely heavily on agriculture for their livelihoods.

CHAPTER THREE

Muhammad – 'the Seal of the Prophets'

You may be forgiven for thinking that the Prophet Muhammad was a myth, such was the grand scale of His many achievements and personal attributes. Surely He was a man, but no ordinary man. His persona eclipses the likes of Alexander the Great in terms of military genius and the likes of Aristotle in terms of wisdom. He was an unparalleled social reformer, an intense lover and devoted father. This chapter reflects on the personal pains and stresses Muhammad endured in His early years and some of the momentous events that mark His Prophethood. I have also briefly touched upon the significance of the Prophet's Ahadith and the controversy surrounding their collection.

MUHAMMAD'S EARLY YEARS

To describe the Prophet Muhammad's early life as tragic is an understatement, but Muslims must accept this as the will of ALLAH and part of ALLAH's scheme of things in His grand design. Muhammad was born in Mecca into the powerful tribe of the Quraysh in the year 570 AD. His father Abdullah, son of Abd al-Muttalib, died when Muhammad was still in His mother's womb. Muhammad's mother, Aminah bint Wahb, died when He was only six years old. Muhammad was therefore orphaned at a very early age and deprived of the love and affection of His parents.

A few years after His birth and during the lifetime of His mother Aminah, Muhammad was entrusted to a Bedouin foster-mother, Halimah al-Sa'diyyah, it being the custom then of Arab tribes such as the Quraysh to have their new-born babies cared for and nursed by foster mothers. Tradition has it that during His stay with His foster parents the young Muhammad while playing with his foster brothers was seized upon by two Angels who appeared as men in white, who cleansed His heart with what appeared to be snow. The spiritual message conveyed by this incident is that Muhammad was destined to be no ordinary man but the Beloved of ALLAH, chosen to convey the Divine Message to humanity till eternity.

Following the death of His mother, His paternal grandfather, Abd al-Muttalib of the Hashimite Clan and a leading figure in Mecca, cared for Muhammad. But Abd al-Muttalib soon passed away and it was Muhammad's uncle and later protector, Abu Talib, who reared Him to adulthood. Abu Talib was a respected leader of the Quraysh and a successful merchant, but more significantly he was the father of Ali (Muhammad's son-in-law and the fourth Rashidun Caliph).

In addition to being a shepherd boy minding sheep, Muhammad at the age of 12 accompanied His uncle on a trade journey to Syria. This trip is viewed with significance as Islamic tradition holds that during this trip a Nestorian Monk called Bahirah, based on his keen observation of the young boy, predicted that Muhammad was going to be a prophet in the future. Islamic tradition therefore holds out that during Muhammad's early years there were indications that Muhammad was destined to lead an extraordinary life.

In Mecca as a young man, Muhammad was known as al-Amin, 'the trustworthy'. He inspired confidence in others due to his sincerity, honesty, integrity and strength of character. It was because of these personal attributes that Muhammad, then aged

25, was called upon by a wealthy female merchant named Khadijah bint al-Khuwaylid to take a caravan to Syria. This would result in a dramatic turn of events for Muhammad, not only for His personal life but also for His Prophetic mission. So impressed was Khadijah with Muhammad's commission and the reports from her manservant Maysara, who accompanied Muhammad on the expedition, that she proposed marriage to Him. This Muhammad accepted. Khadijah was older than Muhammad at the time of the marriage; tradition has it 15 years older. She was a widower having lost two previous husbands. But she was intelligent, wealthy and loved Muhammad not least for His reputation in Mecca, but also by His good character and truthfulness.

They had six children together, two sons, Qasim and Abdullah (both of whom died in infancy) as well as four daughters, including Fatimah, who married Ali; they became the proud parents of Hasan and Husayn. (In the second civil war that engulfed the Caliphate, Husayn and his family were murdered at Karbala.) Muhammad's marriage to Khadijah was not intended by Him to be one of economic convenience. Far from it, Muhammad made no personal gain for Himself from Khadijah's wealth but instead gave alms to the poor from the family income and continued to be a merchant, leading a simple life.

Muhammad never remarried while Khadijah was still alive. He was a devoted husband and a loving father to His children. The Prophet Muhammad was no sexual predator, as has been alleged over the years by extreme right-wing opponents and some feminist groups.

As years went by, Muhammad's standing in Mecca steadily grew, and He was often called upon to arbitrate in matters of dispute. On one such occasion, prior to His Prophethood, Muhammad's prowess would come to light. With the Ka'bah falling into a state disrepair, the Quraysh had taken the decision to rebuild portions of it. However, soon bitter infighting developed among the Clans, threatening to break the fragile unity of the Quraysh about which Clan should have the honour of positioning the Black Stone. (Tradition has it that initially the Stone was white and had been sent down to Earth as a gift/sign from Heaven.) Muhammad, then in his mid-thirties, was called to arbitrate. Considering the context of the situation, in what can be described as nothing short of brilliance, Muhammad advised that the Black Stone should be placed in the centre of a cloak with a representative of each Clan holding the edges of the cloak and jointly lifting the Stone into place. This solution preserved the unity of the Clans in this noble enterprise.

Despite the modest comforts of His normal everyday life, Muhammad became increasingly disturbed by the malaise in Mecca, with its idol worship, prevailing social injustice, economic exploitation, disparity of wealth and self-destructing tribal feuds. This state of affairs is referred to as Jahiliyyah (pre-Islamic ignorance). Muhammad would seek answers to this chaos by resorting to mountain retreats. It was during one of these retreats in the month of Ramadan, in around 610 AD, that Muhammad then aged forty, underwent an extraordinary experience that marked the first of a series of Divine Revelations that continued for the next 23 years of His Prophetic life, culminating in the Holy Qur'an. (This is discussed in more detail in Chapter 1).

There was nothing new about the revelations received by Prophet Muhammad. The Holy Qur'an confirms the Holy Books that preceded it namely, the Zabur (Psalms) revealed to Prophet Dawud (David), the Tawrat (Torah) revealed to Prophet Musa (Moses) and the Injil (the original Gospel) revealed to Prophet Isa (Jesus). The monotheist religions have one central theme at their core: the worship of the one true God. The Holy Qur'an does, however, disassociate itself from the subsequent corruption and distortions that later found their way into the preceding Revealed Books as narrated in **Chapter 5, Al-Ma'idah, Verses 13–16**: *'Because they broke their Covenant, so We distanced them (from Us) and hardened their hearts. They distort the meaning of the (revealed) words and have forgotten some of what they were told to remember; you (Prophet) will always find treachery in all but a few of them. Overlook this and pardon them: ALLAH loves those who are kind. We also took a Covenant from those who say, 'We are Christians,' But they too forgot some of what they were told to remember, so We stirred up enmity and hatred among them until the Day of Resurrection, when ALLAH will* *tell them what they have done. People of the Book! Our Messenger has come to make clear to you much of what you have kept hidden of the Scripture, and to overlook much [you have done]. A light has now come to you from ALLAH, and a Scripture making things clear, with which ALLAH guides to the ways of peace those who follow what pleases Him, bringing them from darkness out into light, by His will, and guiding them to a straight path.'*

The Divine Texts preceding the Holy Qur'an were compromised to further the political and religious establishments that later followed. While it is universally accepted that the Revealed Texts preceding the Holy Qur'an were Divinely inspired, it is equally accepted by religious scholars of different religious persuasions that human intervention is clearly apparent. This is evident by the numerous variants in the Bible that were found across Christendom throughout the ages. The 'Reformation' in Europe was essentially a response to Catholic religious orthodoxy/bigotry of the time. Up until the 16th century the Bible was only found in its Latin, Greek and Hebrew translations which were the exclusive monopoly of the European religious establishments. Following the Reformation, the Bible was translated into native languages but then its dissemination was controlled by the political establishment of their time.

THE BATTLE OF BADR: A DECISIVE VICTORY

Incensed by the increasing number of converts to Islam and consequently, the threat the Prophet Muhammad posed to the Meccan socio-political order, Muslims were increasingly being persecuted by the ruling elite in Mecca. The vast majority of them had no choice but to escape, literally with their lives. In their haste they were forced to leave behind much of their wealth and possessions. The Prophet and His Sahabah (closest companions) were among the last to make their escape. They chose to migrate to the city of Yathrib (later renamed Medinah–tun–Nabi or Medina). Their decision to migrate was inspired by the second Pledge of Aqaba made in 622 AD. This flight from persecution is referred to as the Hijrah.

In turn the ruling Quraysh in Mecca confiscated the belongings that the Muslims had left behind. This inevitably caused resentment among the exiled Muslims against their former Meccan rulers. But then Medina was strategically placed on the caravan-trading route between Mecca and Syria, and Mecca was desperate to secure her trading routes. Discontent was at boiling point. Full-scale armed engagement was inevitable. But the Prophet Muhammad refrained from armed attack. This stance He maintained until He received a revelation invoking Muslims permission to fight. This is narrated in **Chapter 22, Al-Hajj, Verse 39:** *'To those against whom war is made, sanction is given (to fight), because they have been wronged: – And verily, ALLAH is indeed able to give them victory.'*

It must be emphasised here that the Prophet was not a man who actively sought bloodshed. He was not a man of the sword, as some right-wing propagandists, or for that matter so-called Islamic extremists, have made the Prophet out to be. Far from it, during the 10-plus years the Prophet preached in Mecca, Muslims were forbidden to fight their Meccan persecutors despite the many transgressions directed against the Muslim community. Armed strife with the Meccans from within Mecca would definitely have meant annihilation for the small community of Muslims.

Forced into exile along with His many fellow Muslims, the Prophet changed tack. He now had permission to fight in the cause of ALLAH. As events unfolded, the Prophet Muhammad proved to be a brilliant strategist. He seized the initiative to bring the trading routes to and from Mecca under His control. To impress the message to the Meccan rulers that trade caravans passing near Medina now faced serious danger, the Prophet dispatched raiding parties periodically to ambush caravans travelling along the main commercial trading routes in and out of Mecca.

As chance would have it, in 624 AD, a large caravan was making its way from Syria to Mecca headed by Abu Sufyan. He was Chief of the Banu Abd-Shams Clan of the Quraysh tribe, making him one of the most powerful rulers of Mecca. A small force of only 313 ill-equipped Muslims set out to meet the caravan under the command of the Prophet Muhammad. They camped at the wells of Badr. Fearing an attack from the Muslims, Abu Sufyan sent message to Mecca to come to his aid. The Meccans rulers responded by assembling a large fighting force of more than 1000 well-equipped men, including 100 horses and a large number of camels. They began their march to Badr.

In the meantime, Abu Sufyan changed the route of his caravan to put it out of reach of the Muslims. He then sent message that the trade caravan was safe and advised that the Meccan force should return back. Those commanding the force refused to accept this advice, for this was their opportunity to crush the Muslims once and for all and they would do so in battle, or so they thought, particularly Abu Jahl, who was among the prominent leaders of Mecca. He viewed this as an opportunity to consolidate his position in Mecca as the ruler who subdued the Muslims. But as it transpired, they all underestimated the religious zeal of the Muslim force.

As regards the two ill-matched forces, the Holy Qur'an narrates this in **Chapter 3, Al-Imran, Verse 13**: *'There has already been for you a Sign in the two armies that met (in combat); One army was fighting in the Cause of ALLAH; and the other made up of disbelievers. With their own eyes (the former) saw (the latter) to be twice their own numbers, but ALLAH strengtheneth with His succour whom He wills. Herein verily is a lesson for all with eyes to see.'*

The Prophet Muhammad strategically placed His men by the wells of Badr, which meant that the Quraysh would have to fight for water. Prior to the battle, conditions were imposed by the Prophet upon the Muslim fighters on rules of armed engagement. Women were not to be harmed, nor were children or old people. No harm was to be done to men who worked in the field. Trees were not to be cut down. Muslims were ordered only to strike against those who had expelled them and enriched themselves with their possessions.

In keeping with battle tradition, the battle of Badr too began with single combat, with both sides producing their champions. Hamzah, Ali and Ubaydah ibn al-Harith represented the Muslims, while Utba, Shayba and al-Walid ibn Utba represented the Meccan force. The Meccan champions did not stand a chance against the likes of Hamzah and Ali. Utba, the father of Hind, who was the wife of Abu Sufyan was brought down by Hamzah, while Utba's son, al-Walid (Hinds brother), was killed by Ali's sword.

Soon after this the battle began in earnest. The Muslims fighting that day clearly understood that this was a make or break situation for them. Defeat would mean certain death for all of them. The Meccans were in no mood to take prisoners. For the Muslims their backs were against the wall. It was a kill or be killed scenario.

The situation as it presented itself to the Muslim force was an extremely desperate one. Defeat was not an option. What started out to as a raid on Abu Sufyan's caravan turned into a battle of survival for the religion of Islam, and the Prophet Muhammad knew it. Inspired with religious zeal, however, the Muslims fought with discipline and vigour. Many former Muslim slaves found themselves fighting their one-time Meccan masters on an equal footing to the death. By midday the Meccan force, despite regrouping themselves a number of times, finally fled in disarray, leaving many prominent Meccans dead on the battlefield, including Abu Jahl. The Meccans had clearly underestimated the Muslim force in its ability to execute an effective battle strategy.

So decisive was the Battle of Badr that it is mentioned in the Holy Qur'an. In **Chapter 3, Al-Imran, Verse 123** it states: *'ALLAH had helped you at Badr, when you were Helpless; Then be mindful of ALLAH, so that you may be grateful.'*

With regard to the Meccan war captives, they were handled with remarkable mercy. Inspired by Revelation, the Prophet Muhammad adopted a humane policy towards them. The captives were not to be ill-treated in any way. Many of the captives were close relatives of Muslims. Those who could pay a ransom were freed. The poor and the old were freed without ransom. Those captives who could read and write were charged with teaching Muslims in order to gain their freedom. This humane and tolerant treatment brought dividends as many captives voluntarily converted to Islam.

Lessons can certainly be learnt from this. Once victory is realised, vengeance should not be actively pursued. Rather efforts should be taken to exemplify the truth of your beliefs, establishing moral ascendancy over your opponent.

If the Prophet's enemies considered Him a spent force that could be brushed aside with relative ease, the victory at the wells of Badr changed all that. The Prophet Muhammad was now a man to be reckoned with. No more was He a Meccan exile but instead a major leader of the Hijaz. The success at Badr also enhanced His position in Medina, allowing Him to subdue his opponents there. These were the Jewish Tribes of Banu Qainuqa, Banu Nadir and Banu Quraiza. Not only did they stand accused of spreading discontent in Medina against the Prophet, but they also plotted to kill Him. The tribe of Banu Quraiza went to the extent of conspiring with the Meccan army in 627 AD during the Battle of the Ditch in a siege that almost brought down Medina. This was despite the fact that they pledged themselves to the Constitution of Medina.

The deaths of many of the Meccan ruling elite at Badr helped to consolidate Abu Sufyan's position as the undisputed leader of Mecca. It therefore became imperative upon him to seek military engagement with the Muslims. Naturally the Meccans sought retribution for their humiliating defeat at the wells of Badr. More so, Hind had a death-score to settle with Hamzah, the man who killed her father, Utba. Battle preparations were made in earnest, with Meccans calling upon Bedouin tribes to join them in their war against the Muslims. History records that the Meccans exacted their revenge in the Battle of Uhud in 625 AD.

THE CONQUEST OF MECCA:
THE TURNING POINT

In 628 AD, in the sixth year of the Hijrah, the Prophet Muhammad set out for the Ka'bah with around 1400 unarmed Muslims to perform Umra (a short pilgrimage). Notwithstanding their defeat in the Battle of Uhud, the Muslims in Medina were emboldened after a subsequent abortive Meccan siege in what came to be known as the Battle of the Ditch, despite being overwhelmed by the enemy's superior numbers of 10,000 men. The Muslims must surely have felt that ALLAH was on their side. Dressed in their white pilgrimage attire, they approached Mecca, stopping at a place called Hudaibiyah. It was a tactical move on behalf of the Prophet, for He knew that the Quraysh as guardians of the Ka'bah would not slaughter unarmed pilgrims, as this would cause outrage among the tribes and nomads of Arabia. But then it was also unlikely that the Meccans would simply allow Muslims to enter Mecca, for that would surely amount to severe humiliation on their part. Plans were therefore put into effect to prevent this. Khalid bin al-Walid (Khalid) was dispatched with a contingent of armed horse riders to stop the Muslims from entering Mecca. What followed was an intense standoff. Consequently, an agreement was reached between the Quraysh and the Prophet. This agreement has come to be known as the Hudaibiyah Agreement.

The conditions in this agreement would in turn set the stage for the conquest of Mecca, although it did not appear so at the time of signing the agreement. In fact, so disheartened were the Prophet's Companions with this agreement that it risked mutiny. The conditions of the Hudaibiyah Agreement were that Prophet Muhammad and His followers would return to Medina without performing the Umra at the Ka'bah on that occasion (thereby saving face for the rulers of Mecca). But the next year Muslims would return to Mecca as pilgrims and remain for no more than 3 days to perform the religious rites of the Umra around the Ka'bah unhindered. Furthermore, members of the Quraysh who had become Muslims and emigrated to Medina would be returned to Mecca on demand, but no such reciprocity applied to the Quraysh in respect of Muslims taking refuge in Mecca.

There would also be a truce for 10 years between Mecca and Medina. Muslims could go to Mecca and Ta'if, while the Quraysh could make trips to Syria through Muslim areas. Each party would remain neutral in the event of a war between the other and a third party. The Bedouin tribes were free to choose to make an alliance with either Mecca or Medina. Finally, as part of the truce neither party could attack any tribe nor ambush any caravan or injure any individual associated with either of them. Breach of the truce would render the agreement void.

What really incensed the Prophet's closest companions was that the truce meant that Muslims could no longer raid the Quraysh trade caravans, in effect ending the economic blockade of Mecca. Further cause for humiliation was when the Prophet Muhammad waived any reference in the Hudaibiyah Agreement of Himself as the Messenger of ALLAH but instead as the son of Abdullah.

The Prophet, however, was understandably keen to establish a truce with Mecca. He did not want further battles or bloodletting with them, but more importantly, He wanted to gain access to the Ka'bah. This would allow for a propaganda strategy in winning the hearts and minds of the Meccans. Crucially, with the agreement allowing Bedouin tribes to form alliances with Medina, abandoning their old alliances with the Quraysh, the tribe of Banu Khuza'ah sided with the Muslims. The Banu Bakr tribe, on the other hand, who were antagonistic towards Banu Khuza'ah, remained with the Quraysh. Significantly, soon after the Hudaibiyah Agreement, many non-Muslims embraced Islam, including Khaled. He would later prove to be an asset as a military strategist and commander.

In November of 629 AD, one of the clans of Banu Bakr launched a surprise night-time attack on Banu Khuza'ah in their own territory, allegedly with the aid and assistance of the Quraysh. Though members of the Banu Khuza'ah took refuge in the sacred precincts of the Ka'bah, they were still butchered there. This single incident would ignite a storm across Arabia, resulting in the surrender of Mecca. The Banu Khuza'ah appealed to the Prophet. Realising that the Hudaibiyah Agreement lay in tatters and that the Prophet would respond by seizing this opportunity to His advantage, Abu Sufyan hastily went to Medina to plead with the Prophet Muhammad that the truce was still in force. But the damage was already done. The conditions of the Hudaibiyah Agreement were breached and the truce was now void. Realising that the balance of power was about to change in the Hijaz, many other tribal leaders pledged their allegiance to the Prophet Muhammed.

In January 630 AD, in the month of Ramadan, in the eighth year of the Hijrah, the Prophet Muhammad set off for Mecca at the head of a large military contingent numbering more than 10,000 men. The Quraysh had no means of repelling such a large Muslim army, and Mecca had no alternative but to capitulate to the Muslims. The Meccans feared that the Muslim army would enter Mecca and exact revenge that would result in a bloodbath. Realising this, Abu Sufyan made his way to the Muslim Camp that was situated just miles away from Mecca. Upon embracing Islam, he left for Mecca to warn its inhabitants of the impending massacre that he believed would befall them, despite a promise to the contrary by the Prophet Muhammad. In fear of their survival the Quraysh barricaded themselves indoors. Approaching Mecca from all directions, the Muslim contingent, however, entered Mecca without incident.

The Prophet Muhammad declared a general amnesty. Despite having been ridiculed, persecuted and finally forced into exile eight years earlier, the Prophet did not exact vengeance. It was not His purpose to do so. His principal objective was to cleanse the Ka'bah of the idols housed in it. To the deafening cries of 'ALLAHU AKBAR' (ALLAH is the Greatest) the Prophet Muhammad smashed the idols placed in and around the Ka'bah. With this definitive act of defiance against the old order, paganism and idolatry were banished from Arabia.

With the conquest of Mecca, again the Prophet proved that He was not a man of the sword. Despite having the opportunity to crush His Meccan persecutors and put an end to potential political rivals, the Prophet ordered His Muslim army not to exact revenge. No one was to be harmed and no closed doors were to be forced. By commanding so, the victory over Mecca was permanent. Having consolidated His power over Mecca and Medina, the stage was set for the banner of Islam to spread across the Hijaz and beyond the Arabian Peninsula.

In hindsight the Prophet's decision not to avenge His former enemies proved to be a disastrous oversight in the context of the second Fitna (civil war) that engulfed the Caliphate after His death, for it was Abu Sufyan's son Mu'awiyah who founded the Umayyad dynasty and whose successive Caliphs ruled the expanding Islamic Empire between 661 till 750 AD. Crucially, it was Mu'awiyah's son Yazid I, who upon succeeding his father as Caliph, orchestrated the massacre of the Prophet's grandson Husayn, together with his family, at Karbala in 680 AD. Consequently this effectively brought to an end any claim by the Hashemite Clan, i.e., the Prophet's immediate household and blood relatives to the Caliphate. This murderous affair also marks the principal schism between Muslims that has persisted throughout the ages namely, that of Shi'ite and Sunni Islam, and continues today. This is discussed in more detail in Chapter 4.

HADITH AND ISLAM

The Hadith narrate the actual sayings and actions of the Prophets Muhammad. With numerous collections of Ahadith (plural of hadith) being undertaken during the second century Al Hijri, six collections have been widely regarded by Muslims through the ages as being authoritative, with two of them being regarded as authentic in their entirety. They are the Sahih al-Bukhari (collected and compiled by Abu Abdallah Muhammad bin Isma'il al-Bukhari) and Sahih al-Muslim (collected and compiled by Muslim ibn al-Hajjaj). The other four collections, though being held in high esteem are not recognised as authentic in their entirety. These four collections of Hadith are the Sunan Abi Dawud, Sunan Ibn Majah, Jami At-Tirmidhi and Sunan an-Nasa'i.

The importance attached by the Muslim world to these six authoritative collections should not be underestimated, for after the Holy Qur'an the Ahadith are the principal source of Shari'ah law, customs and practices. On many important issues the Holy Qur'an simply states the principles, while it is the Ahadith that provides details of their application. For example, while the Holy Qur'an requires Muslims to offer Salah, observe Sawn and pay Zakat it does not specify the manner and form by which these are to be carried out. It is from the Sunnah of the Prophet Muhammad that we derive the details. This is narrated in **Chapter 16, An–Nahl, Verse 44** of the Holy Al Qur'an: *'(We sent them) with Clear Signs and Scriptures. And we have sent down the Message unto thee (Prophet) too; That thou mayest explain clearly to men what is sent for them, that they may reflect.'*

Unlike the verses of the Holy Qur'an that were compiled into a single volume within a few years of the Prophet Muhammad's death, the Ahadith were, on the other hand, collected more than 200 years after His death. Given the long period of oral transmission before the Ahadith came to be written down and collected, it is alleged by critics that there was every possibility that some of the Hadiths mingled fact and myth, truth and error into one big smelting pot. Furthermore, with the ongoing power struggles within the Caliphate there was a real opportunity for spurious Hadiths to support rival positions, schisms and grievances. Notwithstanding this, the scholars engaged in collecting the Hadith, went to great lengths in establishing the reliability of the chain of transmitters. In fact, an entire science thoroughly investigating the character and background of each transmitter to identify the strength and weakness of the chain of transmitters was developed. Consequently, the numerous Hadiths were graded into varying degrees of reliability in terms of trustworthiness of the sources, multiple references and the chain of verbal succession, among other things. The grades are sahih (sound), hasan (good) and the da'if (weak). This obsession with examining the chain often overshadows the importance of taking into account the content of the numerous Hadith and their compatibility with the Holy Qur'an.

THE FAREWELL SERMON

In 632 AD, in the 10th year of the Hijrah, leading a large number of pilgrims, the Prophet Muhammad set out for Mecca from Medina to perform the annual Hajj. Sadly, this would turn out to be the Prophet's last pilgrimage. The rituals set down in the Prophet's farewell pilgrimage form the established rituals of the Hajj. On completion of the Farewell Hajj the Prophet, believing that His death was near, took the opportunity of addressing the

Ummah on the plains of Arafat to surmise His Prophetic Message in what has come to be known as the Farewell Sermon. It must be remembered that the Farewell Sermon is not Divine Revelation comparable to the verses of the Holy Qur'an. Nevertheless, its impact on the Muslim psyche cannot be underestimated.

Praising and thanking ALLAH, the Prophet said:

'O people, listen to my words carefully for I know not whether I will meet you on such an occasion again.'

'O people, just as you regard this month, this day, this city as sacred, so regard the life and property of every Muslim as a sacred trust. Remember that you will indeed appear before God and answer for your actions.'

'Return the things kept with you as trust (Amanah) to their rightful owners.'

'All dues of interest shall stand cancelled and you will have only your capital back. ALLAH has forbidden interest, and I cancel the dues of interest payable to my uncle Abbas ibn Abdul Muttalib.'

'O people, your wives have certain rights over you and you have certain rights over them. Treat them well and be kind to them for they are your committed partners and committed helpers.'

'Beware of Satan, he is desperate to divert you from the worship of ALLAH so beware of him in matters of your way of life.'

'O people, listen carefully! Let all your feuds be abolished. All the believers are brothers. You are not allowed to the things belonging to another Muslim unless he gives it to you willingly.'

'O people, you are all descended from Adam and none is higher than the other except in obedience to ALLAH. No Arab is superior to a non-Arab. Between Muslims there are no races and no tribes. Do not oppress and do not be oppressed. '

'O people, reflect on my words. I leave behind two things, the Qur'an, revealed by ALLAH which is light and guidance and my example and if you follow these, you will not fail.'

'Listen to me carefully! Worship ALLAH and offer Salah; observe Sawm in the month of Ramadan; pay the Zakah and perform the Hajj.'

'O people, be mindful of those who work under you. Feed and clothe them as you feed and clothe yourselves.'

'O people, no prophet or messenger will come after me and no new faith will emerge.'

'*All those who listen to me shall pass on my words to others and those to others again.*'

The Prophet Muhammad then asked the multitude of people assembled, '*Have I conveyed the Message of ALLAH to you, O People?*' The tens of thousands that had gathered answered in one voice, 'You have, and ALLAH is the witness.' As the Prophet finished delivering His sermon the following revelation came to Him as narrated in **Chapter 5, Al-Ma'idah, Verse 3**: '*Today I have perfected your religion for you, completed my favour upon you and have chosen for you Islam as your religion.*'

In the backdrop of an Arabia plagued with tribal allegiances and blood feuds, the Farewell Sermon was nothing short of revolutionary, for it tore away at divisive tribal allegiances that had formed the bedrock of Arabia, reiterating that all Muslims were part of the same one Ummah and united in faith. While Muslims are reminded not to be persecuted, at the same time, they are warned not to transgress. The Sermon's emphasis on the status of spouses, that they both have rights and obligations to one another, was a radical departure from the norm at the time. Emphasis was also put on treating the weak in society with compassion. To truly appreciate the magnificence of the Farewell Sermon with respect to social reform it is worthwhile noting that it was delivered in the context of the seventh century, when Arabia was only just emerging from 'Jahiliyyah' (pre-Islamic ignorance), when Europe was sunk in the Dark Ages and when old empires were crumbling.

PROPHET MUHAMMAD: KHATAM-AN-NABIYYIN

The Prophet Muhammad is the last of ALLAH's Apostles. He is referred to as Khatam-an-Nabiyyin (the seal of prophethood). No Messenger will appear after Him. No new monotheist Faith will emerge after Islam. The Prophet makes this clear in His Farewell Sermon. Further, the Holy Qur'an in **Chapter 33, Al-Azhab, Verse 40 narrates**: '*Muhammad is not the father of any of your men, but (he is) The Messenger of ALLAH and the Seal of the Prophets: and ALLAH has full knowledge of all things.*'

What distinguishes Muhammad from the other preceding Prophets is that while they were sent to a chosen people/nation, the Prophet Muhammad was sent by ALLAH to all mankind as stated in **Chapter 34, Saba, Verse 28**: *'We have not sent thee (Muhammad) But as a Messenger to all mankind, giving them Glad tidings, and warning them (Against sin), but most men know not.'*

With the Message of Islam being universal in its appeal, it is only natural that the Messenger communicating the Divine Message be the universal Prophet. Furthermore, of the Divine Books, the Holy Qur'an is the last of the Divine Revelations. Again ALLAH makes a covenant with mankind through Muhammad by revealing to the Prophet that Islam is the chosen religion as narrated in **Chapter 5, Al-Ma'idah, Verse 3** above. This narrative is further supported in **Chapter 48, Al-Fath, Verse 28**: *'It was He Who sent His Messenger with Guidance and the Religion of Truth, to make it show that it is above all (other) religions. ALLAH suffices as a Witness.'*

From a political perspective, in the interests of maintaining unity and integrity in the Ummah, it was imperative that the Prophet Muhammad was clearly accepted and firmly established as the last of the chain of the true Prophets in accordance with Divine Revelation. This would act as a natural deterrent on false apostasy claims. Nevertheless, shortly after Prophet Muhammad's death, Abu Bakr spent most of his time as Caliph battling against false Prophets in what has come to be known as the Apostasy wars and won. The false prophets included Musaylimah, Tulayha and Aswad Ansi who sought nothing but political power.

In summarising, it should be stressed that Muslims by no means worship the Prophet Muhammad in any manner, shape or form. All worship is for ALLAH alone, the unseen one true God. There are those who claim that the Prophet established a new religion in his lifetime. Nothing could be further than the truth. The Prophet Muhammad is not the founder of Islam. The term Mohammedanism is a misconception and highly offensive to Muslims of understanding.

Certainly however, Muslims revere Muhammad as the Prophet of Islam and Messenger of ALLAH sent to all mankind till eternity. Both as man and Prophet, Muhammad embodies virtues of patience and tolerance. For Muslims across the globe, He serves as an exemplary role model. His traditions (collections of Hadith) inspire Muslims not to submit to persecution but at the same time not to transgress. They teach Muslims to fight for their rights but in a coordinated manner with force being appropriately directed as a last resort and only in self-defence. Devout Muslims irrespective of nationality strive to lead their lives within the spirit of the Prophet's hadith.

Any misrepresentations concerning the Prophet Muhammad therefore, naturally inflame emotions, particularly among young impressionable Muslims. But such non-constructive propaganda defiling the Prophet Muhammad is often orchestrated in the name of exercising freedom of speech. For some right-wing politicians and intellectuals, drumming up Islamophobia brings for them media attention and fame; in fact for some it is a source of their livelihood and political stratagem. While freedom of speech should challenge our intellect, at the same time it is only fair and proper that caution should be exercised that such freedom does not serve as a source of propagating distorted facts aimed at furthering vested political/commercial interests. For instance, the amateur film 'Innocence of Muslims', produced in the US, which depicted the Prophet Muhammad with ridicule and contempt, portraying Him as a fraud, womaniser, homosexual and a madman, sparked numerous spontaneous demonstrations in September 2012 against US diplomatic missions across the Muslim world and beyond. These demonstrations reflected the anger and underlying current of resentment of Muslims against what they perceive to be continued attempts by vested Western interests to belittle and discredit the Prophet of Islam. What caught the attention of the global media and US policy makers were the images of widespread anti-US protests in more than 20 countries, from the Middle East to South-East Asia, as well as North Africa. There were also comparatively less violent protests in the cities of London, Paris, Antwerp and Sydney though they did result in scuffles with the police with several arrests. Previously, the book, 'Satanic Verses' and later the Danish cartoons portraying the Prophet Muhammad as a terrorist had also inflamed emotions across the Muslim World.

While these violent protests were widely criticised in numerous commentaries as being orchestrated by so-called Muslim extremists, global Muslims are unwilling to acquiescence and therefore, prepared to reject vested right-wing propaganda belittling the Faith of Islam. While previous US and Western governments have distanced themselves from such anti-Islamic rhetoric nevertheless, there is a common consensus among the vast sway of Muslims that more can be done by Western governments today to tackle such outrageous and bigoted actions by right-wing extremists. Then again, the tragic attack on 7 January 2015 that witnessed terrorists' storm the offices of the satirical magazine Charlie Hebdo, however, takes matters too far. Such an extremist response demonstrates a level of intolerance that is not condoned in Islam. This horrendous attack, without a doubt, surely transgresses limits.

CHAPTER FOUR

Succession and the Seeds of War and Division

The Death of the Prophet: An Ummah in crisis

So colossal was Muhammad as Man, Prophet and Messenger that upon His death on 12 Rabi'ul-Awwal of the 10th Hijrah (8 June 632 AD), the matter of appointing a Khalifah/Caliph (successor) in terms of providing leadership to the Islamic community became a very real and crucial issue. The Prophet Muhammad left no male heir. The tribal tradition of blood inheritance was consequently ruled out. More importantly, the Holy Qur'an gave no definitive guidance on the question of how a successor was to be chosen after the Prophet Muhammad's death. Nor was there any scope for the Prophet's companions, or anyone else for that matter, to claim leadership as a new Prophet since the Prophet Muhammad was proclaimed by ALLAH as the last Prophet: 'Khatam-an-Nabiyyin' (the last of the chain of the true Prophets).

With the Prophet's death the infant Islamic community was in a state of loss and shock, so much so that many in the community found it difficult to come to terms with the reality of the news. In the midst of the confusion and commotion it was the Prophet's closest companion, Chief Counsellor and father-in-law, Abu Bakr, who brought a sense of purpose and direction. While addressing the crowd that had gathered before the Prophet's humble dwelling he declared, *'Whosoever worshipped Muhammad, let him know that Muhammad is dead, but whosoever worshipped ALLAH, let him know that ALLAH lives and cannot die'.*

On the question of who should be the Caliph there was initial disagreement between the Ansar (Muslims of Medina who received and helped the Prophet after His migration from Mecca and were mainly members of the Medinite tribe of Kharaj) and the Muhajirin (followers of the Prophet who migrated from Mecca with, before and after Him to Medina), both claiming that the office should go to one of them. At one stage the Ansars suggested that there should be two Caliphs, one from each. In the interests of maintaining solidarity, Umar flatly rejected this proposition. Any such course of action would surely have fragmented the Islamic community. In the course of discussions (which were taking place at the courtyard of Banu Sa'idah) Abu Bakr, at the initiative of Umar, was consequently unanimously elected as the first Caliph of Islam following a public bay'ah (pledge) at the Mosque the next day. A significant factor behind Abu Bakr's election was the fact that the Prophet Muhammad Himself appointed Abu Bakr to lead the congregational prayers during His last illness. Had any of the Prophet Muhammad's sons survived Him the issue of succession would surely have taken an entirely different direction, having profound consequences in its aftermath both for the immediate community of Islam and the expansion of Islam into the rest of Arabia and beyond. Even if Ali had reservations in the election of Abu Bakr as the first Khalifah (Caliph), Ali's integrity and love for Islam is evidenced by the fact that he did not declare open opposition/hostility to Abu Bakr's Caliphate in the interest of the infant Islamic State.

Shi'ites however, have a seriously disturbing take on the circumstances surrounding the election of Abu Bakr. They allege that Umar had threatened to burn the house of Fatimah (daughter of the Prophet) unless her husband Ali, along with his supporters, went to the Mosque to pledge allegiance to Abu Bakr. Sensing Ali and his supporters might pose a threat to the election of Abu

Bakr, Umar, along with some men, stormed into Fatimah's house and while breaking open the door injured the child in Fatimah's womb, as a consequence of which the baby boy was stillborn. All this was happening while the Prophet's body was lying in state awaiting burial. To add to the grief of losing her beloved father and loss of her baby, Abu Bakr went on to refuse Fatimah her right of inheritance to the land of Fadak. These overbearing experiences of tragedy and treachery took their toll on Fatimah's health, and she died exactly 75 days after the death of her father, the beloved Prophet Muhammad.

It is chronicled that Fatimah refused to make peace with Abu Bakr and Umar and instructed her husband on her deathbed to bury her in secret without informing Abu Bakr, the first Caliph. This Ali did and as result, the exact location of Fatimah's burial place is still disputed today. Had Ali and his supporters at that moment engaged in armed conflict to secure the Caliphate for himself, the resulting strife would have stopped the spread of Islam in its tracks. Fatimah's stillborn child was the first casualty of the schism that would later metamorphose into the Fitna (civil war) that would engulf the early Caliphate, culminating in the gruesome murder of another of Fatimah's sons, Husayn, at Karbala alongside his family at the hands of the militia of Yazid I, who was the grandson of the former ruler of Mecca, Abu Sufyan.

There is an important lesson for Muslim rulers to learn from this. Ali's magnanimous character allowed him to concede his claim to the Caliphate knowing full well that any armed opposition to Abu Bakr's election as Caliph at that time would have destroyed the infant Islamic community. Today, oppressive Muslim rulers in the Middle East and beyond unfortunately doggedly hold on to power, refusing to relinquish it in favour of transparent democratic institutions and processes despite mass protests, and in response they are willing to kill peaceful protesters by unleashing deadly force. Worse still, tyrants like the Syrian President, Bashar al-Assad, would rather see the systematic destruction of Syria in terms of colossal infrastructural damage, the death of hundreds of thousands of Syrian non-combatants including tens of thousands of children than step down from power. Within the spirit of true

Islam there can be no justification whatsoever for this greed for power.

There is some perplexity surrounding the circumstance of the Prophet Muhammad's death, centred on the following hadith. Narrated by Aisha in **Sahih al-Bukhari Volume 5, Book 59, Hadith 713** that the Prophet in his ailment in which he died, used to say, *'O' Aisha! I still feel the pain caused by the food I ate at Khaibar and this time, I feel as if my aorta is being cut from that poison'*. This particular hadith has been subject to intense scrutiny and debate. Depending upon the way it is interpreted, it can have tremendous ramifications. In fact, it could potentially prove highly divisive and provocative. A brief exploration of some of the issues arising will illustrate the point. There is plenty of material on social media where attempts have been made to link this hadith to **Chapter 69, Al-Haqqah, Verses 41-52** of the Holy Qur'an (mentioned in Chapter One). These social media critics claim, while trying to reconcile the hadith with these verses of the Holy Qur'an, that the Prophet suffered the wrath of ALLAH at the time of His death. Shi'ites however, seek to emphasize that the Prophet Muhammad died a 'martyr's death', having been poisoned as a result of a conspiracy by those vying to claim the Caliphate, uprooting any potential claim by Ali from becoming the first Caliph, taking advantage of the Prophet's illness prior to His death. But then again, it could be argued that both controversial views are nothing more than an attempt to justify ignorance with logic that distorts the truth. One could put the case that the Prophet simply died of an illness that exhibited the symptoms of heart disease.

After his election, Abu Bakr settled the question as to where the Prophet's body should be buried. Recalling the words of the Prophet, *'No prophet dieth but is buried where he died'*, the grave was dug in the floor of the room of Aisha (the Prophet's widow and daughter of Abu Bakr) near the couch where the Prophet Muhammad was lying. (Referring back to the Shi'ite view on the Prophet's death, the decision to bury the Prophet Muhammad's body in Aisha's house was taken to consolidate Abu Bakr's own position.) Consequently, the Prophet Muhammad was buried on the night of 14 Rabi'ul-Awwal in the year of the 10th Hijrah. The Prophet's burial therefore, taking place following the election of Abu Bakr as Caliph.

Centred on the Prophet Muhammad's burial place today sits the grand palatial compound of the al-Masjid an-Nabawi. It is revered by Muslims as the second holiest site in Islam after Masjid al-Haram in Mecca, which houses the Ka'bah. Buried alongside the Prophet are two of His closest companions, Abu Bakr and Umar. It is widely accepted by Muslims that a fourth burial place has been set aside for the Prophet Isa (Jesus) who Muslims believe will come at the End of Time to kill the Dajjal (Anti-Christ) and establish ALLAH's rule on Earth. This is discussed further in chapter five.

Abu Bakr, Umar ibn al-Kattab (Umar), Uthman ibn Affan of the Umayya clan (Uthman) and the Prophet's cousin and son-in-law, Ali ibn Abu Talib (Ali), are referred to as the righteous/rightly-guided Caliphs: 'Khulafa' Ur Rashidin'. They had all heard the revelations from the Prophet himself and been guided by His example. Each served in turn as Caliph. However, with the exception of Abu Bakr, who died from illness, the remaining three Rashidun Caliphs died violent deaths, not in war, but as a consequence of conspiracies manifesting themselves in murder and assassinations.

ABU BAKR (632–634 AD)

Abu Bakr was indeed a great man. He succeeded in playing a crucial role at a critical time following the announcement of the Prophet's death on Earth. A close trusted friend and confidant of the Prophet, Abu Bakr was also among the first to embrace Islam. He is commonly referred to as al-Siddiq, meaning 'the Truthful'.

Abu Bakr was born into a noble family belonging to the Quraysh tribe of Mecca. A thriving cloth merchant, he was one of Mecca's richest merchants, but following his conversion he dedicated his wealth to the cause of Islam. Many slaves who had embraced Islam and were consequently tortured for doing so, including Bilal, were purchased by Abu Bakr from their masters and given their freedom.

Abu Bakr accompanied the Prophet Muhammad on the flight from Mecca to Medina. He also fought alongside the Prophet on many military campaigns, including the Battle of Badr, the Battle of Uhud and the Battle of the Ditch.

Following Abu Bakr's election as Caliph, his acceptance speech can be said to have laid the foundation of democratic accountability required of leaders in that they are trustees of the people over whom they govern. Abu Bakr is recorded as having said, *'I have been elected your Ameer, although I am not better than you. Help me, if I am in the right; set me right if I am in the wrong; obey me as long as I obey ALLAH and His Prophet; when I disobey Him and His Prophet, then obey me not.'* Ironically, leaders in the Arab world and the wider Muslim Ummah demand the absolute obedience of their citizens and subjects either following their election or ascension to the throne

A major achievement of Abu Bakr's brief two-year rule was the victory over the 'false prophets' in what are referred to as the Apostasy Wars. Among these false prophets, Musaylimah proved to be the most dangerous. He claimed that he was also in receipt of a Divine Mission reducing, among other things, the number of compulsory daily prayers, as well as relaxing the duty to fast and the paying of zakat while laying claim to half of Arabia. Misjudging Abu Bakr's political and military prowess, a considerable number of tribes that were hostile to Islam joined ranks with Musaylimah. Initially, the Muslim armies faced defeat. But under the brilliant command of Khalid ibn al-Walid (Khalid), the army of Musaylimah was defeated and after fleeing the battlefield was hunted down and killed.

After the Prophet's death, Abu Bakr realised that the Muslims had to be united under a common enterprise of military expeditions. He launched military campaigns against the Sassanid Empire and Byzantine Empire, setting in motion a trajectory that continued on with Umar and Uthman so that within just a few decades of the Prophet Muhammad's death the Islamic Empire would become one of the largest in history.

Following the deaths of numerous Qurra (those who could

recite the Qur'anic verses from memory) at the Battle of Yamamah against Musaylimah in 632 AD, Abu Bakr, on the insistence of Umar, commenced the task of bringing together all the Divine revelations, both written and oral, into one volume in what later became the Holy Qur'an. This task he entrusted to Zayd Bin Thabit. It was imperative to do so to prevent the emerging Ummah to split on religious-political lines.

Sunni Muslims believe that the Divine revelations were written down as one single manuscript and presented to Abu Bakr. The Holy Qur'an was therefore compiled within one year of the death of Prophet Muhammad when most of His closest Sahabah (companions) were still alive. Prior to his death, Abu Bakr gave this manuscript to Umar and remained with him throughout his rule as the second Righteous Caliph. Prior to his death, Umar gave the manuscript to his daughter Hafsah, who was a widow of the Prophet Muhammad. Uthman's official codex was subsequently prepared from the copy kept with Hafsah.

Securing a political alliance, Abu Bakr was also the Prophet Muhammad's father-in-law. Prior to his death, Abu Bakr nominated Umar to succeed him as the subsequent Caliph.

UMAR ibn AL-KATTAB (634–644 AD)

Umar was not one of the early converts to Islam. After his initial hostility to Islam and while on a personal mission to kill the Prophet Muhammad, Umar embraced the Faith in 616 AD upon reading verses of the Holy Qur'an. So tremendous was his spiritual awakening that Umar would later prove to be one of the staunchest defenders of the Faith. Sunni Muslims revere Umar with the title al-Farooq meaning 'one who distinguishes between right and wrong', believed to have been bestowed by the Prophet Muhammad himself. Born in Mecca into the Banu Adi Clan of the Quraysh Tribe, Umar's father was Khattab ibn Nufayl, who was famed for his intelligence and ruthlessness.

Umar is particularly remembered for his personal attributes. He is known for being tough, bold and a strict disciplinarian. A gifted orator, with his intelligence and overpowering personality he took over his father's mantle as 'arbitrator among tribes'. These personal attributes allowed Umar to become one of Prophet Muhammad's Chief Advisors, and he was also closely associated with Abu Bakr. Like Abu Bakr, Umar too was the Prophet Muhammad's father-in-law. The Prophet was married to Umar's daughter, Hafsa. During his rule as the first Righteous Caliph, Abu Bakr relied greatly on Umar and consequently nominated Umar to succeed him as the second Caliph.

Following a siege by Muslim forces that included those of Abu Ubaidah and Khalid, the city of Jerusalem was surrendered by its then Patriarch, Sophronius, to Caliph Umar. Under the terms of the treaty of surrender, referred to as the Umari Treaty, no churches were to be razed to the ground, while security of life and property were guaranteed. The inhabitants of Jerusalem were captivated by Umar's simple demeanour as he entered the city, not as a conqueror with pomp and grandeur but a simply-clothed rider on camelback with a single aid. This was in stark contrast to the bloody massacre unleashed upon the Muslim and Jewish inhabitants of Jerusalem by the First Crusaders when they took the city in the name of God and Christendom.

Many of the military campaigns undertaken during Caliph Abu Bakr's rule and also briefly during Umar's rule (including conquests of northern Arabia, Syria and parts of Persia) were under the able command of Khalid. His popularity in the Muslim community was rising considerably and Khalid was publicly known as Sayf-ullah, 'Sword of ALLAH'. However, his increasing popularity meant that the Muslim community was attributing military victories to the personality of Khalid. Umar upon becoming Caliph, consequently dismissed him from supreme command of the Muslim Forces in 634 AD on the contention that it is ALLAH that gives victory to the Muslims with Abu Ubaidah being appointed as the new commander-in-chief of the Islamic army. Khalid was later relieved from military service, in 638 AD. In reality there was a potential source of friction between Umar as Caliph and Khalid as Supreme Commander of the Muslim Forces, or at least their supporters, if Khalid had been allowed to continue in his position.

Umar's rule is credited with a series of lightning conquests, which included victory against the powerful Sassanid Persian Empire, in addition to the conquest of Egypt, Syria and Jerusalem. The Muslim forces were by now a well-disciplined and successful military machine.

The Persian Military campaign, however, subsequently proved fatal for Umar. With the Persians suffering successive defeats in the Battles of Qadisiya, Chesipon, Jalula and finally in the Battle of Nihavand in 642 AD, the Persian Empire could no longer offer effective resistance (its King, Yazdgard, fled, only to be killed in 651 AD during the rule of Caliph Uthman). The conquest of Persia brought with it many captives who were consequently sold as slaves, including Umar's assassin. His name was Abu Lu'lu', also known as Firoz. While Umar was leading the morning prayers Firoz repeatedly stabbed Umar with a dagger, seriously wounding him. Umar died some days later after succumbing to his injuries in the month of Muharram, 24 Al-Hijri and was buried by the side of the Prophet Muhammad. On his deathbed Umar appointed a six-man committee to elect his successor from amongst themselves rather than himself expressly nominating a successor. The Committee members were Uthman ibn Affan, Abd al-Rahman ibn Awf, Ali ibn Abu Talib, Sa'd ibn Abi Waqqas, Zubayr ibn al-Awwam and Talha ibn Ubayd Allah. (The latter two would subsequently entice Aisha to go into battle with Ali in what has come to be known as the 'Battle of the Camel' for what they perceived as Ali's failure to bring Uthman's assassins to justice quickly enough).

The Committee had asked Ali to become Caliph on the condition that he would follow the Holy Qur'an, Sunnah and Seerat-e-Sheikhain (the way of the first two Caliphs), to which Ali replied he would follow the Holy Qur'an and Sunnah. He argued if the previous Rashidun Caliphs had followed these, the subsequent requirement became obsolete. If they had not, then he had no intention of following their example. Uthman, however, agreed to accept this condition in its entirety without question. Some sources claim the Committee elected Uthman by default, as Ali refused to accept the conditions imposed upon him, including the condition that he should not proclaim a Hashemite dynasty. The irony in all this is that following the assassination of Ali and the subsequent murder of Ali's son Husayn and his family at Karbala, it was relatives from Uthman's clan that established the Umayyad dynasty. Unlike the rightly guided Caliphs, the Rulers of the Umayyad Empire ruled like kings, enforcing dynastic succession rather than ruling as Deputies of the Prophet.

UTHMAN ibn AFFAN (644–656 AD)

Uthman was born into the wealthy Banu Umayya Clan of the Quraysh Tribe and belonged to the same clan as Abu Sufyan. Uthman's father, Affan, died while Uthman was still young, positioning him to take up his father's thriving business with a large inheritance. A nephew of the Prophet Muhammad, Uthman was also among the first to give his allegiance to Umar after his election as Caliph.

Uthman's role as Rashidun Caliph is highly controversial, as there are two competing views put forward by Sunni and Shi'ite scholars. To begin with, Sunni Islam believes that during deliberations among the six-man committee set up by Umar to appoint his successor, Uthman actually favoured Ali as the next Caliph and Ali favoured Uthman. Shi'ites argue on the other hand that with the exception of Ali and Zubayr, the remaining committee members were in fact relatives of Uthman, and Ali actually protested the composition of the Committee. It is alleged that the Committee was a deliberate ploy by Umar and Uthman to prevent Ali from being the Caliph. Shi'ite Islam further believes that on the Prophet Muhammad's return to Medina from the His last Hajj in 632 AD, the Prophet stopped at a place called Ghadir Khumm (Pond of Khumm) addressing the people there and nominating Ali to be His political and spiritual successor. The Sunni branch of Islam denies this.

Uthman's succession as the third Rashidun Caliph had in it the seeds of civil war. His rule was a watershed in the chronicles of the expanding early Islamic State, for unlike his predecessor

Umar, Uthman's leadership by comparison was weak, for he lacked political maturity, sowing the seeds of the Fitna (civil war) that ensued.

Sunni Islam, however, views Uthman in a more positive light. Significant military gains and conquests of new territories are attributed to the reign of Uthman, including much of North Africa and Cyprus, including subjugating Persian Sassanid provinces that rebelled following the death of Umar.

Though Uthman was married to two of the Prophet's daughters at different times, namely Ruqayyah and subsequently after her death to Umm Kulthum, earning him the title of 'Possessor of Two Lights', Shi'ites argue that this did not outrank or supersede Ali's blood ties with the Prophet, as Ali was married to the Prophet's only surviving daughter, Fatimah, from the Prophet's first marriage to Khadijah at the time of the His death. Ali also happened to be the Prophet's first cousin, belonging to the same clan as the Prophet, namely the Banu Hashim. Furthermore, Hasan and Husayn, the Prophet's beloved grandsons, were Ali's children from his marriage to Fatimah.

The single most important act that signifies Uthman's rule is the transcription of the standardised text of the Holy Qur'an and its subsequent dissemination. This he entrusted to Zayd Bin Thabit at the head of a committee which prepared the official codex from the copy kept with Umar's daughter, Hafsah, but in the dialect of the Quraysh. Copies of the official codex were then sent to different provinces of the expanding Islamic State. In doing so Uthman ordered that all unofficial copies of the Holy Qur'an should be gathered and destroyed. This opened the door to charges against Uthman of engineering the Holy Qur'an by deliberately omitting Qur'anic verses with explicit references to the virtues of the Prophet's Family, with particular reference to Ali. There is, however, no concrete evidence to substantiate this allegation, as Ali made no attempt to introduce a new standardized copy of the Holy Qur'an when he became Caliph. The Quranic Verses commonly sighted as being omitted are those that make up Surah al-Nurayn and Surah al-Wilayah.

The true reason behind the anti-Uthman movement is

disputed among Shi'ite and Sunni Muslims. Nevertheless, a common thread emerges from historical texts. To consolidate his power base Uthman installed and retained members of his own tribe to positions of military and political prominence in key provinces. These included Egypt, Syria, Kufa and Basra. This rapid rise to prominence of men of the Quraysh, who had until the conquest of Mecca by the Prophet Muhammad in 630 AD been bitter enemies against Islam, was naturally giving rise to resentment amongst the Muhajirun and Ansars. This Uthman failed to address, among other things, by retaining Mu'awiyah as governor of Syria who was the son of Abu Sufyan.

Discontent among the Muslims in the provinces of the expanding Islamic State was reaching boiling point over the strong rule imposed by the governors appointed by Uthman. There were grievances over new taxes being introduced to replace war booty, as the pace of conquests had been slowing down since 650 AD. Exploiting increasing tensions between the Hashemite and Umayyad Clans of the Quraysh, a growing movement was emerging demanding the ouster of Uthman as Caliph. In response to the claims of misrule by the governors of the various provinces, Uthman did take initiatives to investigate these allegations. In an attempt to quell this movement, he called upon his governors to attend a Council in 654 AD. The following year, Uthman called upon those who had any grievance to assemble at Mecca for the annual Hajj, promising to address their legitimate grievances. This provided Uthman with a temporary respite, but the propaganda had by then spread far and wide and the conspiracy against Uthman had become deeply rooted.

The situation was becoming increasing desperate in Egypt. Similarly, Kufa and Basra were becoming a centre of revolt. In 656 AD contingents of rebels from these provinces marched on Medina, subsequently besieging Uthman in his house. Uthman shied away from allowing his supporters to engage with the rebels in armed conflict, as he did not want Muslims to shed the blood of other Muslims for the sake of his Caliphate. In a desperate move the rebels later stormed the house, murdering Uthman while, it is understood, he was reciting the Holy Qur'an.

In an attempt to save her husband, Uthman's wife Naila tried to shield him from his attackers, but she was wounded herself. This single murderous act sowed the seeds of civil war that would later fragment the Muslim Ummah. Uthman was subsequently buried quietly in fear that the rebels who were still in Medina would desecrate his body.

ALI ibn ABU TALIB (656–661 AD)

Ali was the son of Abu Talib, a prominent member of the Tribe of Quraysh belonging to the Hashemite Clan. His father was the Prophet Muhammad's Uncle, making Ali the Prophet's first cousin. Both had a common grandfather, namely Abdul Muttalib. Ali's mother Fatimah bint Assad also belonged to the Hashemite Clan, making him a descendant of Ibrahim's (Abraham's) son Isma'il (Ishmael). A brave warrior, Ali participated in many battles during the time of the Prophet, including the Battle of Badr, Uhud, Khaybar and Hunayn. For his brilliance in battle the Prophet Muhammad conferred on Ali the title of Asadullah, meaning the 'Lion of ALLAH'. Famed for wielding a bifurcated sword, he is also loved and revered by Muslims for his courage, wisdom, knowledge on Islamic Jurisprudence, deep loyalty to the Prophet Muhammad, equal treatment of all Muslims, compassion and strength of character.

On the eve of the Prophet's flight to Medina, Ali lay under the blanket in the Prophet Muhammad's bed, thwarting an assassination plot to kill the Prophet. Ali was also among the very first to embrace Islam.

Following the assassination of Uthman a state of confusion and anarchy prevailed in Medina. Rebels against Uthman's rule were still in Medina and looked to Ali to take the reins of the Caliphate. Ali initially refused this offer by the rebels. They then turned to Talhah and Zubayr to accept the role of Caliph, but they too refused this. Faced with an ultimatum by the rebels and on the insistence of prominent companions of the Prophet Muhammad, Ali subsequently accepted the role of Caliph. Talhah and Zubayr gave their pledge to Ali, along with the people of

Medina, though Talhah and Zubayr would later allege that they did so reluctantly.

Soon after becoming the fourth Rashidun Caliph, in an attempt to consolidate his own position, Ali sought to root out growing Syrian and Persian influence in the Ummah. Going against the advice of learned counsel, Ali ordered that those provincial governors either appointed by or retained by Uthman should be dismissed, replacing them with his trusted aides. Most of them were successful in taking charge of the provinces. However, Mu'awiyah, who was kinsman of the slain Uthman, and was appointed governor of Syria by Umar and retained by Uthman, refused to acknowledge Ali as Caliph and therefore refused to vacate his position as governor. On the contrary he implicated Ali as an accomplice in Uthman's murder for his neglect in apprehending and punishing Uthman's murderers. As events subsequently panned out, it was apparent that Mu'awiyah was only interested in establishing his own dynastic rule and was in no mood to relinquish power. Furthermore, Mu'awiyah had managed to successfully raise a strong army to back his challenge to Ali's Caliphate.

THE FIRST FITNA (CIVIL WAR) IN ISLAM: THE RISE OF SHI'ITE ISLAM

In the meantime, enraged with Ali's inability to bring the murderers of Uthman to justice, Talhah and Zubayr approached Aisha, daughter of Abu Bakr and widow of the Prophet, to rally support against Ali. Aisha, grieving the death of Uthman and angered at the subsequent election of Ali as the new Caliph, also demanded revenge for Uthman's death. Consequently, they succeeded in raising an army. Sensing a challenge to his leadership, Ali too raised an army. The two armies met at Basra in what is known as the Battle of the Camel, marking the beginning of the first Fitna (civil war) in Islam.

During the course of the battle, fierce fighting took place, resulting in the death of many Muslims. Facing defeat, Talhah and Zubayr fled the battlefield and Ali's army took the upper hand.

As a mark of victory Ali severed the hamstrings of the camel Aisha was riding on and had her sent back to Medina, after which she withdrew from active frontline political participation. This victory helped to consolidate Ali's rule over the Ummah, with the exception of Syria. Meanwhile, Ali moved his capital to the garrison city of Kufa in present-day Iraq.

To undermine Ali's authority, Mu'awiyah started a propaganda campaign instigating the people to rebel against Ali's Caliphate. Whether it was an oversight on behalf of Ali or not, there was little chance Mu'awiyah was going to relinquish power so readily to a new governor appointed by Ali, given that Mu'awiyah was in charge of a large battle-hardened army. Furthermore, Mu'awiyah's submission to Ali would surely mean the ascendancy of the Hashemite Clan as opposed to the Umayyad Clan in the affairs of the expanding Islamic State. Ali, however, was reluctant to expand the civil war, as this would lead to the death of many Muslims on both sides. Ali therefore, opened lines of communication with Mu'awiyah, hoping to gain his allegiance. But this did not yield any results. Consequently, when war became inevitable between Ali and Mu'awiyah both were making preparations for armed engagement.

The two armies met at Siffin near the Euphrates. After initial skirmishes, the main battle began in the month of Safar, 37 Al-Hijri. This armed engagement is known as the Battle of Siffin. Within a few days of heavy fighting which resulted in both sides sustaining large casualties, Mu'awiyah's army was on the verge of being routed. In order to avoid a crushing defeat, Mu'awiyah hatched an ingenious plan by placing copies, as well as pages, of the Holy Qur'an on the spearheads of his front ranks. This caused confusion and disagreement among different factions of Ali's army and reluctantly he had to recall his forces.

Following cessation of hostilities, it was decided by the warring factions that the matter of the Caliphate should be put to arbitration. While Ali was in favour of arbitration to prevent further bloodshed, to Ali's disappointment however, Abu Musa Ash'ari was chosen to represent him while Amr ibn Aas represented Mu'awiyah. Not everyone in Ali's army was in favour of arbitration, especially when they had been close to victory. Among those who opposed arbitration they later came to be known as Kharijites, meaning 'those who withdrew'. Branding Ali as a traitor for failing to wage jihad against the Umayyad usurpers, the Kharijites came out of Ali's armed coalition and subsequently rebelled against Ali's rule. In the Battle of Nahrawan that followed, Ali crushed their rebellion with only a handful managing to escape with their lives, but they swore to avenge this with Ali's death. (The Kharijites were staunch opponents of Uthman's rule and included many Bedouin tribal leaders, as well as, the Prophet's closest friends and relatives who were absolutely determined to uphold the religious traditions that they viewed as conforming to the Prophet Muhammad's teachings. They are alleged to have been behind the murder of Uthman and the instigators of Ali's election as Caliph who subsequently allied themselves with Ali fighting alongside him at the Battle of the Camel and Siffin).

The arbitration did not go in favour of Ali and the armed conflict between Ali and Mu'awiyah resumed. Following the fall of Egypt to Mu'awiyah, rebellions against Ali broke out across the Ummah. Taking full advantage of this, Mu'awiyah's armies overpowered those rebellious cities, bringing them under Mu'awiyah's rule. In the backdrop of this Ali was attacked by a Kharijite, Abdur Rahman ibn Muljam with a poisonous sword while he was leading the dawn prayer at the site of the present-day Grand Mosque in Kufa. A few days later in the month of Ramadan, 40 Al-Hijri, the last Rashidun Caliph died from his wounds.

There are different opinions over where Ali was buried. Some believe that fearing his enemies might desecrate his grave, Ali asked his closest friends and relatives to bury him in secret. Most Shi'ites accept that Ali was buried at the site of the Tomb of Imam Ali in the Imam Ali Mosque in the Iraqi city of Najaf. However some Afghans maintain that Ali's body was taken and buried in the Afghan city of Mazar-e-Sharif at the famous Blue Mosque or Rawze-e-Sharif.

In the immediate aftermath of Ali's death, his son Hassan succeeded his father, but shortly afterwards he capitulated to

Mu'awiyah, who had marched an army into Iraq to unseat Hassan's Caliphate. Mu'awiyah in the meantime declared himself as the Caliph and in doing so founded the Umayyad dynasty of Caliphs. Subsequently, in the month of Safar, 50 Al-Hijri, Hassan was murdered after being poisoned by one of his wives at the instigation of Mu'awiyah, and the Hashemite claim to the Caliphate passed to Husayn ushering in the second Fitna.

THE SECOND FITNA (CIVIL WAR) IN ISLAM: THE MARTYRDOM OF HUSAYN

Upon his death in 680 AD, Mu'awiyah appointed his son Yazid I as his heir and successor. Refusing to recognise Yazid I as Caliph, the Shi'ites urged Husayn to claim the Caliphate. In response to their call, Husayn set out for Kufa but was intercepted by the forces of Yazid I at Karbala. Refusing to pay allegiance, Husayn, along with his family and small band of followers, were mercilessly killed in the skirmish that followed, with their bodies being decapitated. In Husayn's martyrdom Shi'ite Islam found a sense of purpose and direction as a force of rebellion. Even today Shi'ite Muslims across the globe commemorate the tragic events at Karbala, drawing strength and inspiration from the belief that the military skirmish that resulted in the murder of their third Imam (paving the way for the establishment of the Umayyad dynasty) will be redeemed by the awaited twelfth Imam, who they believe to be the Mahdi bringing peace and justice to the world at the end of times. In fact, a study of Shi'ite tradition reveals how all the preceding eleven Imams died violent deaths, being killed either by the sword or by poison, and ironically by Muslims of the non-Shi'ite affiliation. Sadly, this political feud manifests itself even today in the proxy wars being fought out in the Middle East between Shi'ite Iran and its affiliates and the Sunni powers in the region headed by Saudi Arabia.

Shi'ites argue that Ali should have been the immediate successor to the Prophet Muhammad and that he was unfairly denied the Caliphate three times before. They believe that the head of the Muslim Community or Ummah should be a descendant of the Prophet. Shi'ites believe that the Umayyad Caliphs were usurpers of the Caliphate, imposing dynastic succession ruling as kings rather than Deputies of the Prophet failing to govern in accordance with the Holy Qur'an and the Prophetic traditions. For the Shi'ites, the Caliph who they term the Imam is also the spiritual representative of the Prophet on earth with the capacity to interpret Divine Law.

The first and second Fitnas in Islam threatened to undermine everything the Prophet Muhammad had tirelessly struggled to achieve. After the assassination of Ali, ironically it was descendants of the Prophet's bitterest enemies that ruled the Islamic Ummah, beginning with Mu'awiyah (who was Abu Sufyan's son), and had established the Umayyad dynasty. Critics argue that Uthman was no doubt partly responsible for this and blame should be apportioned to him.

The Prophet Muhammad's vision of a democratic Caliphate was effectively handicapped with the establishment of the Umayyad dynasty. Dynastic rule is contrary to any notion of a Caliph, who should rather be a representative of the Ummah. This is evidenced by the fact that the Prophet Muhammad did not expressly appoint a named successor despite the fact that the Prophet knew in His heart that He was approaching the end of His life on Earth, as evidenced by His Farewell Sermon. No doubt the Prophet had done this to avoid any allegation of partiality that might splinter the infant Islamic community after His death. But more importantly, by not appointing a named successor Prophet Muhammad intended to sow the seeds of elected representation. This was centuries before any semblance of democratic values was practised in Europe.

Sunni scholars argue that Shi'ite Islam is at odds with elective representation. Shi'ites scholars counter this with the argument that political and religious authority should be vested in the most learned on Islamic Jurisprudence. They point to the Sunni despots in the Middle East who live in magnificent splendour, out of touch with the populace over whom they rule, ruthlessly repressing demands for political pluralism. In fact, they claim that Iran (which is predominantly Shi'ite) is the only democratic

Muslim majority state in the Middle East.

Islam requires Muslim rulers not to be tyrannical. They are on a par with the rest of the population over whom they govern. It is the duty of every Muslim to overthrow tyrannical despots, for they rule not in the way of Islam. At the very core of political Islam lies elected representation. The Middle East is infested with predominantly Sunni despots who purport to rule in the name of Islam yet have deviated from the principles set out by the Prophet Muhammad. If we take the example of the Rashidun Caliphs, they did not separate themselves from the populace by living in luxury and grandeur. In fact, it is well documented that all the Rashidun Caliphs led ordinary lives and were accessible to the people they governed. They all worked tirelessly to uplift the poor and the destitute. Abu Bakr in his acceptance speech went so far as to give permission to the Ummah to remove him should he fail to rule in the way of the Holy Qur'an and the Prophet's Sunnah.

The Arab Spring of 2011 was a reaction to decades of despotic rule. It ignited in Tunisia, quickly engulfing North Africa and the Middle East. Despite stiff resistance by entrenched dictators and their military establishment, the struggle for democratic freedoms and processes continues to reassert itself in the way of true Islam. It would be premature to conclude that the Arab Spring is effectively dead despite the military coup against a democratically elected President in Egypt and the brutal repression carried out by the Syrian and Bahraini Regimes on its peoples. It can be argued that the Arab Revolt is currently experiencing a watershed and what it needs is a renewed revival of the inspiration that sparked the uprising.

Though the Arab Spring will be discussed in more detail in later chapters, it is important to note here that it is imperative that any Islamic Renascence is not hijacked by both the political and military 'Old Guard' sitting on the fringe lying in wait.

CHAPTER FIVE

The End of Times: The Islamic Narrative

Judgement Day in the Holy Qur 'an and the Hadith

The knowledge of the Final Hour is with ALLAH alone. This is narrated in the following verses of the Holy Qur'an:

Chapter 7, Al-A'raf, Verse 187: *'They ask thee about the (final) Hour – when will be its appointed time? Say: 'The knowledge thereof is with my Lord (alone): None but He can reveal as to when it will occur. Heavy were its burden through the Heavens and the Earth. Only, all of a sudden will it come to you.' They ask thee as if thou wert eager in search thereof: Say: 'The knowledge thereof is with ALLAH (alone), but most men know not.'*

Chapter 31, Luqman, Verse 34: *'Verily the knowledge of the Hour is with ALLAH (alone). It is He who sends down rain, and He who knows what is in the wombs. Nor, does anyone know what it is that he will earn tomorrow. Nor does anyone know in what land he is to die. Verily with ALLAH is full knowledge and He is acquanited (with all things).'*

Chapter 33, Al-Azhab, Verse 63: *'Men ask thee concerning the Hour: Say, 'The knowledge thereof is with ALLAH (alone)': And what will make thee understand? It may be that the Hour is nigh!'*

Chapter 41 Fussilat, Verse 47: *'Unto Him is referred (All) knowledge of the Hour. And no fruit burst out of its sheath, nor does a female conceive nor bring forth, but with His Knowledge. The Day that ALLAH will calleth unto them, 'Where are the Partners (Ye attributed) to Me?' They will say, 'We do assure Thee that not one of us is a witness for them.'*

And the Final Hour is sure to happen, there is no doubt thereof as stated in the following verses of the Holy Qur'an:

Chapter 20, TaHa, Verse 15: *'Lo! The Hour is surely coming. But I will keep it hidden, that every soul may be rewarded for that which it striveth (to achieve).'*

Chapter 22, Al-Hajj, Verse 7: *'And verily the Hour will come: There can be no doubt about it, or about (the fact) that ALLAH will raise up all those who are in the graves.'*

Chapter 34, Sabah, Verses 3-4: *'Those who disbelieve say, 'Never to us will come the Hour', say, 'Nay! But most surely, by my Lord, it will come upon you; – by Him Who knows the unseen, – From Whom is not hidden an atom's weight in the Heavens or on earth: Nor is there anything less than that or greater, but it is in a clear Record: That He may reward those who believe and work deeds of righteousness: for them is forgiveness and a sustenance most gracious.'*

Chapter 40, Al-Ghafir, Verse 59: *'The Hour will certainly come: Therein there is no doubt: Yet most men believe not.'*

While the exact timing of the Final Hour is not specifically mentioned in the Holy Qur'an, nevertheless there are signs and tribulations mentioned in many Ahadith by which the devout may foresee the coming of the Hour. The Holy Qur'an does however describe the Final Hour in apocalyptic terms in **Chapter 81, At-Takwir, Verses 1-14:** *'When the sun (with its spacious light) is folded up; when the stars fall, losing their lustre; when the mountains vanish; when the she-camels, ten months with young are left unattended; when the wild beasts are herded together; when the oceans boil over with a swell; when the souls are sorted out (like with like); when the female (infant) that was buried alive is questioned – for what crime she was slain; when the Scrolls are laid open; when the sky is torn away; when the Blazing Fire (hell) is kindled to fierce heat; and when the Garden is brought nigh; (Then) every soul will know what it has put forward.'*

It is narrated from Abu Huraira **(Sahih Al-Bukhari, Volume 1, Book 2, Belief, Hadith Number 47)** that one day while the Prophet Muhammad was sitting with a group of people, a Bedouin came to the Prophet and asked Him about 'Iman' and Islam. Then he asked, 'O Messenger of ALLAH, when will the Hour be established?' The Prophet replied, *'The answerer has no better knowledge than the questioner, but I will tell you about its portents. When a slave (lady) gives birth to her master; when the shepherds of black camels start (boasting and) competing with others in the construction of higher buildings. The Hour is one of the five things which no-one knows except ALLAH.'* Then the Prophet is reported to have recited **Chapter 31, Luqman, Verse 34**, mentioned above.

After the Bedouin took his departure from the Prophet, He said to those gathered around him, *'Call him back'*, but when the people went out to call him, the Bedouin was nowhere to be found. The Prophet then said, *'That was Jibrael (Gabriel), who came to teach the people their religion.'*

Other Sahih Hadith pertaining to the Final Hour includes the following:

It is reported from Anas **(Sahih Al-Bukhari, Volume 1, Book 3, Knowledge, Hadith Number 81)** that the Prophet said, *'Among the signs of the Hour are the following: (Religious) knowledge will decrease and ignorance will prevail; fornication (illegal sexual intercourse/having sex with someone not married to) will be prevalent; the number of women will increase, until one man will look after fifty women.'* By knowledge, here we can assume the knowledge and wisdom in the Truth of Tawhid and all that it stands for.

Again, it is narrated by Abu Huraira in **(Sahih Al-Bukhari, Volume 9, Book 88, Afflictions and the End of War, Hadith Number 237)** that the Prophet said, *'The Hour will not be established till: (1) two big groups fight each other whereupon there will be a great number of casualties on both sides and they will be following one and the same religious doctrine, (2) about thirty Dajjals (liars) appear, and each one of them will claim that he is ALLAH's Messenger, (3) the religious knowledge is taken away (by the death of religious scholars), (4) earthquakes will increase in number (5) time will pass quickly, (6) trials and afflictions will appear, (7) Al-Harj (ie killing)* *will increase, (8) wealth will be in abundance ... so abundant that a wealthy person will worry lest nobody should accept his Sadaqa, and whenever he will present it to someone, that person (to whom it is offered) will say, 'I am not in need of it,' (9) the people compete with one another in constructing high buildings, (10) a man when passing by a grave of someone will say, 'Would that I were in his place,' (11) and till the sun rises and the people will see it (rising in the west) they will all believe (embrace Islam) but that will be the time when: (As ALLAH said), 'No good will it do to a person to believe then, if he (or she) believed not before, nor earned good (by performing deeds of righteousness) through his (or her) Faith.'*

And the Hour will be established while two men spreading a garment in front of them but they will not be able to sell it, nor fold it up; and the Hour will be established when a man has milked his she-camel and has taken away the milk but he will not be able to drink it; and the Hour will be established before a man repairing a tank (for his livestock) is able to water (his animals) in it; and the Hour will be established when a person has raised a morsel (of food) to his mouth but will not be able to eat it.'

These portents of the Final Hour are often referred to as the lesser or early signs. It is not uncommon – in fact it is convenient – to adopt an escapist perspective on the Final Hour, denying any possibility of its relevance in our lifetime. However, even the Prophet Muhammad did not know of its exact timing. We are already witnessing many of the lesser signs of the Final Hour. Many have come to pass; some are ongoing, while others are yet to happen. Also among the lesser signs is the rejection of the moral values of the Holy Qur'an, where despite the fact that the Holy Qur'an is read, the knowledge and wisdom it contains will not be practised; religion will be used as a means for profit and gain; worship performed for show; the mosques being full of people but they will be empty of righteous guidance; so-called Muslims (hypocrites) will be in the majority, while real scholars and sincere Muslims will be in the minority. Liars will be believed at the expense of truthful people. Gains will be shared out only among the rich, with no benefit for the poor. Furthermore, unrepresentative regimes will enforce tyrannical rule.

Astronomically speaking, a study of the above hadith also suggests that the end of times will be marked by destruction on a cosmic scale. Arguably it could involve a super-massive gamma ray burst. The beam itself will be very wide by the time the wave hits the earth and there will be no warning as it travels at the speed of light. It will deplete the ozone layer in the upper atmosphere, allowing harmful UV radiation to hit the ground. It may alternatively be a coronal mass ejection from our own star, the Sun, which will have the potential to destroy civilization as we know it.

The major signs include the emergence of the Dajjal (the false Messiah), the appearance of the Mahdi, the rightly guided leader of the Muslim Ummah who will fight the tribulations of the Dajjal; the second coming of Isa (Jesus), son of Mary who will kill the Dajjal; the havoc created by the 'tribes' of Ya'jooj and Ma'jooj (Gog and Magog); the three Landslides, one in the east, one in the west and one in the Arabian Peninsula; the Smoke; the rising of the Sun from the west; the manifestation of the Beast; the Holy Qur'an will be taken up into heaven, and the Fire which will drive the people to their final gathering place. When the first of these major signs appear, the others will come soon after in quick succession. There is however, no definitive authority on the exact sequence in which all these greater signs will appear.

During the course of the rest of this chapter we will briefly touch upon some of the major portents of the Final Hour.

THE DAJJAL: 'The accursed one'

It should be noted that the word Dajjal does not appear in the Holy Qur'an. It does however; appear in various Ahadith collections, including the two Sahih Collections, Al-Bukhari and Al-Muslim.

Certainly, we cannot literally accept the common metaphorical descriptions of the Dajjal. To do so would be an absurdity – a distortion of logic and rationality. A rational approach to the subject suggests that the Dajjal will be an enterprise exhibiting several facets operating on multiple levels. First and foremost, the Dajjal will be an individual – a charismatic global political leader. In the Christian Apocalypse he is described as the 'Anti-Christ'.

The Dajjal will also represent a global cultural phenomenon having the power to manipulate all streams of media information. The Dajjal as an ideology will command global economic supremacy. Ahmad Thomson, in his book *Dajjal*, has explained the phenomenon of the Dajjal with three aspects. There is Dajjal the individual, Dajjal as a global social and cultural phenomenon and Dajjal as an unseen force.

As an individual the Dajjal will have global reach with the power to draw the masses to his cause. He will be conceived from global economic chaos, socio-political upheaval and lack of moral values. Today the global economy is essentially based on unethical accumulation of capital based on riba (interest) manipulated by financial institutions and vested stakeholders. Riba is forbidden in Islam. The very rich thrive while the middle and working classes find their financial circumstances constrained. With Europe and the United States slowly coming out of a deep recession we are looking at interesting times ahead. History teaches us that economic chaos often produces despots who impose tyrannical rule.

A master liar, deceiver and manipulator, his sight will be constrained to that of evil. To get an understanding or realisation of the Dajjal, he will embody the traits and circumstances of both Napoleon and Hitler but on an unprecedented scale. The Dajjal will seek global conquest and therefore, naturally be in command of a mighty military force. No place will remain unscathed except, according to numerous Ahadith, the holy cities of Mecca and Medina. Some will argue that the platform for the arrival of Dajjal, the individual is already under way.

ALLAH will test our faith through the portents of the Hour, including the tribulations of the Dajjal. One important fact is that the Dajjal will seek the destruction of the followers of the three Abrahamic faiths, not just Islam, pitting one against the other. Symptomatic of this, the Dajjal will raise the stakes with regard to the 'Holy Land' provoking anguish and ultimately a destructive conflict centring on the holy sites in Jerusalem. Arguably a careful study of global geopolitics is indicative of a trajectory that will ultimately culminate in this Fitna that will encompass the hijacking of the religion of Islam by irrational and reactionary forces (to be used as a tool to confront the West and their alliances and out of the ashes of this devastating conflict will arise a so-called new world order like a phoenix from the fire.)

THE MAHDI: 'One Man to unite them all'

The Mahdi (the 'guided one') will be no prophet but an exemplary and rightly guided political leader. He will restore justice and fairness under Qur'anic guidance, overcoming injustice and oppression. Though the Mahdi is not specifically mentioned by name in the Holy Qur'an, in the Tirmidhi and Abu Dawudh Hadith collections however, the Prophet Muhammad is recorded as describing the Madhi as a man from His Household ('Ahl Al-Bayt'), ie a descendant of Husayn, son of Ali and His daughter Fatimah. He will have the same name as the Prophet, while the Mahdi's father's name will be the same as the Prophet's father, ie Abdullah.

As recorded in the Hadith of Ahmad Ibn Hanbal and Ibn Majah, the Prophet states that ALLAH will inspire the Mahdi, preparing him to carry out his task successfully. Though his rule will be brief, only seven years, within that time, nevertheless, the Mahdi will confront the many tribulations of the Dajjal. The Mahdi will unify Muslims under one political-religious banner and that is 'One Ummah'. He will also face many battles, including confrontations in Syria and the battle for the conquest of Palestine. In order to achieve fairness and justice in the world, just as Jesus had overturned the tables of the money changers at the Temple Mount, so too will the Mahdi strike out against a global economy based on greed, interest (riba) and economic disparity. It is the mismanagement of resources that is the prime cause for much of the poverty in the developing world today. Having dismantled the economic power houses of the Middle East, the Muslim Ummah will enjoy a period of prosperity accessible to all. It is pertinent to emphasise here that many of the tribulations of the Dajjal will precede the arrival of the Mahdi.

In Shi'ite Islam, the Mahdi has become central to religious-political belief. The majority of Shi'ite Muslims believe that the Mahdi is Muhammad al-Mahdi, the Twelfth Imam, who was born in 869AD and was hidden by ALLAH. He is still alive but has been in occultation waiting the time that ALLAH has decreed for his return. Sunni Islam however, believes that the Mahdi will be born into an ordinary Muslim family but will be Divinely inspired.

It comes as no surprise then that over the centuries various individuals have claimed to be the Mahdi. The notion of a Mahdi as a redeemer who will establish a universal social order based on justice overcoming oppression has lent itself to various interpretations leading to different claims by individuals during the course of Islamic history. They include Mirza Ghulam Ahmad, who founded the Ahmadiyya Movement. This movement has proved limited in scope and reach as mainstream Sunni, as well as, Shi'ite Islam does not recognise Mirza Ghulam Ahmad of Qadian as the true Mahdi. Followers of the Ahmadiyya Movement can be found in West Africa, the US and Europe with sizeable adherents being of Pakistani descent.

Given the mandate of the 'true Mahdi' it is very likely that his imminent arrival will be met with by a violent reaction not by the West, contrary to what many Ulamas advocate, but rather ironically by the Muslim Ummah itself. Today, the political and economic elite, as well as the religious establishment of the Muslim Ummah, stands to be the Mahdi's greatest adversary. The reasons being, amongst others, that the Mahdi will seek to unite Muslims under one political-religious banner, thereby advocating the eradication of the divide between Shi'ite and Sunni Islam. This is unlikely to go down well with Shi'ite and Sunni powers in the Middle East given the hostile polarity between them. He will also strike at the heart of the financial system employed by much of the Muslim Ummah where the disparity in economic wealth between the elite and the majority of the population is ever increasing. But most important of all, the Mahdi will call for the abolition of tyrants and despotic leaders in the Muslim Ummah who exercise power over their respective populations through coercion and undemocratic processes. It goes without saying that in order to confront the many tribulations of the Dajjal the Mahdi must have the support of a united Muslim Ummah. Consequently, the present mind-set of the Ummah needs to start changing. Faith in justice, equality, fairness, unity and rationality must be ingrained and exercised by Muslims rather than allowing reactionary forces to manipulate the Faith of Islam such as in the form of ISIL and Al-Qaeda. Any Muslim leader who advocates perpetuating division and conflict within the Muslim Ummah itself can never rightly claim to be the true Mahdi.

It is a common misconception among extremists that the arrival of the Mahdi can be expedited somewhat by perpetrating terrorist acts on the streets of major Western cities and/or provoking an artificial conflict between the West and Islam. From a practical interpretation of the Islamic texts the true Mahdi is likely to be revealed in the midst of a renewal of the Faith when the religion of Islam will undergo a rational intellectual debate challenging orthodox and extremist narratives akin to an Islamic Renascence. It is within this backdrop during the Hajj, when the world's media will be focused on the annual pilgrimage, that the Mahdi is likely to reveal himself/be discovered.

It is extremely unlikely that the true Mahdi will proclaim himself by seizing the Grand Mosque that houses the Ka'bah in Mecca by armed insurrection as was tried on 20 November, 1979 (1 Muharram 1400AH) when at the turn of the new Islamic century around 300 armed men seized the Grand Mosque. With the head of the armed siege, Juhayman ibn Muhammad ibn Saif Al-Utaybi, proclaiming his brother-in-law, Muhammad ibn Abdullah Al-Qahtani as the Mahdi, they held the Grand Mosque for almost two weeks anticipating that their actions would ignite an armed conflict within the region that would spur on Divine intervention that would usher in the prophesised apocalypse. The armed siege was nonetheless, brought to an end by Saudi security forces backed by a small team of French commandos, the National Gendarmerie Intervention Group (GIGN), on 3 December 1979, with hundreds of casualties including soldiers, militants and civilians. The military assault on the Grand Mosque (the holiest site in Islam) was endorsed by fatwas extracted from leading religious clerics of the time.

The true Mahdi will be Divinely inspired to lead the fight against the tribulations of the Dajjal, who will also precede the second coming of the Prophet Isa (Jesus) discussed below. It is important to note that the true Mahdi and the Prophet Isa will share the same political and military platform in the fight against the Dajjal. In this context, the present cannot influence future events when the future is already pre-ordained. Rather it is the future that will influence present events.

ISA (JESUS): 'The Second Coming'

From a study of the Hadith collections of Al-Muslim, Ahmad Ibn Hanbal and Ibn Majah, the second coming of Isa (Jesus), son of Mary will occur after the appearance of the Dajjal (Antichrist) and the emergence of the Mahdi (the 'guided one'). Isa will descend in the midst of wars being fought between the armies of the Mahdi against the armies of the Dajjal. Isa's descent will be marked with Divine manifestations so that He may be recognised. He will then join the Mahdi forces in their wars against the Antichrist. Eventually, it will be Isa and not the Mahdi who will destroy the Antichrist in battle, following which everyone from the 'People of the Book' (Jews and Christians) will follow Isa. In the Christian Apocalyptic narrative this final battle is referred to as the 'Battle of Armageddon'. Isa will assume leadership of the worldwide community of Islam since the Mahdi would have passed away by then. In Islamic Belief, Isa is considered to be a Prophet of Islam, He will therefore, uphold the teachings and laws of Islam. Consequently, there will be only one Ummah, ie the Community of Islam. It is narrated in numerous Ahadith that Isa will break the crosses (symbols of the crucifixion), outlaw the consumption of swine and abolish the Jizya tax.

This assumption of leadership by Isa is unlikely to be a smooth one, as the second coming of Isa, from an Islamic perspective, will absolutely undermine the institution of the Vatican and its vested stakeholders. Isa will set the record straight namely, that He was neither the son of God nor crucified on the cross, confirming the Qur'anic narrative. It is for this reason that Isa's second coming will be marked by Divine manifestations.

During Isa's rule peace and security will prevail on earth. It will usher in a period of abundant wealth and prosperity. During Isa's time as well, the tribes of Ya'jooj and Ma'jooj (Gog and Magog) will manifest themselves creating havoc on earth. By ALLAH's command these tribes will be destroyed. Isa's rule will be for around forty years, during which time He will marry. Upon His death Muslims will perform the Islamic funeral prayer for Him and then bury Him in the city of Medina in a grave that has been left vacant beside the Prophet Muhammad at the al-Masjid an-Nabawi alongside the rightly guided Caliphs Abu Bakr and Umar.

YA'JOOJ AND MA'JOOJ (GOG AND MAGOG):
'The Scourge of Mankind'

At-Tabarani, on the authority of Abdullah ibn Amru, reports that the Prophet Muhammad stated that Ya'jooj and Ma'jooj are descendants of Adam. Again Ibn Kathir on the authority of Abu Sai'd Al-Khudri reports that the Prophet mentioned that Ya'jooj and Ma'joog will represent two nations. From the Hadith collections of Tirmidhi it is apparent that they will be enormous in terms of numbers with multitudes of weapons dispersing themselves across the globe consuming the world's natural resources and creating havoc on earth. They will appear during the time of Isa (Jesus) after the destruction of the Dajjal. They are currently encased behind a barrier (whether that barrier is physical or metaphorical is a matter of conjecture). Isa, son of Mary, will pray to ALLAH to dispel this evil. ALLAH will respond to the supplication of Isa by inflicting a plague among Ya'jooj and Ma'jooj that will destroy them. It is then that the Final Hour will be near at hand.

The end of days figures in the other two Abrahamic Faiths too.

Judeo-Christian sources consist mainly of the Book of Daniel, Ezekiel, and the Book of Revelations, as well as some scattered sources within other books of the Old and New Testaments.

PART II

'When the people fear their government there is tyranny;
when the government fears the people there is liberty.'

Thomas Jefferson
Founding Father and former President of the United States of America

'When authoritarian rule starts to crumble from within its fall is inevitable'

The Author

'*The essential rationale of an Islamic renascence is that:*

All citizens of the Muslim Ummah (irrespective of race, religion, caste or creed) have an inalienable right to choose and elect their rulers through free, fair and transparent elections and to effectively hold them to account.

All citizens are equal before the law and have a right to demand that their elected representatives provide them with viable and credible opportunities to gain economic emancipation.

The national wealth is held in trust for the benefit of all citizens and no dynasty must be allowed to control that wealth.'

The Author

CHAPTER SIX

Contemporary Islam and the Rise of Militancy

Western foreign policy has actively provoked an extremist response from a passionate enemy unable to channel its frustration into constructive opposition (due to a lack of access to democratic processes); it has instead found an outlet to express its anguish in the form of terrorism. Without condoning terrorism in any manner, shape or form, let us examine this observation, for it is important to critically analyse the sense of hurt and anguish felt by many in the Islamic world surrounding the perceived persecution faced by the Muslim Ummah. It is only then that we can begin to embark upon a rational counter-narrative (as discussed in chapters seven and eight) to the radical interpretation of Islam employed by extremist groups such as ISIL and Al-Qaeda, based upon which they seek to justify their acts of terrorism.

THE ISRAELI-PALESTINIAN CONFLICT

At the very heart of the resentment lies the animosity between Israel and the Palestinians. Much of the anger largely results from the continued growth of illegal Israeli settlements on occupied Palestinian territory, Israel's disproportionate use of force against

Palestinian protesters, the stranglehold siege of Gaza, reports of torture of Palestinian detainees being held without charge or trial, and the unrelenting support of successive US administrations in favour of Israel with no clear sign of a sustainable Peace Process in the offing. Anguish also lies over the status of the Old City of Jerusalem, for it is a city sacred to Muslims across the globe, because it contains the Noble Sanctuary (Haram Al-Sharif) encompassing the Dome of the Rock (which houses the foundation/ascension stone) and the Al-Aqsa Mosque (al-Masjid al-Aqsa), which marks the third holiest site in Islam. Muslims firmly believe the ascension stone marks the place from where the Prophet Muhammad ascended to Heaven on 'The Night Journey' commonly referred to as the 'Mi'raj'. The Miraj is also associated with 'Isra' the journey of the Prophet from the city of Mecca to Jerusalem. This is narrated in the Holy Qur'an in **Chapter 17, Al-Isra, Verse 1** where it states, *'Exalted is He who took His servant by night from the Sacred Mosque (al-Masjid al-Haram) to the farthest Mosque (al-Masjid al-Aqsa), whose surrounding We have blessed to show him of Our signs. Indeed, He is the Hearing, the Seeing'*.

For many US Presidents and their administrations, trying to effect a peace deal between the two belligerents is often only a foreign policy box-ticking exercise resulting in no meaningful outcome, for they crave the financial and voting support of Zionist organizations, their allies and the Jewish lobby. The whole Palestinian issue could be resolved if US politics were kept out of the equation, as once remarked by former US President Harry S. Truman. It is as true today as it was then.

The blockade of the Gaza Strip by Israel was triggered by the capture of Gaza by Hamas in June 2007 following violent clashes with rival Palestinian faction Fatah after President Mahmoud Abbas dismissed the Hamas-led government, declaring a state of emergency. The blockade has resulted in appalling living conditions for its almost two million inhabitants, with sanctions sucking the life out of Gaza, forcing its inhabitants to rely on a network of underground tunnels for supplies. The blockade has however galvanized support for their plight both within and beyond the Muslim World. With Israel labelling Hamas as a terrorist organization committed to its destruction it has always argued that the blockade is essential to prevent Hamas from obtaining weapons and to limit Hamas fired rocket attacks from the Gaza Strip on its cities.

Despite this, under international pressure to lift the blockade following the deadly 'Gaza freedom flotilla' raid, Israel started easing restrictions back in June 2010, allowing only strictly civilian goods to enter Gaza. Nevertheless, assessments carried out in January and February 2011 by the United Nations Office for the Coordination of Humanitarian Affairs (UNOCHA) of the effects of the measures to ease the access restrictions concluded that they did not result in a significant improvement in people's livelihood. In June 2012 it reported that 44% of Gazans were food insecure and 80% aid recipients, with 35% of Gaza's farmlands and 85% of its fishing waters being totally or partially inaccessible due to Israeli-imposed restrictions.

In this context, it is important to stress that the worst form of persecution is to perpetuate another's poverty. Though Israeli authorities deny any wrongdoing, the reality on the ground is a desperate one for the inhabitants of Gaza, particularly for the children. The isolation of the Gaza strip has been further exacerbated by restrictions imposed by the Egyptian authorities on the Rafah border crossing (the main gateway for Palestinians in Gaza to the outside world), allowing it to remain open only for an extremely limited number of days (the longest period being for the month of Ramadan in 2018). The Egyptian authorities claim that the border has been largely sealed since 2013 in order to fight armed groups involved in an insurgency in the Sinai which they accuse Hamas of aiding. Compounding an already desperate situation, the almost two million residents of Gaza suffer from acute power shortages, with electricity blackouts of between 18-20 hours a day affecting basic services. With Hamas-controlled Gaza's only power plant out of commission, Gaza's inhabitants are dependent upon electricity from Israel and Egypt.

In April 2017, as a consequence of the increasing power struggle between Hamas and the West Bank-based Palestinian Authority, the later refused to pay Israel for electricity it supplied to Gaza in an attempt to reassert control by putting pressure on Hamas. In January 2018, following a reconciliation deal between these two Palestinian factions signed in Cairo in October 2017, the Palestinian Authority resumed payments to Israel, but the power supply is still substantially less than what is required. Many residents in Gaza have had to resort to backup generators to keep their house lights and refrigerators on during blackouts. Given the dire situation in Gaza it is often said to be 'the world's largest open air prison'.

Despite the reconciliation agreement setting up a new unity government between Hamas and the Palestinian Authority to bring the hostility between the two to an end to show a united front in any future peace negotiation, the Israeli Prime Minister, Benjamin Netanyahu, was quick to dismiss this move, making it clear that Israel will be unwilling to negotiate as long as Hamas was in this unity government unless it met certain preconditions including Hamas' disarmament.

On 14 May 2018, 58 people were killed, including many teenagers, by Israeli soldiers along the border fence separating Gaza with Israel. On the same day the United States opened its Embassy in Jerusalem, which coincided with the 70th anniversary of the founding of the state of Israel which Palestinians call the 'Nakba' (the day of catastrophe). The Gaza Health Ministry also reported that 2,700 Palestinian demonstrators were injured — at least 1,350 by gunfire. It was a continuation of the campaign of demonstrations that had begun several weeks before, staged by Palestinian refugees to demand their right to return to their homes in what is now Israel, and also to protest at Israel's economic blockade of Gaza. Israel defended its actions by claiming it was protecting its border against terrorists and that it had thwarted squads of armed Hamas fighters taking advantage of the commotion from launching an attack on the border fence potentially to carry out strikes in Israel. Interestingly, there were no reports of Israeli soldiers being shot with live ammunition during the skirmish. Israel's use of lethal force against mostly unarmed Palestinian protesters, including women and children, created widespread international anger.

However, on 15 May 2018 the US shielded Israel at the UN Security Council, when at an emergency session on the border violence it blocked the release of a draft statement reportedly expressing the Security Council's 'outrage and sorrow at the killing of Palestinian civilians exercising their right to peaceful protest'. But then on 18 May 2018, the UN Human Rights Council voted 29-2 with 14 abstentions approving an independent inquiry into the deaths of the Palestinians (the US and Australia voting against the move). It was reported that the UN High Commissioner for Human Rights, Zeid Ra'ad al-Hussein, told the meeting there was 'little evidence that Israel tried to minimise casualties' that day and that the 'stark contrast in casualties on both sides was... suggestive of a wholly disproportionate response' by Israel with one Israeli soldier being reportedly wounded by a stone. He further stressed that many of the Palestinians injured and killed in the protests were 'completely unarmed and shot in the back, the chest, in the head and limbs with live ammunition'. Furthermore, he claimed there was no justification for the use of lethal force by Israeli forces (based only on the fact that some of the demonstrators threw Molotov cocktails, used slingshots to throw stones, flew burning kites and attempted to use wire-cutters) as there appeared no imminent threat to life or deadly injury to them. The Israeli ambassador to the UN in Geneva, Aviva Raz Shechter, claimed that Israel did try to minimise casualties when defending its borders against terrorists in Gaza who used human shields, accusing the Council of indulging in the 'worst form of anti-Israel obsession' and stating that the vote would not change the situation on the ground. Reportedly, the inquiry is due to report back in March 2019.

On 2 June 2018, the United States voted against a Kuwait-drafted UN Security Council resolution calling for 'the consideration of measures to guarantee the safety and protection of the Palestinian civilian population in the Occupied Palestinian Territory including the Gaza Strip'. The US Ambassador to the UN described the resolution as 'grossly one-sided', pinning the blame on the 'terrorist group Hamas for the awful living conditions in Gaza'. However, ten countries, including Russia and France, voted in favour of the draft resolution. The United Kingdom, Poland, Netherlands and Ethiopia abstained. In fact, the United States, a staunch ally of Israel, was the only country in the UN Security Council to vote against the draft resolution. Shamefully the United States, in turn, was the only country to vote in favour of a revised draft resolution it submitted subsequent to the Kuwait-sponsored motion at the UN Security Council. This second vote saw eleven countries abstaining and three rejecting it. The US-sponsored motion omitted references to Israel's use of force and protecting Palestinians but rather demanded Hamas and other Palestinian groups to cease 'all violent activity and provocative actions' in Gaza, again shielding Israel.

All too often we hear of civilian deaths resulting from frequent Israeli airstrikes against what Israeli Defence Forces (IDF) term 'terror activity sites' responsible for firing rockets into Israel from Gaza. This results in cries for revenge against Israel by Hamas that often take the form of rocket attacks, so there appears no end to this vicious cycle of killings, as will be discussed later.

In May 2011 the United States President, Barack Obama, made official the long-held but rarely stated US support for a future Palestinian state based on borders and lines that existed before the 1967 Middle East war alongside mutually agreed (negotiated) land swaps. The President nonetheless reiterated the United States commitment to Israel's security as 'unshakable' and said 'every state has the right to self-defence, and Israel must be able to defend itself – by itself – against any threat'. The Israeli reaction to the pre-1967 border proposition was naturally predictable, coming in its usual uncompromising stubborn rhetoric. Prime Minister Benjamin Netanyahu claimed that the 1967 lines were key to Israel's security. The Prime Minister also refused to work with any Palestinian government that would include Hamas in the negotiations, calling them the 'Palestinian version of al-Qaeda'. But surely, the way forward to securing a credible and sustainable peace cannot be realised by making unrealistic demands prior to starting negotiations. Hamas too needed to lower the ratchet on its anti–Israeli rhetoric.

The President of the Palestinian Authority, Mahmoud Abbas, undertook efforts in September 2011 following an impasse in negotiations with Israel over its settlement building activities in the West Bank and East Jerusalem to secure a vote at the United Nations on Palestinian statehood. A successful application for full membership in the United Nations, however, requires a recommendation from the United Nations Security Council and a two-thirds majority in the United Nations General Assembly. As a permanent member of the Security Council, the United States made it abundantly clear that it would veto any such recommendation for United Nations membership, while Britain and France remained undeclared. The US went as far as threatening to withdraw United Nations funding if the bid on Palestinian statehood became successful. Interestingly, United States law bars funding by the US to any United Nations Body that grants full membership to Palestine before a peace agreement between Israel and the Palestinians is reached. Accordingly, in October 2011, when the United Nations Educational, Scientific and Cultural Organisation (UNESCO) voted to recognize Palestine as a full member, the US withdrew around $60 million in financial support to it. It must be emphasized here that UNESCO membership has no formal bearing on any bid for Palestinian statehood.

The Obama administration argued that Palestinian statehood without a negotiated peace agreement with Israel would isolate Israel internationally and deal a major setback to Israeli-Palestinian peace prospects. Mr Abbas however, stressed that it was necessary for Palestinians to assert the legitimacy of their claim to territory under pressure from Israeli settlements and that they had no choice, believing that negotiations had run their course. Consequently, the bid for United Nations membership was a logical conclusion to the stalemate. The US insisted, however, that Hamas must denounce its use of terror and accepts Israel's right to exist.

What transpired in the end was that despite the threat of a US veto, Mr Abbas submitted a letter requesting United Nations membership for Palestine to its Secretary-General Ban Ki-moon. The Secretary-General handed the request over to the UN Security Council, which in turn placed the application before its Committee on the Admission of New Members for their recommendation. The Committee, however, was unable to make a unanimous recommendation back to the Security Council with respect to the request for Palestinian membership in the United Nations. The Palestinian bid fell short of the nine 'yes' votes necessary for the resolution to pass the UN Security Council. The US was, as a result, spared from using its power of veto, which ran the risk of alienating the Muslim world on a crucial policy decision that would have opened itself up to criticisms of hypocrisy and double standards by opposing the self-determination of Palestinians, yet supporting uprisings in Libya, Egypt and Syria.

The fact remains that the US was and still is prepared and willing to exercise its power of veto on the issue of Palestinian statehood. So much so that when again in late November 2012, Mahmood Abbas returned to the UN, this time to upgrade Palestinian membership from an 'observer' to a 'non-member state', the US exercised its veto, this time at the General Assembly of the UN. Among the 193 member states of the General Assembly, 138 voted in favour and 9 against with 41 abstentions, which included the United Kingdom and Germany. Nevertheless, it was enough, and Palestine now enjoys the same status at the UN as the Vatican. More crucially it will be able to gain access to the International Criminal Court (ICC), not only to pursue claims of war crimes against Israel but also for Israel's ongoing settlement building on occupied territory. Should Palestine choose to do this, Israel and the US with President Trump at its helm will no doubt retaliate, with crippling financial implications.

Prime Minister Benjamin Netanyahu of Israel both naturally and predictably dismissed the General Assembly vote, calling it 'meaningless', and claimed that it 'won't change anything on the ground'. He must have meant it, for within days of the vote the Israeli government announced that it would go ahead with building new settlements. Recently, in response to reports that the

Palestinian Authority was seeking to prosecute Israel for alleged war crimes in the International Criminal Court (ICC) the US administration in September 2018 announced the closure of the PLO office in Washington, D.C., with the US National Security Advisor, John Bolton, threatening the ICC with sanctions if it carries out investigations into Israel.

The continued building of Israeli settlements with impunity on occupied Palestinian territories is a source of much resentment by Palestinians and is proving to be a major obstacle to peace efforts. This was indicative of the US-sponsored peace talks, which began in July 2013 under the stewardship of US Secretary of State John Kerry and resulted in the tendering of resignations by the Palestinian peace delegation in November 2013, blaming Israel for sabotaging the peace talks by approving the construction of new settlements on occupied territories (West Bank and annexed East Jerusalem). It may be worth noting that Article 49 of the Fourth Geneva Convention provides that an occupying power is forbidden from transferring part of its own civilian population into the territory it occupies. United Nations Security Council Resolution 446, adopted on 22 March 1979, concerning the issue of Israeli settlements in the 'Arab territories occupied by Israel since 1967, including Jerusalem', determined 'that the policy and practices of Israel in establishing settlements in the Palestinian and other Arab territories occupied since 1967 have no legal validity and constitute a serious obstruction to achieving a comprehensive, just and lasting peace in the Middle East'. The resolution was adopted by 12 votes to none, with 3 abstentions, from Norway, the United Kingdom and the United States of America.

The International Court of Justice considers these settlements in the occupied territories as illegal too, as do some Western powers. Yet Israel continues to expand existing settlements, in addition to settling new areas in the form of settlement outposts. Successive Israeli governments have always emphasized that all settlements are legal and consistent with international law.

Despite the settlements' illegality, ironically Israeli firms operating in these illegal settlements continue to engage in international trade, mainly in fresh fruits and vegetables, with considerable exports to Europe securing substantial revenues. Though Israel and the EU have trade agreements, surely this cannot be intended to benefit goods produced on illegal settlements in the occupied territories? Furthermore, EU firms, including British businesses, have extensive commercial involvement in illegal Israeli settlements, particularly in construction. In 2012, the European Union began working on guidelines for labelling Israeli products exported to Europe that were manufactured in the West Bank. Then in January 2016, the European Union made clear its position that farm and other products made in Israeli settlements must not be labelled as 'Made in Israel' but labelled as coming from the settlements, with European Union Foreign Ministers reiterating that the European Union does not recognize Israel's occupation of the West Bank, Gaza, East Jerusalem and the Golan Heights captured in the 1967 Middle East war, the labelling policy being intended to distinguish between goods made inside the internationally-accepted borders of Israel and those made outside. Predictably, the Israeli government reacted strongly to this and suspended contact with European Union Bodies involved with peace efforts with the Palestinians. Shrewdly, Israel nevertheless insisted that it was retaining bilateral relations with all European Union countries. In doing this, while retaining trade links with the European Union, Israel sought to use this as a pretext to undermine the European Union's desire for a more active role in seeking to effect a peace between Israel and the Palestinians.

In any case, this move by the European Union is likely to have a limited impact only, mainly affecting fresh produce estimated by the Israeli Economy Ministry to be about $50 million which is around a fifth of the $200–300 million worth of goods produced in the settlements each year. This compares relatively insignificantly to the $30 billion of goods and services Israel exports to the European Union annually. Despite this, Israeli Ministers have criticized the European Union's stance on labelling as amounting to a boycott of Israel similar to the Boycott, Divestment and Sanctions Movement, popularly known as the (BDS) movement that was initiated in 2005 by a coalition of Palestinian NGOs.

BDS, inspired by the campaign to end apartheid in South Africa, has continually gained support, particularly among universities and unions in Europe and the United States. It calls for non-violent pressure on Israel through boycott, divestment and sanctions until it complies with international law by meeting three demands namely, ending its occupation and colonization of all occupied lands and dismantling of its wall; recognizing the fundamental rights of the Arab-Palestinian citizens of Israel to full equality and respecting, protecting and promoting the rights of Palestinian refugees to return to their homes and properties as stipulated in United Nations General Assembly Resolution 194 (III).

It is understandable that the US and particularly Israel are apprehensive of a unilateral declaration and subsequent recognition by International Bodies of Palestinian statehood, as this would threaten both US and Israeli interests. It would undermine accepted frameworks for peace based on negotiated agreements in which the US no doubt wishes to see itself as a major player. Understandably perhaps, many Muslims across the Muslim world perceive the unrelenting support in favour of Israel by some Western powers, in particular by the US, as not only injustice to the plight of Palestinians but by extension an underlying antipathy to Islam and Muslims which feeds substance to the rhetoric that the 'West is at war with Islam'.

Ironically, while despotic regimes in the Middle East express their support for the oppressed Palestinian people these regimes themselves enforce an iron grip on their own populations, denying them their civil liberties. In this regard, power politics is surely the art of the possible. And yet when Israeli airstrikes pounded Gaza in November 2012 in response to rockets fired by Hamas into Israeli cities, those despotic regimes could only muster calls demanding a ceasefire to the bloodshed.

It was Egypt's then new democratic government that seized the initiative to broker a ceasefire between Hamas and Israel, which came into effect on 21 November 2012. The preceding eight days of airstrikes and rocket attacks left more than 150

Palestinians and five Israelis dead, mostly civilians, in what Israel called 'Operation Pillar of Defence'. Hamas claimed victory over the ceasefire, claiming that Israel had indirectly recognized Hamas on a political level when up until then Israel had branded Hamas a terrorist organization. The Egyptian President's credibility in brokering the ceasefire later proved to be a pretext for Mohamed Morsi to grant himself sweeping new powers in the name of safeguarding national security, which he subsequently had to relinquish however, following clashes between pro and anti-Muslim Brotherhood activists that rocked Cairo in December 2012. Following months of political stalemate and a failing economy, the Egyptian military finally ousted Mohamed Morsi from power on 3 July 2013, suspending the constitution in what can only be described as a military coup against Egypt's first democratically-elected President.

Despite efforts by US Secretary of State John Kerry starting in mid-2013 to effect a peace deal between Israel and the Palestinians, violence nevertheless again erupted in the summer of 2014. With the Fatah-dominated Palestinian Authority in the West Bank and Gaza-controlled Hamas forming a 'national unity government' in April 2014, Israel reacted furiously by suspending peace talks with the Palestinian Authority demanding that they nullify their agreement with Hamas. (The Israeli political establishment, in contravention of the Oslo Accords signed in 1993, that recognized Gaza and the West Bank to be an inseparable territorial unit, has increasingly sought to separate the Gaza Strip from the West Bank as part of any future political settlement, the intention being to integrate regions of the West Bank it considers to be of value as a part of Israel.) Two Palestinian teenagers were shot dead by Israeli police in May 2014 while demonstrating against Israel's Independence Day, and tensions between the two sides further escalated after the abduction and killing of three Israeli teenagers from the settler community in the West Bank in June 2014 (that Israel blamed on members of Hamas), and the subsequent suspected revenge killing of a Palestinian teenager in Jerusalem by burning him to death at the beginning of July 2014. Compounding the situation, in searching for the abducted teenagers as part of a 'collective punishment' Israel carried out search operations resulting in the arrest of hundreds of West Bank Palestinians (many without charge or having no connection to the kidnappings) with a series of Israeli air strikes which killed several members of Hamas, in response to which Hamas launched rocket attacks against Israel. Consequently, serious violence broke out between the two belligerents.

According to a report published by UNOCHA on 4 September 2014, between 8 July and 26 August 2014, Israeli airstrikes and the naval bombardment of Gaza (including an Israeli ground invasion) resulted in more than 2100 Palestinians being killed, mostly civilians, of whom 501 were children when Israel launched Operation 'Protective Edge' to stop rocket fire from Gaza into Israel and to destroy Hamas' military capability. The Israeli bombardment was played out in front of the global media, which reported on the deaths of women and children, as well as the catastrophic destruction of infrastructure in Gaza with approximately 18,000 housing units being destroyed or severely damaged, rendering more than 100,000 Palestinians homeless. More than 10,000 Palestinians were wounded. Also according to the UNOCHA more than 500,000 Palestinians in Gaza were displaced at the height of the hostilities, with around 110,000 remaining internally displaced and taking refuge in United Nations Relief and Works Agency (UNRWA) emergency shelters and with host families following the ceasefire of 26 August 2014. On the other hand, 71 Israelis were killed, of whom 66 were soldiers. Reportedly, damage to Israeli infrastructure was comparatively negligible despite the more than 4000 rockets that were fired from Gaza during the conflict (with less than 10 percent striking Israeli residential areas). What caused anguish within the Muslim Ummah was the fact that all this was happening in the Muslim holy month of Ramadan with the global media covering the deaths of children on a daily basis.

What took many Muslim living in the West by surprise was the 'limited response' by Western European governments in condemning the attack on Gaza in terms of the overwhelming attacks carried out by the Israeli military machine. Furthermore, the US President's rhetoric that 'Israel had the right to defend itself' against rocket attacks in response to which the Israeli military used disproportionate force against the Gaza strip, as evidenced by the loss in civilian lives and substantial destruction to infrastructure, frustrated the patience of ordinary Muslims across the Ummah who were wishing for a peaceful and speedy resolution to the conflict.

Sadly, what is equally deeply disturbing but often overlooked by media reports is the continuing trauma suffered by Gaza's inhabitants, particularly children who have lost their loved ones, as well as families that have lost their livelihoods, rendering them dependent on aid to sustain themselves. The destruction to schools and other educational establishments, including disruption to utility supplies such as water and electricity, denying Gazans the dignity of ordinary civic life, is also distressing and humiliating to Gaza's inhabitants.

The worst form of persecution and the most potent way to weaken an enemy is to break their self-respect and dignity by ensuring that they remain in a constant state of poverty and fear. This, the Israeli political and military establishment has surely endeavoured to achieve with its repeated military incursions into Gaza. In this context, between 27 December 2008 and 18 January 2009, in a previous Israeli ground offensive into Gaza called Operation 'Cast Lead', again in response to rocket fire from the Gaza strip (allegedly provoked by an earlier Israeli incursion into Gaza on 4 November 2008 that killed half a dozen Hamas militants), an estimated 1400 Palestinians were killed (mostly civilians), some 5000 were injured and many maimed for life, with extensive damage being done to Gaza's civilian infrastructure. It was reported by Amnesty International that some 300 children were killed. The Israeli army, however, stressed that most of those killed were not civilians and that they do not deliberately target civilians.

There is an important observation to make here. History teaches us that when a population is faced with continued persecution, this radicalises their resolve to such an extent that they start thinking they have nothing to lose by fighting back.

If the international community has not realised this with respect to the Palestinians aspiration to achieve statehood, then that is regrettable.

With unemployment in Gaza hovering around 45% and simmering tensions between Gazans and Israel reaching fever pitch due to the continued blockade and the lack of any progress on peace talks, the potential of another conflict between the two belligerents is very much a reality. The UN Secretary General, Ban Ki-moon, while visiting Gaza on 28 June 2016, commented 'the closure of Gaza suffocates its people, stifles its economy and impedes reconstruction efforts. And for this collective punishment there must be accountability'. However he urged both Israeli and Palestinian leaders to take courageous steps for a lasting two-state solution. Should the present dire situation continue, the UN Secretary General went on to state that 'it would feed anger and despair increasing the danger of a new escalation of hostilities'.

An interesting observation was made by the UN Special Coordinator, Nickolay Mladenov, while briefing the Security Council on 30 June 2016. He stated, 'Palestinian frustration cannot be washed away; it cannot be vanquished by aggressive security measures, arrests or punitive home demolitions… But nor will the violence and terror, fuelled by resentment, bring about a Palestinian state'.

For any peace process to have a real chance of success, both Gaza and the West Bank must be treated as one viable territorial entity that would be governed by a single, democratic government based on the rule of law, with an independent judiciary and economic freedom. Both Palestine and Israel must be allowed to be viable independent states having full control of their respective ports and security. Should, on the other hand, Israel reject the Oslo Accords and demand that the West Bank be included as a part of Israel, in what many observers are beginning to describe as a 'one state reality', whereby Israel would offer its Palestinian inhabitants local autonomy with improved security and economic incentives while retaining most of the West Bank, the prospects of a two-state solution and a sustainable peace would be critically undermined. It is difficult to see how this so-called one-state reality would work in practice because Israel would then have to tackle the contentious issue of addressing what political rights the Palestinians in the occupied West Bank would have in terms of their eligibility to vote in elections to the Israeli Knesset and the right of such Palestinians to be elected as members of the Knesset. If on the other hand, the Israeli government were to deny Palestinians in the occupied West Bank the right to vote or participate in the political process in a one-state reality, then the end result would be nothing less than instituting a policy of apartheid. As the only democracy in the Middle East, Israel will find itself increasingly isolated from the international community for running an apartheid state akin to South Africa during its apartheid history on the treatment of blacks.

Interestingly, there three categories of Palestinians for Israel. First there are Palestinians (Israeli Arabs) who remained in Israel after the 1948 war who have Israeli citizenship and can vote in both national and local elections. Then there are Palestinians from East Jerusalem, who are considered 'permanent residents in Israel' but do not have Israeli citizenship and are only allowed to vote in municipal elections and not in the national elections for the Knesset. To make things worse for the 420,000 Palestinians living in East Jerusalem, following the ratification of the controversial 'Breach of Loyalty' Bill by the Knesset on 7 March 2018, the Israeli Interior Ministry now has the power to seize residency permits of Palestinians in East Jerusalem deemed to be a threat to the state of Israel. This new law effectively seeks to impose upon the Palestinians an obligation of loyalty to an occupying power. And finally there are Palestinians who are 'resident' in occupied territories of the West Bank and Gaza, who are not allowed to participate in either national or municipal elections but are restricted to voting in Palestinian Authority elections.

According to a recent article published on the Jewish Virtual Library, around 21% of Israel's more than 8 million citizens are Arabs, of which 81% are Muslims enjoying equal voting rights and currently holding ten seats in the Israeli Parliament, the Knesset. A report issued in January 2016 by the Palestinian Central Bureau of Statistics (PCBS) puts the number of Palestinians living in the

Gaza Strip and the West Bank at 1.85 million and 2.9 million respectively. By the end of 2020, the report estimates that the number of Palestinians in present-day Israel, the West Bank and Gaza will likely equal if not surpass the number of Jews by 2020. It is difficult to see, therefore, how the current Israeli political establishment will accord equal voting rights to all Palestinians in a one-state reality. This raises the question of how the Israeli power elite will accommodate this demographic realism. Even if Gaza were to be excluded from Israel's one-state reality, the Palestinians of the occupied West Bank will still represent a significant proportion of the population. It is for this reason that Israeli policy makers have encouraged aggressive settlement building in the West Bank.

Though Britain does not officially recognize Palestine as a state, on 13 October 2014, the United Kingdom Parliament called upon its government to recognize the state of Palestine alongside the state of Israel – the aim being to recognize two states whose peoples enjoy equal rights. MPs voted by an overwhelming majority on the motion to recognize Palestine (274 for, 12 against). Though the vote was symbolic it nevertheless marked a shift in the political landscape following the failure of peace negotiations and the bitter conflict in the Gaza strip earlier that summer. Even staunch supporters of Israel within the Conservative party chose not to oppose the motion that was brought by the Labour backbench MP Grahame Morris. Like many Conservative MPs, Prime Minister David Cameron abstained from the vote rather than voting against the motion, reiterating nevertheless that the vote would not affect Britain's foreign policy on the matter.

On 30 October 2014, Sweden became the first EU Member State in Western Europe to officially recognize the state of Palestine. While the Palestinian leadership welcomed the move, Israel summoned Sweden's ambassador to protest and express its disappointment. The United States cautioned Sweden against recognition, calling it 'premature' and making the point that a Palestinian state could only come through a negotiated solution between Israelis and Palestinians. Given the fact the any constructive dialogue between Israel and the Palestinians has been seriously undermined following the election of US President Donald Trump in November 2017 and the re-election of Benjamin Netanyahu in March 2015, as illustrated below, it is now imperative that the EU as a whole officially recognises an independent sovereign Palestinian state alongside the state of Israel.

All too often in various media reports we see both the Israeli and Palestinian leadership blaming each other for failing to engage in any meaningful dialogue for a sustainable peace accusing each other of undermining any peace initiative. Only a two-state solution can guarantee a democratic Israel in the distant future. A single binational state with an equal number of Jews and Arabs will not remain democratic but will rather fester apartheid. Both sides are nevertheless blameworthy for perpetuating hostilities and mistrust between them, for you cannot shake hands with clenched fists! While with so many stakeholders involved, it may be difficult to take decisive decisions. The ultimatums for peace must be rooted not in any partisan US foreign policy but in the hopes and aspiration of the peoples of both Israel and Palestine.

Netanyahu's election victory in March 2015 and his refusal to work for a two-state solution that formed part of his election rhetoric are quite revealing. Not only does it match the policies of the Likud Party but in the absence of any renewed negotiations sponsored by the West between the two belligerents since the failure of John Kerry's diplomatic initiative, a one-state reality would appear to represent Netanyahu's political strategy. Especially when back in 2016 the political leadership in the United States, Europe and most of the Middle East were focused on other contentious matters including the military intervention by Russia in the Syrian civil war, the desperate situation in the Syrian city of Aleppo that threatened to ignite another Cold War between Russia and the West, Iraqi attempts to oust ISIL from Iraq's second largest city of Mosul and the potential descent of Yemen into a failed state with Saudi Arabia leading a military coalition against (Shi'ite) Houthi Rebels who had forced President Abd Rabbuh Mansoor al-Hadi (previously Vice President to former President,

Ali Abdullah Saleh) to flee to Saudi Arabia.

As a result of the Arab Spring of 2011 and its political fallout, the Middle East has witnessed curious developments, with countries aligning themselves on the lines of the 'Shi'ite-Sunni divide', which has allowed Israel to cunningly ally itself with Saudi Arabia and other Sunni authoritarian regimes in the region against Iran and Syria contrary to the dichotomy of the Arab-Israeli conflict of the past. With Hamas being labelled a 'terrorist organization' by both Israel, Egypt and the United States the 'Palestinian question' is for the time being not crucial to Israel's security and its relationship with the Sunni Arab states in the region. The reality on the ground following the Arab Spring of 2011 has forced the political dynamics in the Middle East to enter a new phase that may very well see Europe taking the lead on seeking to support the Palestinian issue by recognizing the demand for Palestinian statehood. This is however, subject to the caveat that far-right wing parties across Europe, particularly in France and Germany, don't disrupt any concerted European effort to promote the Palestinian cause.

However, following Donald Trump's victory in the United States Presidential Elections in November 2016, any hopes of a Palestinian state as part of a viable two-state solution appear to have been diminished, especially any claim by the Palestinians that the West Bank and East Jerusalem should form part of any future Palestinian state. Mr Trump is viewed by the political elite in Israel as supporting the building of Jewish settlements in the West Bank and East Jerusalem (occupied territories), long condemned by successive United States administrations. In fact, the far-right Israeli Education Minister, Naftali Bennett, was reported by different media streams as having stated that with the election of Donald Trump, 'the era of a Palestinian state is over'. Benjamin Netanyahu's relationship with Donald Trump in the context of Israel's relationship with the Palestinians will no doubt be closely looked upon by political analysts.

On 22 December 2016, the United Nations Security Council passed resolution 2334 calling for an end to illegal Israeli settlements after the United States 'refused' to veto it. In fact, the resolution demanded that Israel 'immediately and completely cease all settlement activities in the occupied Palestinian territory, including East Jerusalem' and reaffirmed that 'the establishment of settlements by Israel in the Palestinian territory occupied since 1967, including East Jerusalem has no legal validity and constitutes a flagrant violation under international law and a major obstacle to the achievement of the two-state solution and a just, lasting and comprehensive peace '. The United States is well known to veto such resolutions, sheltering Israel from condemnatory resolutions. However the United States Ambassador to the United Nations argued (only weeks prior to Donald Trump taking the oath of President) that the resolution reflected an international consensus that the growth of Israeli settlement-building had come to threaten the viability of a Palestinian state in any future peace deal. The resolution was indicative of the reality on the grounds that settlement growth had been accelerating. The United States Ambassador went on to state: 'the settlement problem has gotten so much worse that it is threatening the two-state solution'. She also criticized Israeli Prime Minister Benjamin Netanyahu's support for settlement expansion, saying, 'one cannot simultaneously champion expanding settlements and champion a two-state solution that would end the conflict'.

Interestingly, the resolution was put forward for a vote on the 22nd of December to the 15-member Security Council by New Zealand, Malaysia, Venezuela and Senegal a day after Egypt withdrew the draft resolution following arm-twisting by Israel and the United States President-elect Donald Trump, who had spoken with Egyptian President Abdel-Fattah al-Sisi. Both Israel and Mr Trump had called on the United States to veto the measure. Remarkably, the resolution was adopted with 14 votes in favour with the abstention of the United States. (A United Nations Security Council resolution requires 9 votes in favour and no vetoes by any of the permanent members namely, the United States, France, Russia, United Kingdom or China to be adopted).

Naturally the Israeli government and its ambassador to the

United Nations reacted angrily to the resolution and criticized the stance taken by the United States, ignoring the fact that the other 4 permanent members did not veto either. Israel, in a furious backlash, described the resolution as 'shameful', 'disgraceful' and 'an abandonment of Israel'.

Then on 28 December 2016, United States Secretary of State John Kerry went out of his way to explain why the United States did not veto the resolution. He argued that the current settlement building activities by Israel in the West Bank were undermining the viability of a two-state solution and therefore any prospect for peace. He also criticised the coalition government of Benjamin Netanyahu as the most 'right wing' oriented in Israel's history, saying it was not interested in finding a two-state solution to Israel's conflict with the Palestinians but 'believed in one state: a greater Israel'. In fact, he warned that the rapid expansion of settlements in the occupied territories meant that 'the status quo is leading towards one state and perpetual occupation'. Mr Kerry went on to emphasise, however, that President Obama was committed to Israel's security and to the peace process, but despite best efforts over the years, the two-state solution was in serious jeopardy. Interestingly, though supporting the Security Council resolution the United Kingdom's Prime Minister's Office subsequently condemned Secretary Kerry's critical evaluation of the Israeli coalition as being the most right-wing in Israel's history, stating that it was 'inappropriate to attack a democratically-elected government of an ally'. The Prime Minister's Office also highlighted that the settlements were far from the only problem in the conflict and in particular, the people of Israel deserved to live free from the threat of terrorism, with which they have had to cope for too long.

In January 2017 a Peace Conference took place in Paris under the auspices of French President François Hollande. Had Marine Le Pen and her National Rally political party gained power, France's commitment to a viable two-state solution was likely to go in the same direction as the United States following the election of Donald Trump.

As was anticipated on a visit by Israeli Prime Minister, Benjamin Netanyahu, to Washington, D.C. on 15 February 2017, US President Donald Trump signalled that the US was not solely committed or wedded to a two-state solution. This is a significant departure from US foreign policy since the Oslo Peace Accords of 1993. During the joint press conference it became apparent that the US and Israel were seeking to achieve a comprehensive peace that would bring in 'new allies' of Israel in the Middle East. It will be interesting to see how the US and Israel's new allies in the region put pressure on the Palestinian leadership to accept a peace other than the two-state solution. The threat of cutting off aid to the Palestinian Authority by its major donors including the US and Saudi Arabia unless it accepted their planned Middle East peace proposal could prove to be a game changer. (In January 2018, the United States President threatened to cut off aid to the Palestinian Authority unless it recommenced peace talks with Israel, this after Donald Trump recognized Jerusalem as the capital of Israel. Earlier, the United States Ambassador to the United Nations, Nikki Haley, had already threatened that the United States would cut funds to the UNRWA, the United Nations agency for Palestinian refugees, unless the Palestinian Authority went back to the negotiating table).

It may be worth noting that the UN Relief and Works Agency (UNRWA) provides Palestinian refugees with health care, education and social services in the West Bank, Gaza strip, Jordan, Syria and Lebanon. Regrettably, in a move supported by Israel, in a statement on 1 September 2018, the US Department of State declared that it would be cutting all further funding to the UNRWA which it deemed to be 'fundamentally flawed'. The Department claimed that the US had been shouldering a very 'disproportionate share' of the UNRWA costs and that the international community should contribute more. It further criticized the way UNRWA was expanding the number of refugees eligible for assistance expressing disagreement over which Palestinians can indeed be classified as refugees. This argument plays into the bigger picture over which Palestinian refugees have a right to return to homes they fled following the

1948 Arab–Israeli war. Given UNRWA involvement, cutting off aid to the organization from its largest donor will have a profound effect on the assistance it provides to the most desperate, fragile and vulnerable. Critics have argued that this latest move by the US makes a mockery of humanitarian assistance, citing that it has done nothing more than to use humanitarian aid as a weapon.

In October 2017, an interim agreement was concluded in Cairo setting up a new unity government between Hamas and the Palestinian Authority to bring the hostility between the two to an end to present a united front in any future peace negotiation. However, again the Israeli Prime Minister Benjamin Netanyahu was quick to dismiss this move making it clear that Israel will be unwilling to negotiate as long as Hamas was in it unless it met certain preconditions including its disarmament and that Gaza be placed under the full security control of the Palestinian Authority, including border crossings.

With the intention of getting the United States to recognize the 'entire' city of Jerusalem as Israel's 'eternal capital', members of the Israeli ruling coalition had called on Donald Trump to act on his election pledge to move the United States Embassy from the coastal city of Tel Aviv to Jerusalem. Such a move would overturn decades of United States foreign policy and surely prove contentious to any prospect of a future peace deal, as Palestinians have earmarked East Jerusalem to be the capital of any future Palestinian state. But then on 6 December 2017, Donald Trump defied global opposition, announcing from the White House to the world that the United States was officially recognizing Jerusalem as the capital of Israel, directing the State Department to start making arrangements to move the United States Embassy there. Though the President did not declare Jerusalem to be the undivided capital of Israel, reiterating that the United States was not taking a position on any final status issues, including the specific boundaries of Israeli sovereignty in Jerusalem, that was little consolation to the chorus of criticism from world leaders, including the United Nations General Secretary, Antonio Guterres, who viewed the United States unilateral declaration prior to any comprehensive final status negotiations between

Israel and the Palestinians as 'jeopardizing the prospect of peace for Israelis and Palestinians'. The British Prime Minister was reported to have also said that Mr Trump's announcement was 'unhelpful in terms of prospect for peace in the region'. The French President, Emmanuel Macron, and the German Chancellor, Angela Merkel, also condemned the move.

In an immediate reaction to the announcement, Palestinian President Mahmoud Abbas reportedly said that the United States had effectively abdicated its role as mediator in the region, while the chief Palestinian negotiator, Saeb Erekat, said that President Trump had 'destroyed any policy of a two-state solution'. Prior to making his announcement, Pope Francis had issued a heartfelt plea to the President to respect the status quo of the city, and to conform to United Nations resolutions. Worryingly, Hamas called for a third intifada.

In the Middle East, the response was universally hostile with Saudi Arabia, Turkey, Jordan, Lebanon and other regional governments criticizing the announcement as jeopardizing the peace process that would escalate regional tensions. For now, both President Trump and the Israeli Prime Minister, Benjamin Netanyahu have however, reiterated that the status quo of 'Haram al Sharif' that encompasses both the Dome of the Rock and the Al-Aqsa Mosque (the third holiest site for global Muslims) would not be altered by the United States recognition of Jerusalem as Israel's capital. For the sake of preventing a violent backlash on an apocalyptic scale let us pray this status quo of Islam's holy sites does remain. For should hawkish elements within Israel's religious and political establishment, emboldened by President Trump's announcement, subsequently take concrete steps to alter the status quo of 'Haram al Sharif', this will surely cause outrage across the Muslim Ummah that Muslim governments will not be able to contain. The harrowing prospect of an Armageddon being unleashed upon the Middle East will become very much a reality. What is already alarming for global Muslims and had proved potentially damaging for renewed peace prospects was the move made by Israeli right-wing politicians in February 2014 forcing a debate in the Israeli Knesset to annex and enforce sovereignty over the Al-Aqsa Mosque compound, which is currently being managed by an Islamic trust and administered by the State of Jordan by virtue of the Jordan-Israeli Peace Treaty of 1994. Furthermore, eager to find evidence of what Israeli authorities believe to be ancient Jewish temples, excavation works are being carried out beneath the Old City of Jerusalem as well as at the Al-Aqsa Mosque compound, posing a threat to the structural integrity of the sacred mosque. All the while elements within the Israeli political establishment wish to fulfil the 'Jewish prophecy' of building the 'Third Temple' at the Al-Aqsa Mosque compound.

This announcement by President Donald Trump has no doubt cast an eye of suspicion on his thought processes, giving ammunition to extremists to reiterate their point that the current political establishment in the United States is increasingly at odds with the Muslim Ummah and fuelling rhetoric that it is also at odds with Muslims and Islam in general. Critics allege that Mr Trump's disdain and mistrust of Muslims appears to be influenced by the radical narrative pursued by extremists and being unable to disassociate this from the vast majority of Muslims who do not support the radical interpretation of Islam as well as, his own ignorance of the true tenants of Islam as a religion of peace. They point, among other things, to the travel ban on a number of Muslim nations, the support of the Saudi regime despite its appalling human rights record and military action in Yemen that has resulted in a humanitarian disaster, the retweeting of far-right extremist tweets, and the dishonouring of US commitments particularly, the Iran nuclear deal.

In fact, it beggars belief that the United States strongly believes that after inflaming emotions across the Arab world and thrusting Arab governments into a precarious position, it can still see itself as a leading neutral arbitrator in any peace negotiations. It appears that Donald Trump, whether wittingly or not, has surely put a spanner in the works. Critics have argued that by recognizing Jerusalem as the capital of Israel the United States, as the world's only superpower, in an attempt to recognize the so-called 'current reality', has sought to legitimize the contentious (illegal) Israeli settlements in East Jerusalem. While the United States considers its decision on Jerusalem as right and just for Israel, Palestinians also have a right to fair and just treatment.

At a summit held in Turkey on 14 December 2017, the Organization of Islamic Countries (OIC) declared East Jerusalem as the occupied capital of Palestine, adding that the 57-member group remains committed to a 'just and comprehensive peace based on a two-state solution'. It called the declaration by Donald Trump 'null and void lacking any legitimacy', as it sought to change the legal status of Jerusalem. At the summit the Palestinian President, Mahmoud Abbas, reportedly stated that the United States had 'disqualified' itself from future Israeli–Palestinian peace talks after proving its 'bias in favour of Israel'.

Then on 18 December 2017 the United States vetoed a United Nations Security Council draft resolution that 'any decisions and actions which purport to have altered the character, status or demographic compositions of the Holy City of Jerusalem have no legal effect and are null and void and must be rescinded in compliance with relevant resolutions of the Security Council'. Interestingly the United States was not named in Egypt's draft resolution, but that did not deter the United States from exercising its veto, preventing the draft resolution from being adopted. The draft resolution was however, backed by the other 14 Security Council members, including many allies of the United States. Observers view this as an increasing isolation of the United States over a sensitive issue that has triggered mass demonstrations in many major international cities in support of the Palestinians. A defiant United States Ambassador to the United Nations, Nikki Haley, however went on to state that the United States had the 'courage and honesty to recognize a fundamental reality'. She added that Jerusalem has been the political, cultural and spiritual homeland of the Jewish people for millennia and that they had no other capital city. But then it will not be out of place to observe that the United States in its aggressive diplomatic posturing is conveniently positioning Israel to gain maximum advantage in any future comprehensive peace plan.

Following the anticipated veto by the United States, the Palestinian leadership in the West Bank called for an emergency special session of the 193-member United Nations General Assembly to pass a resolution calling on Donald Trump to rescind his decision. In a move that critics pointed to as not only amounting to intimidation by the United States but further questioning the United States legitimacy to act as a neutral arbitrator in any future peace initiative, Ms Haley, prior to the vote on the resolution, threatened United Nations member states with possible retaliation if they supported the resolution by cutting off financial aid. Then on 21 December 2017, despite the warning, the United Nations General Assembly adopted resolution (A/ES-10/L.22) titled 'Status of Jerusalem' by voting 128 to 9 against, with 21 absentees and 35 abstentions, declaring 'null and void' any actions intended to 'alter Jerusalem's character, status or demographic composition'. It called on all states to refrain from establishing embassies in the Holy City, demanding that they all comply with all relevant Security Council resolutions and work to reverse the 'negative trends' imperilling a two-state solution of the Israeli–Palestinian conflict. The draft resolution was presented by Yemen (Chair of the Arab Group) and Turkey (Chair of the OIC).

The Minister for Foreign Affairs of the State of Palestine, Riad Al-Malki, reportedly insisted that the emergency session was not called because of any animosity to the United States but rather to make the voice of the vast majority of the international community – and that of the people around the world – heard on the question of Jerusalem/al-Quds al-Sharif. He described the 6 December 2017 decision by the United States President to recognize Jerusalem as Israel's capital, and to move the United States embassy there as an aggressive and dangerous move, cautioning that it could inflame tensions and lead to a religious war that would have 'no boundaries'.

Ms Haley declared that regardless of this vote, the United States would still locate its embassy in Jerusalem. Failing to bully the majority of the United Nations member states into submission from exercising their sovereign right, she then made a subtle threat to the United Nations itself as an institution. She reportedly warned that the United States was by far the largest single contributor to the United Nations and that its contributions were intended to advance its national values and interests, but when such an investment failed, the US government would be obliged to spend its resources 'in more productive ways'.

Recognizing the vote as largely symbolic, the Israeli Prime Minister, Benjamin Netanyahu, was quick to reject this decision of the United Nations, expressing his gratitude to the countries that had abstained and thanking President Trump on his unequivocal position on Jerusalem.

It is, however, interesting to note that 22 of the 28 EU States voted for the resolution, including the United Kingdom, France and Germany as well as allies of the United States in the Middle East, such as Saudi Arabia. Thirty-five countries did abstain including 5 EU States, and other United States allies including Australia, Canada, Columbia and Mexico, although representatives from abstaining countries, including Mexico, used their time on the podium to criticize Trump's unilateral move. Another 21 states were absent from the vote, suggesting Trump's warning over funding cuts and Israel's furious lobbying may have paid off to a limited extent.

To criticize the Israeli government's policy in Gaza and the West Bank including East Jerusalem is not anti-Semitic, as has often been suggested by some media streams and vested interests. (In fact, to suggest otherwise is to belittle what should aptly be condemned as being anti-Semitic). Rather, such criticism is to focus attention to the apartheid policy being directed against Palestinians by the Israeli government. Sadly, what the Israeli–Palestinian conflict has done is to allow more than one generation of Palestinians to know of nothing other than conflict, death and suffering. Families have been torn apart, with many children orphaned, having lost either or both their parents to Israeli air strikes, while parents have had to endure the pain of losing their children and wives of losing their husbands. Not to mention the many thousands of Palestinians who have ended up in Israeli prisons (including children) without recourse to any legal representation. Thousands face hunger and a life of destitution. With Palestinians having to live in a state of perpetual poverty and fear, this has inevitably caused an entire generation to 'hate' their Israeli occupiers. Israel too has suffered with a substantial part of its budget going on defence spending as well as, loss of life, albeit on a much lower scale. If the leadership of either Israel or the Palestinians seek this conflict to fester without any prospect of a viable peace process, we can only hope that the people will eventually rise up and demand that their leaders seek a permanent resolution to this conflict which can only bring peace and economic prosperity to them.

Political sovereignty, it must be stressed, ultimately resides with the people and not the government, whether that government be democratic or autocratic. The longer the international community, particularly the United Nations, fails to effectively work towards a viable and sustainable peace, the greater the risk of extremist narratives becoming entrenched on both sides of the political spectrum.

The time for reconciliation and consensus has arrived. To deny Israel's right to exist as well as the Palestinians' right to statehood is escaping or denying reality. While the International Holocaust Remembrance Alliance (IHRA) definition of antisemitism specifies 11 contemporary examples to include denying the Jewish people their right to self-determination, e.g., by claiming that the existence of the State of Israel is a racist endeavour, which many countries have adopted, to give it balance, what of the Palestinian right to self-determination too, culminating in two independent sovereign states bound by a comprehensive peace agreement? Ultimately, it must be said that it is for the peoples of both Palestine and Israel to agree terms to any sustainable peace agreement. This should entail putting any eventual peace proposal to a referendum

THE HIJACKING OF THE ARAB SPRING

Let us turn our attention to the Arab Spring of 2011 and the contemporary relationship between the West and the Muslim Ummah. Some political scientists have commented that the Arab Spring was a direct consequence of the 2003 United States-led invasion and occupation of Iraq. Such an observation is too simplistic in the light of events as they unfolded. Rather, political analysts should be critically assessing whether the Arab Spring, or as the Iranians preferred to call it, the 'Islamic Awakening', represented the culmination of an ongoing power struggle in the region that threatened the dominance of Sunni Islam in the Middle East from Shi'ite Islam. Though initially, the Arab uprisings, witnessed solidarity across national borders by the masses, particularly among the youth population, protests in the Gulf, in countries such as Saudi Arabia, Bahrain and subsequently in Yemen, quickly took the appearance of a sectarian conflict (with the protests being portrayed by these regimes as a bid by Iran to spur up Shi'ite dominance in the region) which had also been exploited by some Western powers. When the ruling (Sunni) Al-Khalifa family of Bahrain called on the support of Saudi troops in March 2011, albeit under the aegis of the Gulf Cooperation Council (GCC) (a six-nation regional coalition of Sunni ruled countries namely, Saudi Arabia, Kuwait, the United Arab Emirates, Bahrain, Qatar and Oman) to assist in what can appropriately described as a brutal crackdown on the (predominantly Shi'ite) peoples' uprising against its rule, the Western powers took a relatively cautious approach, not only in terms of their public criticism of the crackdown but also the lack of comprehensive Western media coverage of the murders, arrests and disappearances of pro-democracy protesters. The US Fifth Fleet, based in Bahrain, is critical to United States political and military interests in the region, in particular to check any ambitious military moves on the part of Shi'ite dominated Iran.

Curiously, the Arab Spring failed to make any meaningful headway in terms of ushering pluralist democratic electoral reforms to the region's autocratic monarchies. The eight Arab monarchies (the above Gulf Cooperation Countries as well as Jordan and Morocco) have come through unscathed, as opposed to the region's authoritarian republics. The monarchies are far from being constitutional kingships. Rather, the Kings and Emirs wield near-absolute power, naming their cabinets, dictating major domestic and foreign policies, controlling the state's security services and allowing limited authority to Parliaments (where they exist in name only) and the judiciary. This power is exercised through a nexus of loyal extended families. Saudi Arabia took a leading role in propping up many of the monarchies in the region with the Hashemite House of Jordan enjoying resolute promises of support.

Along with Iraq, Bahrain has a sizable Shi'ite population. If we look at the demography of the Middle East, Shi'ites represents a significant percentage of the population in several States. Prior to the Arab Spring of 2011, according to the Pew Forum Report of 2009 on global Muslim population, the percentage of the Muslim population that is Shi'ite in Bahrain was between 65-75%; in Iraq between 65-70%; in Lebanon between 45-55% and in Yemen between 35-45%. The worst nightmare scenario for the West, and in particular Israel, was the fear that the Arab Spring was about to usher in democratically-elected Shi'ite governments across the Middle East, backed by a nuclear weapons-capable Iran, which would have undoubtedly led to nuclear arms proliferation in the region. Arguably that would have left Israel particularly vulnerable in a volatile landscape, certainly changing the political dynamics in the region. The Shi'ites in the Gulf have had a long history of political marginalization, economic deprivation and religious discrimination often compelling many of them to seek empowerment through revolutionary ideologies to challenge the predominantly Sunni monarchies.

In the aftermath of the Arab uprisings, surviving Sunni despots have embarked upon a frantic purchase of conventional weapons to repress any opposition to their rule, be it from an internal or an external source. Prior to the recent 350 billion-dollar arms deal with the United States signed during President Donald Trump's visit to Saudi Arabia in 2017, Saudi Arabia was reportedly already spending billions of dollars purchasing weapons, with the United Kingdom being its principal supplier. Much of that has reportedly found its way into the military offensive against neighbouring Yemen. (Saudi Arabia has been engaged in a military campaign in Yemen since 2015).

What the Arab Spring of 2011 did achieve was to galvanize

a whole generation of Muslims in the region, providing them with an outlet to vent years of resentment against authoritarian rule and corruption. Starting with Tunisia, on 17 December 2010, in a single act of defiance by Mohamed Bouazizi by setting himself on fire in protest against the corruption, and harassment of government officials, the anger and frustration felt by young Tunisians against autocratic rule and failing economic circumstances subsequently spread like wildfire across North Africa and the Middle East. However, 'selective' Western support for freedom and democracy in the Middle East and Northern Africa was perceived by many critics as nothing more than securing their military and economic interests. In fact, post 9/11, it was widely perceived that the oil-rich countries of North Africa and the Middle East were experiencing a new wave of imperialism and empire building by Western powers, who were eager to secure energy supplies as well as establishing their military and political hegemony in that region.

While the Arab Spring may have been subdued for now with the crisis in Syria, disintegration of Libya, suppression of democratic protests in Bahrain and the military coup against Egypt's first democratically elected government, the inspiration behind it is nevertheless still very much alive. The essential rationale is that all citizens of the Muslim Ummah (irrespective of race, religion or creed) have an inalienable right to choose and elect their rulers and to hold them to account. All citizens are equal before the law and have a right to demand that their elected representatives provide them with viable and credible opportunities to economic emancipation. While the national wealth is held in trust for the benefit of all citizens, no dynasty must be allowed to control that wealth.

To ensure that a non-violent people's uprising against a repressive government is successful, the armed forces must refrain from unleashing a violent response. While the police are likely to be politicised, the army should not intervene to suppress a mass upheaval. When peaceful protest is brutally suppressed it will inevitably transform itself into a violent movement. It is poignant to note here the words of former United States President John F. Kennedy when he said, 'those who make peaceful revolution impossible will make violent revolution inevitable'. Recent events in Syria bear testimony to this.

Where the military has refused to support a repressive and corrupt government in light of peaceful mass unrest, those governments have fallen. For example, the authoritarian government of President H.M. Ershad of Bangladesh fell in December 1990 when in the face of mass demonstrations in defiance of a state of emergency the military refused to shoot at protesters. The police were in no position to contain the mass unrest. Similarly, in Egypt on 11 February 2011, President Hosni Mubarak resigned when following deployment of troops in the midst of clashes between the police, pro-Mubarak supporters and anti-government protestors the military refused to brutally suppress an 18-day-long uprising.

On the flip side of this, should elements within the army by themselves now seek to unseat a government without populist support, then that is likely to fail, as evidenced by the attempted coup in Turkey that unfolded on 15 July 2016. The failed coup illustrates that any coup attempt to topple a government must now enjoy widespread public support. When images of the President calling upon the Turkish people to come out onto the streets to convene at public squares and airports to defy the attempted military coup were aired, the coup was set to fail from the outset. Images were beamed across the globe in real time, showing demonstrators in favour of the government of President Recep Toyyip Erdogen storming the Istanbul Ataturk airport despite a curfew being imposed by the soldiers staging the attempted coup. Furthermore, not only did the coup attempt not have the support of many of the military top brass (reportedly it was a fractional uprising in the military with only 20 percent of the country's generals being involved) but the national police remained loyal to the President, preventing the gendarmerie from leaving their barracks, while social media were functional and even a state news channel came back on the air after a brief disruption.

The military coup on 3 July 2013 against Morsi, on the other hand, had both initial widespread public backing and extensive military support. The Egyptian armed forces had earlier issued an ultimatum to the President in the light of large scale anti-government demonstrations across Egypt that centred on Cairo. Ironically, the 2013 military coup was supported by celebrations across Egypt. For them, Mr Morsi failed to meet their expectations, particularly in reviving the economy and ensuring public security, among other concerns. Moreover, Mr Morsi was viewed with contempt by secular forces in particular for his pro-Islamic stance, which was viewed as a credible threat to their secular principles. Mr Morsi's increasingly authoritarian style of leadership was also being seen as at odds with democratic principles.

Having said this, a more 'regulatory approach' is required to sustain any future Arab uprising. With the fall of autocratic regimes must be implemented 'prescriptive criteria' to secure a peaceful transition to democratic processes. The consequence of failing to do so with the first Arab uprising has only led to a more volatile Middle East. This is further discussed below.

In the meantime, it is important to realise that the youth of the Middle East are no longer devoid of education and living in backwater villages and rural towns. With urbanization and increasing access to the internet, the flow of information is no longer in the exclusive control of authoritarian regimes. The younger generation can now share ideas, as well as, manifest their dissent on a global platform.

THE IMPLOSION OF LIBYA

In March 2011, Western powers intervened militarily in Libya with Britain, France and the US taking a leading role to prevent what they believed was a potential massacre of civilians by Colonel Gaddafi's autocratic regime in the Libyan city of Benghazi. Strangely enough, up until then the West, in particular Britain, France and Spain, found it plausible to do business with Gaddafi. Swiftly pushing through UN Security Council Resolution 1973 adopted under Chapter VII of the UN Charter, the Resolution formed the basis for military intervention in the Libyan civil war. It demanded an immediate ceasefire and authorised the international community to establish a no-fly zone and to use 'all means necessary' short of foreign occupation to protect civilians. This consequently took the form of airstrikes under NATO command and the arming of anti-Gaddafi forces, which resulted in the capture and summary execution of Colonel Gaddafi on 20 October 2011, allegedly by National Transition Council (NTC) fighters in his hometown of Sirte, east of the capital Tripoli, after his convoy was attacked by NATO warplanes.

In terms of the financial costs of waging this military campaign it was no doubt a substantial burden on the taxpayers of the lead participating countries. It is reported that the United Kingdom spent 320 million pounds and France 813 million dollars, with the United States spending 1.3 billion dollars. But more importantly and ironically the number of civilian casualties was regrettably high, despite the fact that the legal basis of UN Security Council Resolution 1973 was to protect civilian life. According to the NTC, 30,000 people were killed up until September 2011. All sides to the conflict had inflicted civilian deaths that included government, rebel and coalition forces. Furthermore, Human Rights Watch called on NATO to investigate the numerous civilian deaths resulting from its airstrikes, despite the fact that NATO claimed that it had done everything possible to minimise risk to civilians.

From the start of the campaign there were allegations that the limits imposed by UN Resolution 1973 and by United States law were being violated. At the end of May 2011, Western troops were captured on film by Al-Jazeera in Libya, despite Resolution 1973 specifically prohibiting 'a foreign occupation force of any form on any part of Libyan territory'. The news report did however state that armed Westerners and not Western troops were on the ground. What it boils down to is the semantics of the language used by the media and in UN Security Council resolutions.

Critics of the military campaign allege that the real impetus behind the intervention was regime change, as well as gaining control of Libya's substantial oil reserves and financial capital. As a member of OPEC, Libya was a major oil producer prior to the uprising. In addition, Libya is alleged to have had substantial gold reserves in its Central Bank. Meanwhile, with the fall of Colonel Gaddafi, lucrative deals were signed with Western corporate bodies to develop the infrastructure which was destroyed in the civil war. The General National Forces Alliance (NFA), which was elected by popular vote in July 2012, took over from the NTC as Libya's legislative authority, picking up 39 of the 88 seats in the General National Assembly reserved for political parties. Its real test came on 11 September 2012 when the US Ambassador to Libya and three other consulate staff were killed, allegedly by armed groups taking advantage of the rage that followed airing of the controversial video, 'The innocence of Muslims'. The NFA surely had its task cut out in disarming the many Libyans who acquired arms during the uprising against the former dictator Colonel Gaddafi. In fact, it was reported that the influx of weapons during the course of the 'Libyan Campaign' had helped to consolidate the position of extremist elements operating in the 'Islamic Maghreb'. The fall-out of this is evidenced by the volatile situation in Libya with different armed groups engaging in bitter fighting to secure their power base through the capture of key oil terminals.

Libya is surely a county ripe for rich pickings. With a population of only 6.4 million (less than the population of the city of London) but with a land area of 685,524 square miles (larger than the UK) and with substantial oil reserves, no wonder Libya is being torn apart while different competing militias seek to control large stretches of the country. Taking advantage of the turmoil, criminal gangs are using Libya as a springboard for human trafficking with many of the victims making the perilous journey across the Mediterranean Sea into Europe and many losing their lives in the process. It was reported by the International Organization for Migrants (IOM) that during 2015, 3,771 men, women and children drowned while crossing the Mediterranean in unseaworthy vessels and 77% of these deaths occurred in the Central Mediterranean route mostly used by smugglers operating from Libyan shores. It would not be out of place to say that Libya is today a 'failed state'.

In September 2016, a report by the UK Foreign Affairs

Select Committee found that the consequence of British and French intervention in Libya in 2011 was 'political and economic collapse, inter-militia and inter-tribal warfare, humanitarian and migrant crises, widespread human rights violations, the spread of Gaddafi regime weapons across the region and the growth of ISIL in North Africa'. The report went on to find that the UK government failed to verify the actual threat to civilians posed by Gaddafi's regime, while it selectively took elements of Gaddafi's rhetoric at face value (this arguably fed into the UK government's propaganda machine, reminiscent of the propaganda drummed up by the then Labour government prior to the second Gulf War), while it failed to identify the militant Islamist extremist element in the rebellion. In fact, the UK intervention strategy was, as the report claims, to be 'founded on erroneous assumptions and an incomplete understanding of the evidence'. The Foreign Office, however, rejected these findings, citing that the decision to intervene in Libya was supported by the Arab League and had the backing of a United Nations Security Council resolution. It could be argued that the backing of the Western powers and the Arab League presents no surprise as Gaddafi was deemed by many Arab leaders to be unpredictable and a threat to the international trade of oil from the region as he was toying with the idea of introducing the 'gold dinar' to replace the 'petro-dollar'. As with Iraq, Western powers in post-war Libya too failed to come up with an effective strategy to exercise leadership on stabilization and reconstruction. Similar views were echoed by the former United States President, Barack Obama. Even today Libya does not have one single recognized government. In fact, it risks falling into a fully-fledged civil-war leading to the breakup of the country, much like the situation in Syria.

THE EGYPTIAN DEJA VU

It should be emphasized that despots are only as powerful as their Generals make them out to be. That is why, in those countries where the people had taken to the streets to protest against despotic rule in favour of political pluralism, including Tunisia,

Egypt, Libya, Yemen, Bahrain and Syria, the security forces had clamped down on protesters with deadly force. The fall of a dictator even by popular revolution will therefore, make very little difference unless the army steps aside from political interference. In December 2011 scores of Egyptian protesters were killed and brutally beaten in sporadic clashes with Egyptian security forces for demanding a transition to civilian rule by Egypt's interim military leadership following the fall of Hosni Mubarak earlier in February 2011 (after an 18-day uprising removed him from power). Cairo's iconic Tahrir Square was again the focal point for protest.

The Supreme Council of the Armed Forces (SCAF) appeared in no mood to hand over power to a civilian government at the time without first securing concessions and guarantees for themselves in any future political power structure for Egypt. They played the Western powers with their assurances that the Peace Treaty with Israel was secure with them. (The West will surely demand similar assurances of peace from new regimes that have emerged or are likely to emerge as a consequence of the Arab Spring of 2011). Consequently, upon being narrowly elected with 51% of the vote in the second round of the 2012 Presidential Elections, the new Egyptian President, Mohamed Morsi of the Muslim Brotherhood, stated that he would honour Egypt's Peace Treaty with Israel. Abrogation of the 1979 Camp David accords by Egypt would effectively put Egypt in a state of war with Israel. This is something that even the Muslim Brotherhood sought to avoid. Interestingly enough, Mr Morsi's election victory was achieved despite the fact that the Egyptian Parliament was dissolved only days before by Egypt's Supreme Constitutional Court on the pretext that the Parliamentary elections – won by the Muslim Brotherhood–led Democratic Alliance – were null and void. It may be worth noting that Mohamed Morsi's rival, Ahmed Shafi, who was an ex-general and former Prime Minister under disposed President Mubarak, secured 48% of the vote. Had the Supreme Council of the Armed Forces got its way with Ahmed Shafi winning the Presidential elections, widespread violence would certainly have gripped Egypt back then.

Mohamed Morsi's presidency was effectively undermined from

the start by the military, who were reluctant to hand over total effective power to a civilian government without concessions. In an act of defiance against the military, Mr Morsi, soon after taking power as President, issued a decree recalling Parliament. After a brief session, the Supreme Constitutional Court overturned the decree on 10 July 2012. Mr Morsi agreed not to escalate the situation and to respect the Supreme Court's decision. A subtle power struggle ensued and a new constitution was drafted and subsequently ratified by a referendum in December 2012. In February 2013, President Morsi announced that Parliamentary elections would be held in April of the same year. But that seemed doubtful in light of court rulings on the electoral law and threats of boycott.

Undermining the democratic process, Mr Morsi was effectively forcibly ousted from power on 3 July 2013 by the Egyptian armed forces after they had earlier issued an ultimatum to the President in the light of large-scale anti-government demonstrations across Egypt that centred on Cairo. As part of the coup strategy the military suspended the constitution, appointing Adil Mansoor, the head of the Supreme Constitutional Court, as interim head of state, to be assisted by an interim council until new Presidential and Parliamentary elections were held. Many media outlets were raided and closed, while senior Muslim Brotherhood leaders were arbitrarily arrested, no doubt with the intention of avoiding an organised backlash by pro-Morsi supporters. The Egyptian Army had again proved that despite the downfall of Hosni Mubarak in February 2011 following widely-supported nationwide mass demonstrations, it was still the main power-broker in Egypt and was willing and able to step into the political arena. Ironically, the 2013 military coup was supported by celebrations across Egypt. For them, Mr Morsi failed to meet their expectations, particularly in reviving the economy and ensuring public security, among other concerns. Moreover, Mr Morsi was viewed with contempt, by secular forces in particular, for his pro-Islamic stance, which was viewed as a credible threat to their secular principles. Mr Morsi's increasing authoritarian style of leadership was also being seen at odds with democratic principles.

However, grave concern centred on the violent and bloody

clampdown by the military of pro-Morsi supporters. Hundreds of people were reported to have been shot dead, with many more being wounded, in bloody clashes between protesters loyal to ousted President Mohammed Morsi and security forces. Among the bloodiest clashes, at least 82 protesters were reportedly killed on 27 July 2013 near the Raba'a Al Adiwiya Mosque. Then again on 14 August 2013 hundreds were reportedly killed during a drive to clear protesters' camps, provoking international condemnation but with no real sanctions adopted against the repressive military regime.

The military had declared that elections would be held in 2014 following a referendum on a new charter to replace the so-called 'Islamist constitution' passed during Mr Morsi's presidency. This constitutional referendum took place on 14 and 15 January 2014, with 98% of those who turned out to vote backing a new draft constitution. The turnout was 38.6% of the 54 million eligible voters. Under the new draft constitution political parties are prevented from being formed on the basis of religion while at the same time it empowers the military to appoint the Defence Minister for the next eight years. An uncertain and potentially dangerous period lies ahead, especially with General Abdel Fattah al-Sisi (former director of Egypt's military intelligence and at one time Egypt's military attaché in Riyadh, Saudi Arabia), who effectively deposed Mr Morsi, winning the Presidential elections held between 26 and 28 May 2014 with the Muslim Brotherhood being branded a 'terrorist organisation'. In the light of figures announced by the Presidential Election Commission, interestingly the elections were marked by a relatively low turnout (47.5% of the 54 million eligible voters), and Mr Sisi won 96.91% of the votes cast. In fact, the vote was extended to three days because of the initial low turnout, backed by a threat of a fine for failing to vote. Critics claimed that this was hardly the mandate required to establish Mr Sisi's credibility as a national leader tasked with the job of bringing stability and unity to the country. Nevertheless, as soon as the official results were declared on 3 June 2014, the late Saudi King, Abdullah bin Abulaziz, hailed Sisi's historic win, vowing continued support and calling upon countries to attend a donors' conference to help Egypt overcome its economic difficulties. The Saudi establishment knew all too well that if Mr Sisi was unable to provide security and economic growth, it would not take too long for the Egyptian people to take to the streets again.

During the transitional period following the removal of Mr Morsi's government a massive influx of Gulf aid was pumped into the faltering Egyptian economy. The democratic elections that brought the Muslim Brotherhood to power represented a potent threat to the reign of unelected Sunni despots in the region. Consequently, a reversal of power to the military has obviously played into their fortunes. We are seeing further restrictions on civil liberties as the former General tightens his grip on power. Supporters of the Muslim Brotherhood are being subject to increasing repression, as is any form of dissent. Mr Sisi has vowed to eradicate the Muslim Brotherhood from the Egyptian political scene.

In a dramatic twist, on 29 November 2014, charges against former President, Hosni Mubarak for conspiring to murder hundreds of protesters during the 2011 uprising, were dropped overturning a life sentence received in June 2012 (but was instead serving a three year custodial sentence for corruption). A retrial was however, ordered by an appeals court in June 2015. (Mr Morsi meanwhile, was sentenced to death in May 2015 for organizing a mass prison break during the uprising against former President Hosni Mubarak. On 18 June 2016, he was also sentenced to life imprisonment, having been found guilty on charges of espionage for passing state secrets to Qatar.) In early March 2017 former President Hosni Mubarak was ordered to be freed after Egypt's top appeals courts cleared him over the deaths of protesters in the 2011 uprising while ironically many of the protesters arrested during the revolt were still languishing in Egyptian jails. Finally, on 24 March 2017 Hosni Mubarak left a military hospital in southern Cairo for his home. Mr Mubarak had been residing at the Maadi Military Hospital since 2013 after being transferred there on bail from Torah prison. Egypt is the region's largest Arab state and often argued by political analysts as central to the region's future. What happens in Egypt will have a direct impact on the Middle East. The military coup of 2013 in Egypt is therefore, a stark warning why any second Arab uprising must be a well-organized and prescriptive affair.

Egypt, alongside Israel and Saudi Arabia, views the Muslim Brotherhood both as a physical and ideological threat. In its diplomatic standoff with Qatar, Saudi Arabia demanded that Qatar stop supporting the Muslim Brotherhood. Meanwhile, Egypt alongside Israel is enforcing a continuing siege on the Gaza Strip. Israel views Hamas as a terrorist organisation. This close cooperation between these key players in the Middle East to root out the Muslim Brotherhood and Hamas as terrorist organisations is not only a game changer but a concerted effort by the trio to destroy any credible hostile challenge to their rule. Qatar may be forced to renounce its close economic and political ties with Hamas in the Gaza Strip, which could see Hamas increasingly being isolated both in terms of financial and political capital. This despite the softening of tone by Hamas in its new Charter. Meanwhile, the attempted assassination of the Prime Minister of the Palestinian Authority, Rami Hamdallah, on 13 March 2018 while visiting the Gaza Strip, was firmly aimed at putting a wedge in the relationship between the Palestinian Authority and Hamas to prevent any sustainable reconciliation between the two in a further attempt to isolate Hamas.

Former military strongman Abdel Fattah al-Sisi faced re-election towards the end of March 2018, with the last four years of his rule being marred with accusations of cracking down on all forms of political dissent with brutal force (on the pretext of combatting terrorists) and allegations of torture, abductions and the arrests of journalists. Like many Muslim countries experiencing authoritarian rule, the Egyptian population has been frightened into submission for fear of arrest, torture and enforced disappearances carried out by the state. The widespread reports of rape and sexual assault on female detainees is particularly tragic and deeply concerning. In the run-up to the election all credible opponents to Mr Sisi were intimidated out of the Presidential race, including labour lawyer and human rights activist Khaled Ali and a former senior army general, Sami Anan. Providing a veneer of democratic legitimacy to the election, with only minutes to spare prior to the nominations deadline being passed, a candidate from the pro-government centrist Ghad party, Mousa Mostafa Mousa, put his hat in the ring, otherwise Mr Sisi was set to be the sole officially recognised candidate. Then on 2 April 2018 it was announced that Mr Sisi had won a landslide victory, securing 97.08% of the valid votes cast on a turnout of only 41.5%. Mousa Mostafa Mousa secured just under 3% of the valid votes, while spoiled ballots accounted for 7.27%. In effect, Mr Sisi won 21.8 million votes compared with Mr Mousa's 656,534, less than the 1.8 million spoiled ballots. The fact that Mr Sisi would win an overwhelming majority of the votes cast was never in doubt. With a clear mandate to rule Egypt for another four years it will be interesting to see how Egypt, along with Saudi Arabia, puts pressure on the Palestinian Authority to accept a Peace Plan with Israel so that they can accelerate their shared interests with Israel as Saudi Arabia in particular, seeks to diversify its economy. Given the size of Israel's growing technologically-driven economy the Gulf Cooperation Council countries, as well as Egypt, will be anxious to seek economic cooperation with Israel in addition to jointly confronting the perceived strategic threat to Sunni domination from Shi'ite Iran.

THE SYRIAN CHESS GAME

The crisis in Syria is becoming a frustratingly tough nut to crack. Misgivings by Russia and China in the United Nations Security Council over the motives of the United States, Britain, France and their NATO allies has allowed the Syrian regime to continue the mass killing of Syrian citizens with impunity. For some global players, saving human lives should not entail regime change with a military option. The massacre that took place in the Syrian town of Houla, near Homs, as far back as May 2012, and then in Syria's second city of Aleppo in July 2012, where the majority of casualties were innocent women and children, was a shameful tragedy for the international community, including the United Nations, for their ineptitude to bring the belligerent parties to the negotiating table. It is no secret that both the Syrian government and the opposition are being financially funded and militarily equipped by foreign powers, all with a vested interest in who controls Syria. It came as no surprise, therefore, that the Syrian Foreign Minister, Walid al Muallem, while on a visit to Iran in July 2012, was reported by different media streams to have blamed Turkey, Qatar and Saudi Arabia ('Sunni Axis') for fuelling the rebellion across Syria, resulting in the failure of UN envoy Kofi Annan's peace plan. The mandate for UN Monitors was withdrawn at the end of August 2012. The Sunni Axis on the one side, and Iran and the Hezbollah in Lebanon on the other, appears to be jostling for influence in Syria, with analysts suggesting that the war within Syria is a proxy war based on Shi'ite-Sunni sectarian differences exploited by Western powers. What is deeply disturbing with the Syrian Conflict is the large number of civilian casualties (around 400,000 according to an estimate in April 2016 by Staffan de Mistura, the UN's special envoy to Syria), and the systematic destruction of Syria's infrastructure, not forgetting the 4 million refugees who have fled Syria to the West and to neighbouring countries, including Turkey, Jordan and Lebanon, in addition to the 6.3 million people displaced internally in Syria by the end of 2016. The country is imploding upon itself, as did Libya in 2011.

Strategically, a pro-Western Syrian government is indispensable for any future military strike against Iran, either by Israel or the West. Any such military adventure however, by Israel and the United States in particular, in the direction of Iran within the current geopolitical climate with Russia, Iran and Hezbollah propping up the Assad regime, would no doubt destabilize the region. Policy makers within the United States and Israel therefore need to tread carefully. This is further discussed in the following section.

It was anticipated in diplomatic circles earlier in the conflict that the diplomatic and political stalemate in the United Nations would more than likely take a dangerous turn, resulting in direct military intervention by NATO if the Syrian regime used its alleged chemical weapons stockpiles to suppress its opponents. It was understood in the West that the Syrian government would be extremely reckless should it choose to do so, and therefore unlikely to rely on the support of Russia and China to veto a United Nations Security Council Resolution calling for armed intervention to unseat the regime of Bashar al-Assad. However, despite reports in April 2013 that the nerve agent sarin was used (albeit on a small scale), the West, in particular the United States and the United Kingdom, was cautious not to intervene directly militarily but rather subsequently made it public that they would be arming the Syrian opposition. At the G8 Meeting held in Northern Ireland in June 2013, the Russian President reiterated that Moscow would not be breaching any law if it decided to arm the Syrian government. Russia had stated that it would be providing the Assad regime with advanced anti-aircraft missiles that would seriously undermine efforts to set up a no-fly zone. When, however, in August 2013 another deadly chemical attack was carried out on the outskirts of the capital Damascus in a civilian populated area, it caused an international outcry, with Britain and France calling for immediate military strikes against Assad's regime blaming it for carrying out the attack. However, with MPs in the House of Commons voting against Britain being involved in military action against Syria, the United States and France stepped up the pressure on Bashar al-Assad by drumming up rhetoric in support of limited air strikes against military targets inside Syria. However, Russia, a strategic ally of the Syrian regime, opposed any such military strikes and brokered a solution to the impending crises, persuading the Assad regime to commit itself to destroy its stockpile of chemical weapons. This was then carried out under the supervision of the Organization for the Prohibition of Chemical Weapons (OPCW) as per UN Security Council Resolution 2118.

There was also the fear that should opposition forces get their hands on the government stockpiles of chemical and biological agents, it could prove extremely dangerous, given that reportedly different 'extremist' elements had infiltrated the opposition forces on the ground.

More recently, on 4 April 2017, yet another chemical attack was carried out, this time at dawn on a rebel-held town in the province of Idlib. This killed scores of people, with a large number of casualties being children, allegedly as a consequence of a chemical bomb being dropped by government forces. Distressing scenes of children choking, foaming at the mouth, wailing and unable to bear the pain were beamed across the globe. This continuing use of chemical agents in the Syrian conflict is another chilling reminder of the horrors of chemical warfare, which everyone agrees to be a crime against humanity for which there can be no justification whatsoever. Medical experts on the ground claimed that the attack was likely the result of a nerve agent, such as sarin gas. The following day the United Nations Security Council held an emergency meeting instigated by the United States, the United Kingdom and France, with both the Syrian and Russian envoys denying that Assad's regime launched a chemical attack. Despite the harsh language employed by the United States and the United Kingdom, Russia, Syria's most powerful ally, made it clear it would not support a resolution imposing sanctions against the Assad government. In fact, Russia had in the past used its veto power as a permanent member of the United Nations Security Council at least seven times on Syrian resolutions. The Russian take on this was that the death resulted from gas released when a government airstrike hit a chemical weapons factory controlled by rebel forces. The United States Ambassador to the United Nations issued a stark warning in the direction of Russia and Syria, namely that if the United Nations consistently failed in its duty to act collectively (referring to the Russian veto) it may be compelled to act alone (or in close partnership with its allies). If we accept the allegations made against the Syrian regime being behind the attack, then it would seem that the OPCW had not been successful in destroying all government stockpiles of chemical and biological agents.

Then on 7 April 2017 following another suspected chemical attack by Assad forces on the rebel held town of Khan Sheikhoun in north western Syria killing at least 80 people, many of whom were children, with hundreds suffering symptoms consistent with a reaction to nerve agents, President Donald Trump raised the stakes and ordered a military strike involving United States Navy destroyers firing 59 Tomahawk cruise missiles at the

Shayrat airfield in the western Homs province believed to be the military installation from where the Syrian aircraft responsible for the chemical attack took off. This was the first time since the beginning of the Syrian conflict that the United States had directly targeted Syrian government forces.

Again this prompts the question as to whether the United Nations, particularly its Security Council, is fit for purpose, in terms of its military reach in providing an effective deterrent to the use of chemical weapons on civilians and whether it is in need of urgent reform to reflect the geo-politics of today and not the global political situation of 1945.

Not only that, despite the harsh rhetoric employed by the United Kingdom and the United States in condemning this outrage, the chemical attack took place when the Prime Minister of the United Kingdom was on a visit to Saudi Arabia to further promote and consolidate trade links with a country whose own track record on Yemen is quite disturbing with reports of thousands of civilian being killed by the Saudi military campaign there. As for the United States, this chemical attack had taken place when only a few days earlier the United States President played host to the Egyptian President in Washington, D.C., confirming its strong support of the regime of Abdel Fatah al-Sisi, whose violent crackdown on his own people to silence any opposition to his rule is well documented. This sort of cherry-picking in choosing who to put pressure on in diplomatic circles paints a very interesting picture of political intrigue for any student of political science.

It would appear that the Western powers, despite their differences, have however reacted more effectively over the appearance of ISIL on the ground in Syria, stirring the United Nations Security Council into action and unanimously adopting Resolution 2249. On 20 November 2015, the Security Council unequivocally condemned the terrorist attacks perpetrated by ISIL – also known as Da'esh – (on 26 June 2015 in Sousse, on 10 October 2015 in Ankara, on 31 October 2015 over Sinaï, on 12 November 2015 in Beirut and on 13 November 2015 in Paris, and all other attacks, including hostage-taking and killing, and its capability and intention to carry out further attacks), branding it as a 'global and unprecedented threat to international peace and security', and calling on member states with the requisite capacity to take 'all necessary measures' in compliance with international law to prevent and suppress ISIL's terrorist acts on territory under its control in Syria and Iraq. (It must be recognized, however, that the Resolution was not adopted under Chapter VII of the UN Charter). Consequently, on 2 December 2015 the House of Commons, after a ten and a half hour debate, voted 397 to 223 in favour of extending the United Kingdom's air-bombing campaign into Syria against ISIL, with the government making the point that it had the backing of the United Nations Security Council.

Given the fact that the United Kingdom was joining an already ongoing bombing campaign against ISIL by the United States, France and Russia, the effectiveness of the overall bombing campaign required tactical scrutiny. From a military strategy point of view, it could have been argued that ISIL, given its ability to sustain itself against airstrikes, would have required a ground war to be defeated. However, had NATO or a coalition of countries headed by the United States ultimately resorted to a full-scale ground invasion, Syria would likely have splintered across ethnic lines. Then again, it was unlikely that the United States would have committed itself to any such ground offensive in Syria on the verge of presidential elections.

At the same time, given its historical animosity with the PKK (Kurdish Workers' Party in Turkey which has fought for Kurdish autonomy in Turkey), as well as, the YPG (which Turkey views as an extension of the PKK in Syria that controls much of north-eastern Syria), Turkey is very apprehensive at the idea of a viable sovereign Kurdish State in its backyard that stretches from Turkey into parts of Syria and Iraq. Consequently, in January 2018 Turkish-backed forces entered north-western Syria, capturing villages in Afrin with the Turkish-backed Free Syrian Army (FSA) taking full control of the centre of the city of Afrin in March 2018 and driving out Kurdish forces.

With no end in sight to the conflict, in February 2018 Syrian warplanes pounded Eastern Ghouta, a rebel-held enclave only 10 kilometres east of the capital of Damascus, with at least a thousand dead and wounded, including hundreds of children who were mercilessly killed. So dire was the situation, with 400,000 people being besieged in the enclave, that on 24 February 2018 the United Nations Security Council, after much haggling, passed a resolution calling for a 30-day truce/ceasefire to take effect across Syria 'without delay' (in the absence of a firm date), excepting operations against designated terrorist groups including the Islamic State group, al-Qaeda and the Nusra Front, to allow humanitarian deliveries and medical evacuation. The Syrian government took advantage of this loophole to continue its bombardment of the enclave and also sent in ground troops. The Russian President subsequently ordered a daily five-hour corridor to allow civilians to leave the enclave to take effect from 27 February 2018. By 10 March 2018 Syrian government forces had captured the largest town in Eastern Ghouta, splitting the enclave into three pockets, following which, facing defeat, rebel fighters and their families agreed to be evacuated as part of a Russia-brokered agreement with the exception of the group controlling Douma, Jaysh al-Islam, which continued to hold out. With negotiations stalled, air strikes resumed.

Then on 7 April 2018 dozens of Syrian civilians, many of whom were children, choked to death after a suspected chemical weapons attack struck the rebel-held suburb of Douma. Aid groups blamed the Syrian Air Force for two separate attacks which involved dropping bombs containing toxic substances. Videos posted online by anti-government activists showed lifeless men, women and children sprawled out on floors and in stairwells, many with white foam coming from their mouths and nostrils. The Union of Medical Care and Relief Organizations claimed that many people were treated for breathing difficulties and irritation of the eyes following the first bomb attack. It added that following the second attack patients were brought to hospital smelling strongly of a chlorine-like substance and showing symptoms that included cyanosis, forming of the mouth and cornea irritation. Though this latest atrocity was immediately condemned by the United States and the European Union, with Mr Trump stating that there would be 'a big price to pay' for the attack, Assad's allies, namely Russia and Iran, dismissed allegations of a chemical attack, making a counter-allegation that the reports were 'provocative' and that the United States and its allies were using it as justification for military intervention in Syria against Assad's forces. It further claimed that rebel fighters were already on the verge of leaving the rebel town of Douma under an agreement reached with Russian representatives and there was no need to attack them.

In the meantime, Syria and Russia blamed Israel for launching a missile attack in the early hours of 9 April 2018 against a T-4 airfield in the Homs province, believed to be a base used by Iranian based militias. Israel for its part is determined to prevent Iran from getting entrenched in Syria and seeks to block the flow of arms to Iranian-backed Hezbollah close to the Israeli border in south-west Syria. While the Iranian foreign ministry denounced Israel's actions as 'a violation of the national sovereignty and territorial integrity of Syria', Russia described the raid as a 'dangerous development'.

Disappointingly, but not unexpectedly, the United Nations Security Council failed to agree to adopt three draft resolutions (one drafted by the United States and two by Russia) to determine responsibility for this latest chemical weapons attack when they met on 10 April 2018 with the United States, Britain and France facing off fellow permanent member Russia. With tensions mounting, matched by a war of words, the Security Council again proved inept and unable to bridge the deep divisions and mistrust between the United States and Russia over the conflict in Syria. This effectively gave way to the potential use of military force by the United States and her allies in Syria which materialized on 14 April 2018 with France and the United Kingdom, alongside the United States, launching military strikes aimed at reducing the Syrian regime's chemical weapons facilities. According to a Pentagon briefing, 105 missiles were fired in total, hitting three sites in Damascus and Homs regarded as linked to the storage or testing of chemical weapons. The Russian military for their part claimed that Syrian air defence batteries responded, intercepting 71 of the 103 missiles fired. While this latest military strike by the United States and her European allies sent a clear warning to the Syrian regime that the use of chemical weapons will no longer be tolerated, in real terms it will have very little impact in bringing about a viable political solution to the conflict. In the days leading up to the military strike, given the rhetoric that was coming out of Washington, D.C. and from Russian diplomats, there was a very serious risk of escalation had Russia responded militarily. All the more reason why an early resolution to the Syrian conflict must be actively sought. The United Nations Secretary General, Antonio Guterres expressed his deep concern over the diplomatic standoff and military readiness of the United States and her allies as well as Russia, Iran and Syria when he called for calm, urging all member states to show restraint in 'these dangerous circumstances'.

The civil war in Syria and Yemen has proved particularly useful for the firebrand regimes of the Gulf, for it offers a useful distraction for their own populations away from their own economic stagnation, political repression and lack of political pluralism.

As to finding a political solution to the conflict in Syria, following on from the 'Geneva Communiqué' issued in June 2012 an international conference began in Switzerland in January 2014 known as 'Geneva II', but it failed to make any meaningful progress. The sad reality is that negotiations are decided not at the table but by the fortunes won in battle. The Assad regime has therefore continued to press on with its fighting despite the talks, and so have the rebel fighters. Difficult as it may sound, if a deal is to be reached that does not encompass Bashar al-Assad, then he and his family must be given an exit plan while guaranteeing the Alawite community's security in a post-Assad Syria. If not, should Assad step down, revenge attacks and summary executions against his family and the Alawite community will become widespread, resulting in nothing short of a massacre. The re-election of Bashar al-Assad in June 2014 for another seven years as President was his way of sending a clear message to Western governments that any political settlement must encompass his future. Failure by Western governments to recognize this only complicates matters, especially when the Assad regime has the military and political backing of Russia. This is evident from Russia's military involvement in the Syrian conflict, which has had the effect of placing Bashar al-Assad's forces in control.

Russia for its part has been seeking to bring about a political solution to the conflict. In May 2017, sponsored by Turkey and Iran, Russia launched a diplomatic initiative in Astana, Kazakhstan with an agreement on so-called de-escalation zones (including Eastern Ghouta) which in the main part have been unsuccessful (particularly following the military offensive by Syrian government forces there in early 2018). Then on 30 January 2018 the Syrian National Dialogue Congress was launched in the Russian Black Sea resort of Sochi, with the aim of drawing up a declaration of principles to resolve the Syrian Crises that is yet to see any tangible results.

SANCTIONS AGAINST IRAN

Any protracted armed confrontation between Iran and Western powers over Iran's alleged nuclear programme to develop a nuclear bomb will not only destabilize the Middle East, which is very much already a powder keg, but will predictably send fuel prices rocketing, creating anarchy in the commodities markets. It is extremely likely that the Straits of Hormuz will be transformed into a naval war zone, threatening the supply of a third of global oil supplies. Ultimately, it will be the consumers in the West who will have to bear the brunt of the financial catastrophe that will follow any new protracted military engagement in that region. Consequently, no doubt this will have political overtones in Western domestic politics.

The Western powers will also have to make contingency plans to meet any downturn in oil supplies, unless of course they are confident that they will be able to invade and install a pro-Western government in Iran in very much the same way as they have done in Iraq and Afghanistan, or aid an armed insurgency as they did in Libya. There is substance in the argument that if Iran does develop a nuclear weapon this will usher in a nuclear arms race in the Middle East, but only because Sunni despots will have everything to fear from a Shi'ite nuclear military power in their midst.

There are also potentially serious implications for Israel's security in the region, given the political rhetoric that often comes out of Iran and its military-backed affiliates such as Hamas in Gaza (Hamas up until 1 May 2017 called for Israel's destruction, but still reportedly rejects Israel's right to exist and backs armed struggle against it) and Hezbollah in Lebanon. Conversely, it is argued that if Iran does eventually succeed in making a nuclear bomb, that would bring in a nuclear deterrent in the Middle East. In any case, any military adventure on the part of Israel in the direction of Iran is likely to have dangerous repercussions in the Middle East. Even a surprise military airstrike on Iranian nuclear facilities by Israeli warplanes is very likely to galvanise hatred by Muslims against Israel and her allies in the region and beyond. This will only provide extremist groups with the notion of 'just cause' to recruit new members to carry out acts of criminality against Israeli and Western interests.

With the re-election of cleric Hassan Rouhani in May 2017 as the new Iranian President, it will be interesting to see how he continues to deal with the West with respect to Iran's nuclear programme, particularly with the United States. Prior to becoming US President, Donald Trump repeatedly claimed that the 'deal' struck with Iran was 'the worst deal ever' and was prepared to 'rip up' the nuclear agreement with Iran. Such a move by Donald Trump would appease both Israel and Sunni despots in the region, particularly Saudi Arabia, which fears the establishment of a so-called Shi'ite Empire in the Middle East. Coupled with the United States nuclear standoff with North Korea, this is likely to raise tensions not only in the Middle East but also in South Asia. This explains the recent move in May 2018 by China, North and South Korea and the United States to de-escalate tensions between them over North Korea's nuclear capabilities, culminating in a summit on 12 June 2018 in Singapore between the US President and North Korea's leader Kim Jong Un. The United States believes Iran is responsible for destablising the Middle East by supporting the Assad regime in Syria and backing terrorist organisations like Hezbollah in Lebanon, as well as supporting violent militias that seek to undermine governments in Iraq and Yemen.

Then on Friday, 13 October 2017, Mr Trump threatened to terminate the 2015 Iran nuclear deal if Congress and the United States allies failed to amend the agreement in significant ways. Though announcing to the world that he would not continue to certify the agreement, he stopped short of immediately cancelling United States participation in the agreement. Furthermore, in addition to asking Congress to enact potential new sanctions, the President moved to impose unrelated sanctions by executive actions, including blacklisting the Islamic Revolutionary Guard Corps constituting Iran's elite military unit, which is heavily involved in Iran's trade and business. Such a strategy adopted by the United States can only mean one thing: a prelude to a military confrontation with Iran or an inducement to the Iranian people to bring down the government. With Israel's intelligence minister stating that this move by Donald Trump could 'absolutely' trigger war, it raises alarming prospects. Then again, it could, on the other hand, be a shrewd and calculated move by the President to 'fix' the deal with Iran which would include conducting stricter inspections of Iran's nuclear sites, imposing harsher penalties for Iranian violations, reining in its ballistic missile programme and more importantly, eliminating the so-called 'sunset clauses'.

The collapse of the nuclear deal, however, is not solely dependent upon acquiescence by the United States. This was made clear by the European Union's Foreign Policy Chief, Federica Mogherini, who at a news conference at the European Commission's Brussels headquarters in an immediate reaction to President's Trump's speech in Washington, said the United States has no right to unilaterally terminate the Iran nuclear accord, stating that the agreement was 'effective' with 'no violation of any of the commitments included in the agreement' by Iran. She further said, 'the International Atomic Energy Agency, the IAEA, has verified eight times that Iran is implementing all of its nuclear commitments'. Federica Mogherini also made clear that 'it is not a bilateral agreement. It does not belong to any single country. And it is not up to any single country to terminate it. It is a multilateral agreement, which was unanimously endorsed by the United Nations Security Council', enshrined in United Nations Security Council Resolution 2231 (2015) endorsing the JCPOA (S/2015/545, as attached as Annex B to the Resolution). She was joined by the United Kingdom Prime Minister, Theresa May, French President, Emmanuel Macron and German Chancellor Angela Merkel, who issued a joint statement reaffirming their support for the nuclear accord, which they described as 'in our shared national security interest'.

Having won 57% of the vote in May 2017, Mr Rouhani has for now the populist support to fend off any internal dissent if he wishes to pursue reformist policies. How long he can maintain this is uncertain in the light of the tougher United States stance on the country. Widely reported as being a moderate and a reformer, Mr Rouhani surely has the difficult task of promoting Iran's economic interests for the benefit of its citizens. He must tackle hardliners from within Iran's political establishment, a task that will become an impossibility should the nuclear deal between the P5 +1 and Iran collapse. Iran's political power structure is far from transparent. Without a doubt, Israel will be observing the political vibes within Iran, particularly following the increasing tougher stance adopted by the United States President Donald Trump and the protracted proxy wars being fought out between Saudi Arabia and Iran in the region.

Regrettably, on 8 May 2018 however, as feared by political observers, President Trump announced that the United States would be withdrawing from the JCPOA and re-imposing sanctions against Iran. This went against the advice of its European allies, particularly France, Germany and the United Kingdom. In response, the President of Iran, Hassan Rouhani, reaffirmed Iran's commitment to the nuclear deal, provided the remaining signatories to the JCPOA were willing to remain committed themselves. Initial indications were that the other signatories would honour the agreement, which includes China and Russia.

In the background, frantic diplomatic moves are anticipated to renegotiate the deal to alleviate the concerns of the United States, since the Trump administration made it clear that secondary sanctions would apply to foreign companies (including European Union companies) that trade with Iran. From a practical context the European Union is unlikely to jeopardise its trading relationship with the United States.

The question remains of how far the Iranian leadership will be willing to go to make further concessions when the United States has shown that it is not willing to honour its commitments. Iran must find a way to overcome this crisis without compromising its sovereignty. Though Iran's trade with the European Union has increased significantly following the lifting of sanctions, China, South Korea and Turkey remain Iran's top three trading partners and Iran will surely be seeking trade assurances with them too.

Unsurprisingly, Israel and Saudi Arabia in their reaction publicly supported Mr Trump's withdrawal. Hardliners in the Iranian military and political establishment, emboldened by the withdrawal by the United States, will be hawkishly following developments as they unfold and seeking to undermine the authority of President Hassan Rouhani, who is viewed as a moderate.

There is absolutely no doubt that the collapse of the nuclear deal, followed by increasing international sanctions and the crippling financial cost in pursuing proxy wars with Saudi Arabia, will strain Iran's finances to breaking point, inducing the collapse of the regime. The great danger of course is what comes after it. Should the Iranian people spontaneously come out en masse, demanding the fall of the regime and by extension the current political system, it is inevitable that the Iranian Revolutionary Guard will respond with force. We could see a repeat of the dire situation in Syria replicate itself in Iran. It is indeed in everyone's interest to sustain a long-term agreement. For Iran, it is increasingly important, as its ever-growing youth population seek to reap the financial benefits of the global economy, otherwise the Iranian political establishment is likely to face a domestic backlash. For the West it is imperative that Iran remains committed never to seek, develop or acquire any nuclear weapons. Israel is indeed sceptical of any compromise between Iran and the West, particularly with the United States.

The worst-case scenario from a military perspective is if Iran withdraws from the JCPOA and restarts the uranium enrichment key to making nuclear weapons, and Israel and the United States respond militarily. This would ignite a catastrophic regional war in the Middle East. Ironically, it would be a crisis of the United States' own making. Iran had always insisted that its nuclear programme is entirely peaceful (much to the distrust of Israel), and its compliance with the nuclear deal was verified by the International Atomic Energy Agency (IAEA).

Commencing at 12:01am on 7 August 2018, sanctions were re-imposed on Iran that included restrictions on the Iranian government's access to US bank notes, its freedom to trade in gold and precious metals and the sale or transfer to or from Iran of graphite and metals, as well as unspecified sanctions relating to the Iranian currency. According to US officials, tariffs were also being placed on Iran's automotive sector and the country was prohibited from purchasing US passenger aircraft, while the US would no longer purchase certain Iranian commodities. In his address to the 73rd session of the United Nations General Assembly, on 25 September 2018, Donald Trump confirmed that further sanctions would be imposed in November 2018 taking direct aim at Iran's oil and energy sector, financial institutions connected with Iran's Central Bank, port operators and shipbuilding sectors.

Previously, in June 2017, ISIL claimed its gunmen and suicide bombers carried out an audacious assault in the Iranian capital, Tehran, targeting the Parliament and the tomb of the founder of the Islamic Republic, Ayatollah Ruhollah Khomeini. The attack killed 12 people with dozens injured. The hard-line Revolutionary Guards blamed Saudi Arabia for the attack, adding fuel to the diplomatic spat in the Gulf at the time. The attack was carried out while Saudi Arabia, along with Egypt and the United Arab Emirates, broke diplomatic ties with Qatar over its alleged support for terrorism and close relationship with Iran, which they blame for destabilising the Middle East. The Iranian President, Hassan Rouhani, went on to say, 'The Islamic Republic of Iran will be more determined in the fight against regional terrorism, extremism and violence' in light of the terrorist attack. President Trump, who sided with Saudi Arabia and its Gulf allies against Qatar, issued the statement that 'states [meaning Iran] that sponsor terrorism risk falling victim to the evil that they promote'. This marked the first ISIL attack in Iran, setting the platform for increasing tensions between Shi'ite Iran and Sunni-dominated Saudi Arabia at a critical time in the region.

Some political commentators go on to claim that the diplomatic standoff and blockade by Saudi Arabia and other GCC countries against Qatar will allow Iran to exert its influence on Qatar. If that does ultimately transpire, it would put the GCC on a serious back footer. The GCC cannot afford to antagonise one of its own Member state's (Qatar) especially when the potential of a second Arab Spring cannot be ruled out with absolute certainty. This is particularly true of Saudi Arabia, which is involved in a protracted military campaign in neighbouring Yemen, Shi'ite discontent on its southern border and a general slow-down in economic growth, despite bold moves by the Saudi Crown Prince, Mohammed bin Salman to re-invigorate the Saudi economy.

THE HUMANITARIAN DISASTER IN YEMEN

The conflict in Yemen is not simply a proxy war between regional powers vying for regional domination; it is in fact fast turning out to be a fight for the survival of the House of Saud and its Wahabi narrative. The military offensive began when Saudi Arabia launched an air campaign in March 2015 after Houthi rebels backed by Iran took control of the Yemeni capital, Sana'a, overthrowing President Abd-Rabbu Mansour Hadi in a coup. Fearing for his life, the Saudi-backed president first fled to the southern city of Aden and then to the safety of the Saudi capital, Riyadh. The Saudi war campaign is backed principally by both the United States and the United Kingdom (both permanent members of the United Nations Security Council) who have authorised the sale of billions of dollars' worth of military hardware to Saudi Arabia.

In January 2017 the United Nations Office for the Coordination of Humanitarian Affairs (UNOCHA) estimated that the civilian death toll in the two-year conflict had reached 10,000, with 3 million being internally displaced and 80% of the population on the brink of starvation and in need of immediate humanitarian assistance with a famine slowly gripping the Arab world's poorest nation.

Media reports of the desperate humanitarian situation in Yemen, where thousands of young children as well as babies are dying as a result of malnutrition or through lack of health care (with many of the hospitals being bombed by the Saudi coalition), draws into stark focus the inept inability of the United Nations to effectively intervene to bring the warring parties to the negotiating table or to ensure effective delivery of humanitarian assistance, including the delivery of essential goods to the civilian population in Yemen. A naval embargo imposed by the Saudi-led coalition, fighting around the government-controlled port of Aden and Saudi air strikes on the rebel-held port of Hudaydah have severely reduced imports since 2015. The Saudi coalition has accused the Houthis of using the port of Hudaydah to smuggle weapons and ammunitions and has called for United Nations monitors to be posted there. This is an allegation denied by the Houthis. A lack of fuel, coupled with insecurity and damage to markets and roads, has also prevented supplies from being distributed. Though United Nation Security Council Resolution 2266, adopted in 2016, expressed 'grave distress' at the continued deterioration of the devastating humanitarian situation in Yemen and 'serious concern at all instances of hindrances to the effective delivery of humanitarian assistance, including limitations on the delivery of vital goods to the civilian population of Yemen', in reality this had little material impact on the ground. In the first eight months of 2017, only 21 container ships sailed to Hudaydah, according to port data compiled by the United Nations World

Food Programme and Reuters. By comparison, 54 container ships delivered twice the volume of goods in the same period in 2016. Before the war, 129 container ships reached the port in the first eight months of 2014.

In fact, on 10 March 2017 the United Nations humanitarian chief, Stephen O'Brien, while reporting to the United Nations Security Council, claimed that the world faced its greatest humanitarian crisis since the creation of the United Nations in 1945 with 14.1 million people in Yemen facing starvation with a famine likely to take hold unless there was an immediate injection of funds and an unimpeded access for humanitarian aid. This is in addition to the 2.9 million facing starvation in Somalia, 4.9 million in South Sudan and 1.8-plus million in Nigeria. Furthermore, it was reported by various media outlets in June 2017 that following a visit to Yemen the United Nations Children's Funds regional director, Geert Cappelaere, expressed concern that a serious cholera outbreak was sweeping through the country with the potential to increase to 300,000 cases within weeks without significant intervention. With impoverished parents having little recourse to health care because many of the hospitals and clinics are either closed or destroyed or lack medical supplies, children are invariably the worst affected. Despite these concerns by United Nations agencies, the United Nations Security Council has failed to take credible steps to work towards a peaceful resolution of the conflict.

When ousted President Ali Abdullah Saleh broke off ties with Houthi rebels on 2 December 2017, declaring his intention to do a deal with Saudi Arabia, critics argued that the move would make any resolution to the conflict that much more confusing and precarious. Then two days after this announcement in a revenge attack Houthi rebels shot and killed Mr Saleh in his car during a shootout at a checkpoint on the outskirts of Sana'a, compounding the impasse further. It will be interesting to see if forces loyal to the Mr Saleh will turn on the Houthis making an alliance with the Saudi-coalition.

It would be pertinent to make the point here that it would appear that whenever there is disagreement between the five permanent members of the Security Council, the United Nations is unable to take any effective decision. The time for reform of the United Nations is well overdue, not only in terms of numbers of permanent members of the Security Council but also on the impact of their veto and the requirement to have a unanimous decision by all permanent members, without which a 'substantive' resolution cannot be adopted. The UN would do well to increase the number of permanent members of the Security Council to reflect the increase in the population size of some nations as well as, their political and economic importance and clout. India and Japan would be leading contenders given that India as a country has a population of more than 1 billion (almost a sixth of the global population) and Japan being one of the most populous countries in South Asia, with both countries being global economic powers. Interestingly, not one Muslim country is a permanent member of the Security Council or is likely to be one, despite the fact that a third of the global population will be Muslims by 2050. Rather than having a unanimous vote, a majority vote by permanent members of the Security Council should allow the adoption of a substantive resolution, even where a permanent member vetoes a resolution. Furthermore, the rules and processes in dealing with conflict situations by the United Nations should be revised to reflect the political, military, social-economic and humanitarian challenges that the world struggles to face today following the end of the Cold War, the military role of non-state actors, the rise of reactionary nationalist forces and humanitarian catastrophes culminating therefrom as highlighted throughout this chapter.

OCCUPATION FORCES: ENHANCED INTERROGATION TECHNIQUES

Another serious cause of resentment lies in the allegation that occupation forces in Afghanistan and previously in Iraq, as well as the Israeli army operating in occupied territories in their quest for terrorists, have defiled the sanctity of Muslim homes. They are accused of smashing open front doors of homes in the dead of night and dragging sleeping inmates, including women and children, out of their beds, terrorizing them with deafening shouts and thrusting firearms at them. Children are traumatized, not knowing why these armed men have manhandled their frantic sisters and mothers and taken their brothers and fathers away from them, often for days and weeks, if not months. This raises the question of the number of instances when armed terrorists have actually been apprehended through these raids, while all the time radicalizing opinion against occupation forces.

The West is often accused of providing political and military support to oppressive regimes in North Africa and the Middle East in exchange for economic benefits (oil rights), and often exchanging intelligence resulting in the torture of so-called terrorists. Post 9/11 this form of torture had reportedly taken the form of enhanced interrogation techniques such as water boarding, sleep deprivation and forcing prisoners to maintain agonising positions, amongst others. The plight of Abdel Hakim Belhaj, who played a leading role in the fall of former Libyan dictator Colonel Gaddafi and who for six years fought in the British courts to sue MI6 (amongst others) over his alleged rendition by the CIA in 2004, is a stark example. Files recovered from a government building destroyed during the 2011 US-led war in Libya showed that British spies were complicit in the rendition of Mr Belhaj and his then pregnant wife to Libya from Thailand by CIA officials, having been previously detained by Malaysian officials in Kuala Lumpur. While in Libya he was imprisoned and tortured. In December 2013, a High Court Judge struck out Mr Belhaj's case on the grounds that if it were allowed to proceed it could have potentially damaged British national interests. In fact, the basis of Mr Justice Simon's decision was that it was not within his jurisdiction to decide whether 'the conduct of US officials acting outside the US is unlawful in circumstances where there are no clear and incontrovertible standards for doing so and where there is incontestable evidence that such an inquiry would be damaging to the national interest'.

In October 2014, however, the Court of Appeal ruled that the case should go ahead despite government attempts to resist it on grounds of the 'act of state doctrine', arguing that the courts could not inquire into what happened because it involved a foreign state. The Court of Appeal stated, 'there is compelling public interest in the investigation by the English courts of these very grave allegations. The risk of displeasing our allies or offending other states... cannot justify our declining jurisdiction on grounds of act of state over what is a properly justiciable claim.' It added: 'the stark reality is that unless the English courts are able to exercise jurisdiction in this case, these very grave allegations against the executive will never be subject to judicial investigation'. The government appealed against the decision of the Court of Appeal, with the Supreme Court hearing the appeal in November 2015. But then in June 2016 the CPS decided that there was insufficient evidence to charge MI6 officials in any criminal case. However, in January 2017, the Supreme Court ruled in Mr Belhaj's case that ministers could not claim 'state immunity' or escape trial on grounds of the legal doctrine of 'foreign acts of state', consequently dismissing the appeal and stating that the case could proceed to trial.

There was always the risk however, that the government would refuse to back down and would seek to try the case under the Justice and Security Act 2013, which allows for trials to be held in secret where they involve intelligence and secret documents (civil liberties groups have very often criticized the 2013 Act as a curb on individual liberties as it impedes hearings in the public domain). Given this, the High Court in December 2017 ruled that the case should be heard under section 6 of the Justice and Security Act 2013, as it was a civil matter, finding for the government that the decision by the Crown Prosecution Service not to prosecute a former senior MI6 officer, Sir Mark Allan over his role in their rendition did not directly relate to criminal proceedings. Then the Supreme Court on 22 March 2018 heard an appeal from Mr Belhaj's lawyers arguing that the judicial review of the decision not to prosecute the MI6 officer was a 'criminal cause or matter' and therefore outside the parameters of the 2013 Act. It was their contention that the powers under the Act to hold hearings behind closed doors were granted by

Parliament solely for use in non-criminal proceedings.

Finally on 10 May 2018, after almost six years of protracted court proceedings, the government issued an unreserved apology to Mr Belhaj and his wife, Fatima Boudchar, for the appalling treatment they had suffered as a result of the government's role in 'contributing to their rendition and detention'. The letter of apology from Prime Minister Theresa May was read out by the Attorney General, Jeremy Wright, in the House of Commons, also announcing that Fatima Boudchar would receive £500,000 in compensation and that following mediation with the couple they had withdrawn their legal claim after reaching a 'full and final settlement'. Mr Belhaj had never sought a financial settlement, simply an apology from the British Government. Mr Wright emphasized however, that there was 'no admission of liability'. Consequently, no member of the Blair government and no member of MI6 or any other security establishment will be liable to take responsibility for the 'deeply troubling and appalling treatment' suffered by the couple.

While there can be no justification for torture by a civilized and democratic society, if lessons are to be truly learned then it would have been imperative for the government to provide the Parliamentary Intelligence and Security Committee (ISC) full access to all government papers on Belhaj's case for its inquiry into rendition which was scheduled to report later in the year. Meanwhile, former Prime Minister David Cameron had set up a judge-led Inquiry under Peter Gibson to look into evidence that MI5 and MI6 were colluding in the rendition and torture of British citizens and residents suspected of terrorism. That full inquiry has fallen by the wayside. An interim report was published, but with minimal media coverage. It found that the United Kingdom's intelligence agencies had been involved in rendition operations, and that some of their officers had supported the mistreatment of suspects by assaulting them, depriving them of sleep, hooding and the use of stress positions. The report listed 27 question that remain unanswered.

Then on 28 June 2018, the ISC published two scathing reports titled 'Detainee Mistreatment and Rendition: 2001-2010' and

'Detainee Mistreatment and Rendition: Current Issues'. It found that the British Government had no clear policy on rendition following 9/11 nor recognized the need for having one while concluding that British authorities ignored routine mistreatment by US authorities despite UK intelligence agencies being aware from an early stage that such mistreatment was going on. The reports found that British intelligence officers witnessed prisoners being tortured and played an active role in the rendition of terrorist suspects into the hands of the secret police of brutal regimes knowing that they would face inhuman treatment. The ISC Chairman, Dominic Grieve, regarded as 'inexcusable' the actions of torture and rendition tolerated by the United Kingdom. The ISC recommended a framework to set boundaries within which agencies must operate to prevent them from becoming complicit in torture or rendition (whether by the British state or by allied countries). A major shortcoming behind the publication of these reports, however, was the restrictions imposed by Downing Street on the ISC in calling key intelligence figures from giving evidence as well as politicians, including Jack Straw, who was Foreign Secretary from 2001-2006 as well as being responsible for GCHQ and MI6.

The harrowing reports of abuse perpetrated on inmates at the Abu Ghraib prison in Baghdad by US servicemen and women caused hurt and anguish not only in Iraq but across the Muslim world. Pictures of abuse released in 2004 showed a US private dragging a cowering Iraqi prisoner along the floor with a dog lead. Another showed her smoking a cigarette and pointing a mock gun at a naked prisoner's genitals. Other pictures released in 2004 included naked prisoners being subjected to terrifying taunts by dogs. So horrendous was the abuse that back in 2009, US President Barack Obama undertook to block publication of some graphic images allegedly involving US soldiers 'torturing Iraqi prisoners', fearing that they could provoke a serious backlash against American troops serving in Iraq and Afghanistan at the time. Some of these pictures are reported to depict detainee nudity and images of detainees shackled, as well as pictures of weapons drawn and being pointed at detainees. Until full publication of such pictures is made we will not know their full nature.

In January 2014 a formal complaint was lodged with the Office of the Prosecutor of the International Criminal Court (ICC) in The Hague by Public Interest Lawyers (PIL) and the European Center for Constitutional and Human Rights (ECCHR) calling for an investigation under Article 15 of the Rome Statute of the International Criminal Court into alleged war crimes involving systematic detainee abuse carried out by British troops serving in Iraq. The damning dossier draws on cases of more than 400 Iraqis, representing thousands of allegations of torture, cruel, inhuman and degrading treatment between 2003 and 2008. They range from hooding prisoners to burning, electric shocks, sleep deprivation, noise bombardment, deprivation of food and water, and cultural and religious humiliation. Other forms of alleged abuse include mock executions, sexual assault and threats of rape, death and torture. The British MoD naturally denied that its troops 'systematically tortured' detainees, while the then British Foreign Secretary, William Hague, exclaimed that there was no need for the ICC to investigate these allegations as many of them were either under investigation or had already been dealt with through public inquiries and the UK courts. In May 2014 the Prosecutor of the ICC nevertheless took the decision to conduct a preliminary investigation into the allegations. While some may argue that in the theatre of war it will be extremely naive to think that the invading/occupying army will not perpetrate excesses, this misses the point entirely. UK troops are required to operate within the parameters of international law in conflict situations with respect to detainees. This last point was reiterated by the then British Attorney General, Dominic Grieve, who in completely rejecting the allegation of systematic abuse carried out by British armed forces in Iraq remarked that British troops 'operate to the highest standards in line with both domestic and international law' with the vast majority of the troops meeting that expectation while allegations of abuse were being comprehensively investigated. It will be interesting to observe how events unfold, particularly where Article 17 of the Rome

Statute of the International Criminal Court provides that the ICC may only intervene where no effective investigation was being carried out by the national authorities.

Previously in 2009, the Labour government launched the 'Al-Sweady Public Inquiry' to investigate claims that Iraqi civilians were killed and tortured by British soldiers after a fierce battle in Iraq in 2004 known as the 'Battle of Danny Boy'. During the three-hour firefight 28 enemy fighters were killed and nine were taken for questioning to the Camp Naji military base. It was claimed that there they were mistreated, tortured and executed with bodies being mutilated. In December 2014 the Inquiry concluded that the 'vast majority' of allegations including all the most serious claims against British soldiers were 'wholly without foundation' and 'entirely the product of deliberate lies, reckless speculation and ingrained hostility' from Iraqi witnesses. The Inquiry was critical of the way detainees were blindfolded, strip-searched and not given proper meals, but found such ill treatment had often been unintended and several procedures had since been changed.

This naturally increased demands for legal reforms to protect combat troops serving abroad from future human rights law cases. Potentially, troops that had served in Iraq could have faced up to five probes including a military investigation, an investigation by the Iraq Historical Allegations Team (IHAT), an Iraq Fatalities investigation as well as an investigation by the ICC and a civil claim for compensation.

Following a parliamentary report by the House of Commons Defence Committee in February 2017 condemning his ministry for paying 'ambulance-chasing lawyers' to bring thousands of 'spurious' cases against UK troops, the then Defence Secretary, Sir Michael Fallon, immediately announced that IHAT would be closed in the summer of 2017 with a reduced caseload being transferred to a unit within the Royal Navy Police to be completed by 2018. The parliamentary report branded IHAT 'unfit for purpose' and accused the Ministry of Defence of enabling law firms 'to generate cases against service personal on an industrial level' and recommended that IHAT should be shut down immediately as it had 'directly harmed the defence of the nation'. Almost 3,500 allegations, including murder and torture, were reported to IHAT, the vast majority by Phil Shinner, who was struck off in early February 2017 for reportedly acting dishonestly in bringing false claims made by Iraqis.

Looking at Afghanistan, the year 2012 saw mass public uproar over photos and video depicting US Marines urinating on the corpses of 'insurgents', reports of the burning of the Holy Qur'an by US Forces at a US military base and the massacre of 16 unarmed civilians by Staff Sargent Robert Bales and his immediate removal out of the country, denying Afghan authorities any role in investigating the crime. These events created a deep sense of hurt and contempt against occupation forces.

Reflecting back on President Obama's last year in office, despite announcing his strong intention to close the detention facility in Guantanamo Bay in February 2016 it was unlikely that the US Congress would have approved any such measure, as there was strong resentment by many in the United States over transferring 'suspected terrorists' on its soil. Critics will argue that the President had the opportunity to take credible steps to close the detention facility earlier on during his Presidency but rather had decided to take this initiative in his last year of his Presidency to upstage a Republican-dominated Congress. The Republican Presidential Candidate, Donald Trump, made it clear at the time that he would keep the detention facility in Guantanamo open for business, and now as President he continues to hold that view.

TERROR AND EXTREMISM: THE VIOLENCE OF HATRED

The Norwegian Massacre of 22 July 2011 exposed a (pan-European) neo-Nazi, ultra-far-right agenda based upon an irrational fear that lacks any real sustainable credibility. This extremist ideology threatens to undermine the democratic values and institutions upon which the European Union is based. If it is left unchecked, European Muslims will find themselves victims of their own Exodus in the future. It is not simply making a political issue of multiculturalism in an attempt to woe voters – it goes far beyond that. Giving far-right propaganda a democratic platform will inevitably result in racial tensions. There is no credible evidence to suggest that the vast majority of European Muslims are hell-bent on establishing an Islamic Caliphate in Europe. Far from it, the rational advocates of an Islamic Caliphate would rather prefer the re-establishment of the Caliphate based on democratic ideals and processes in the Muslim Ummah itself, despite the insurmountable challenges in realising this goal, though its establishment will no doubt act as a catalyst to achieving global peace, as well as, facilitating global commerce, acting as an effective counterweight to the global economic domination of China and India predicted by many economists by around 2035.

Post-Cold War, ordinary Muslims are increasingly finding themselves being persecuted, whether that be in the form of ethnic cleansing, as in Bosnia and recently in Myanmar, or foreign intervention to force regime change in order to secure energy supplies such as in Iraq, or lethal force being unleashed by tyrants in order to hang on to their reign on power, as evidenced by the failure of the Arab Spring.

When Muslims have suffered so much and endured such torment for so long, it is ironic that they are losing the moral high ground. With Islam being demonized more often than not by Western media propaganda in the name of freedom of expression, Islam is perceived by the general population in the West as being synonymous with terrorism. This is giving rise to an undercurrent of tension within many national communities, threatening social cohesion. Party political rhetoric that multiculturalism is dead does not help!

Many Muslims living in the West fear that should there be substantial terrorist attacks carried out by ISIL or Al-Qaeda and their affiliates, the backlash both by governments and non-Muslims against the general Muslim population there will be devastating. Indeed, following the massacre at the Charlie Hebdo offices in Paris in January 2015 and the night time Paris attacks in November 2015, the number of anti-Muslim hate crimes has been on the increase, not only in France but in many parts of Europe. The deliberately contorted interpretation of Islam used by extremists to justify their terrorist attacks has caused many Europeans to view Islam as a threat to their national security and Muslims as 'the enemy'.

Since 9/11 and the London and Madrid bombings, some European media streams have based their reporting on stereotypes and have used the actions of terrorists to stigmatize Muslim populations, whether inadvertently or not. Such stereotyping and generalizations about Muslims are negatively impacting Muslim communities in Europe. According to a report published by the European Commission against Racism and Intolerance (ECRI) in 2015, Islamophobia was already on the increase in 2014, often expressed in views that saw Islam as inherently opposed to European values of democracy and secularism, which ignored the reality of Muslim communities. Furthermore, when on 22 July 2011 a fertilizer bomb went off in the Norwegian capital of Oslo in the vicinity of government buildings, followed by the massacre on Utoya Island that resulted in the death of 77 civilians, suspicion quickly fell upon so-called Muslim extremists, and there was an immediate initial backlash against Muslims living in Norway. It was only when it came to light that this was a terrorist act perpetrated by a non-Muslim, in fact by an ultra-far-right wing Norwegian extremist, namely Anders Behring Breivik, that the backlash died down. Subsequently, on 24 August 2012, Mr Breivik was sentenced to 21 years imprisonment, having been found sane and criminally responsible for his actions.

More recently, following the spate of terror attacks in the United Kingdom in 2017, namely the Westminster attack, the Manchester Arena attack and the London Bridge attack, police in Manchester and London have registered a surge in anti-Muslim hate crime. Such hatred took on an extreme manifestation when in the early hours of 19 June 2017 a van was used to drive into a group of Muslim worshippers while on their way home after offering their Ramadan prayers at the Finsbury Park Mosque, killing one of them. The perpetrator of the terrorist attack, Darren Osbourne, is claimed to have shouted, 'I want to kill more

Muslims'. Reportedly, according to his long-time girlfriend, Mr Osbourne had become obsessed with Muslims in the weeks leading to the attack, having watched the BBC drama about the Rochdale grooming scandal not long after the Westminster terror attack. Despite calls for unity from all political parties and religious leaders there appears to be an under-current of Islamophobia in the UK that needs strong and swift intervention by the government. The recent spate of acid attacks on Muslim women in London is of grave concern. More recently hate mail was being circulated in London and other cities in the United Kingdom captioned 'Punish a Muslim Day', with a date for this scheduled for 3 April 2018. Thankfully, the day passed without any major reported incident.

Global Muslims look to the political power structures in Saudi Arabia and the Middle East to embrace democratic norms and values respecting and enforcing individual civil rights and liberties. Despotic regimes in the Middle East, particularly Saudi Arabia, must give way to political pluralism in the interests of promoting democratic accountability and providing leadership to the Islamic World, placing it in an opportune position to face the global economic and political challenges that lie ahead as well as combatting terrorism in the region. As it stands today, the Kingdom of Saudi Arabia ('al-Mamlakah al-Arabiyah as-Su'udiyah') is an 'absolute' monarchy as opposed to a 'constitutional' monarchy, with the King, Salman bin Abd al-Aziz Al Saud (since 23 January 2015), being both the head of state and head of government. Politics in Saudi Arabia practically centres on policy-decisions being made on the basis of consultations between influential members of the Royal Family and the religious establishment, although recently the Crown Prince, Mohammed bin Salman, is increasingly asserting his own personal authority on policy issues in order to implement the 'Vision 2030' Project and consolidate his own power base. The 'Basic Law of Government', issued by Royal Decree in March 1992 serves as the constitutional framework based on the Qur'an and Sunnah, which is subject to interpretation. It sets out among other matters the system of governance, rights of citizens, and powers and duties of the government. Saudi Arabia will always prove contentious for global Muslims, as Islam's two holiest sites are situated on its western frontier.

Recent instances of terrorist attacks against Western interests and its citizens since the tragic events of 9/11 include the Bali nightclub bombings on 12 October 2002 which killed 202 people, mostly foreigners, reportedly carried out by al-Qaeda-linked Jemaah Islamiyah. This was followed by the Madrid commuter train bombings on 11 March 2004, which killed 191 people just three days prior to the Spanish General Elections, carried out by an al-Qaeda-inspired terrorist cell. After that, on 7 July 2005 an alleged Al-Qaeda-inspired cell also carried out a series of coordinated suicide attacks in London, targeting the public transport system during the morning rush hour that claimed the lives of 52 people.

We then have the coordinated shooting and bombing attacks reportedly carried out by Al-Qaeda linked Lashkar-e-Taiba (a Pakistani-based militant organization) across India's commercial capital, Mumbai, killing 164 people between 26 and 29 November 2008. The targets included the 5-star hotels Oberoi Trident and the Taj Mahal Palace and Tower, which were frequented by Western tourists, as well as, the Nariman House, which is a Jewish centre. On 2 September 2013, alleged members of Al-Qaeda linked al-Shabab attacked the opulent Westgate Shopping Mall in Kenya's capital city, Nairobi, also frequented by Westerners, killing at least 62 people. Terrorist attacks have also been carried out by ISIL in Sousse on 26 June 2015, in the Turkish Capital, Ankara on 10 October 2015, on 31 October 2015 over Sinai and on 13 November 2015 in the Lebanese Capital of Beirut. Again on 7 January 2015 and later on 13 November 2015, the French capital, Paris, suffered multiple coordinated terror attacks. On 22 March 2016 a series of deadly terrorist attacks struck Brussels, with two explosions at the main international airport and a third in a subway station at the heart of the city near the headquarters complex of the European Union, killing 32 people. On 29 June 2016 terrorists attacked Kamal Ataturk Airport in Turkey, killing at least 44 people, while on 2 July 2016 terrorists allegedly having links to ISIL targeted a café in Dhaka, Bangladesh, killing 20 hostages, many of whom were foreign nationals. On 14 July 2016, ISIL claimed responsibility for an attack in the seaside city of Nice when a truck charged down a crowded beach promenade as people gathered to celebrate Bastille Day. As mentioned above, in 2017 multiple terrorist attacks were carried out in both London and Manchester, following which ISIL claimed responsibility, though it would appear that the perpetrators were self-radicalized.

In addition to these, there have been a large number of thwarted 'terrorist attacks' against European and US targets since 9/11, the most prominent reportedly being the discovery of a plot in August 2006 to blow up several trans-Atlantic flights. While Western leaders have insisted that there is no correlation between these acts of terror and events happening on the ground in Palestinian-occupied territories, Syria and previously Afghanistan and Iraq, in reality global Muslims do not share the same view. As mentioned in the Introduction, Muslims across the globe share a common psyche, though this manifests itself in different ways. The overwhelming majority of global Muslims, it must be emphasized, condemn such criminal acts as nothing short of atrocities, distancing themselves from such a radical interpretation of Islam. In the meantime, Western media coverage has regrettably always branded these atrocities as 'Islamist'. Such sensationalist headlines give rise to suspicion and mistrust, threatening social cohesion within national communities in the West, while the vast majority of Muslims find such stereotyping offensive.

Before proceeding any further, let us briefly examine some of the perceived historical root causes of mistrust between Muslims and the West. The commercial expansion of Europe in the 17th century brought about by the industrial revolution saw European powers competing with one another to secure monopolies over the supply of spices, tea, silk and other lucrative trade commodities from Asia, Southeast Asia and Africa to Europe. Consequently, over the next few centuries Islamic lands bore the brunt of European colonization. With victory at the Battle of Plassey in 1757, the East India Company under Robert Clive secured a permanent foothold in Bengal, following which the British

Empire was ruling over the entire Indian subcontinent by the 1850s. In 1830 France occupied Algeria, taking Tunisia in 1881. In 1839 the British occupied Aden, and Egypt followed in 1882. Sudan was occupied in 1899. In 1912 the Italians occupied Libya, while the French were in control of Morocco. Following the First World War defeat of the Central Powers, which included the Ottoman Empire, which capitulated on 30 October 1918, it was subsequently divided up among the victorious Allies, drawing the boundaries of the modern Middle East. The League of Nations granted France a mandate to control both Syria and Lebanon, while the British were given Iraq, Transjordan and Palestine. As for Muslim-populated lands in Central Asia, these were absorbed into the USSR.

The claim that Western colonial powers brought civilization in the form of culture and enlightenment to their Muslim colonies is grossly ill-informed and exaggerated. Prior to European colonization, throughout the European Middle Ages, Islamic lands were hubs of innovations and creativity, particularly in the sciences, philosophy and architecture. Magnificent cities such as Cordoba dotted the lands of the Caliphate.

In the years following the end of the Second World War most of the Muslim colonies, including those in Arabia and Northern Africa, gained independence from their colonial masters. Many of these struggles for independence transformed the political mindset of the Muslim World, putting their complete trust in nationalism and secularism.

With China and India emerging as economic superpowers and likely to command almost one quarter of the world's population by 2050, thereby making them the largest global consumer market with an insatiable thirst for energy and natural resources which will surpass the likes of Europe and the United States, the West has every reason to be worried. With current trends, China and India will also be the largest manufacturer and exporter of consumer products, with a vast employable workforce surpassing the entire populations of Europe and the United States. To add to this, the US has a multi-trillion dollar debt (more than 19 trillion dollars as of December 2016). According to the US

Treasury Department, China is the largest foreign holder of United States debt after Japan. Were China to gradually call in its debt holdings in retaliation against increased tariffs on imports of Chinese goods into the US, as well as any move by the United States government against increasing Chinese interference in the South China Sea, the demand for the US Dollar would begin to plummet, disrupting international money markets and affecting United States fiscal policy. While the US dollar is currently the standard currency for most international trade, including crude oil, theoretically speaking such commercial transactions can be carried out in whatever currency the parties involved decide. Should major oil-producing countries conduct transactions other than in US dollars this would have a catastrophic effect on the clout of the 'US Petro-Dollar' and the United States money markets. This may very well be the future consequence of the continuing shift of global economic growth eastwards towards China and India. In fact, the Chinese Yuan (RMB) may potentially replace the dominance of the US dollar in terms of global trade.

The concern for the US is the inevitable economic global clout that BRICS (Brazil, Russia, India, China and South Africa) will command in the near future. Should major oil-producing countries in the Middle East along with BRICS take steps to re-adjust and re-align their economies to enable them to shift their reliance away from the US dollar to conduct trade, the United States economy will indeed be in for a rough ride. In fact, it could be the cause of global conflict as hawkish policy-makers, both in the United States administration and the military, seek to retaliate in the way they are best accustomed to.

The military expenditure of the United States is the highest among all major global military powers. In fact, it was reported in March 2018 that President Donald Trump had approved the largest military budget in US history, 700 billion dollars. As the United States is set to get more involved militarily on the global platform, various facets of its military expenditure will inevitably continue to rise. Should the US economy suffer, then so will its investment in the military. And that is not something the United States will be prepared for.

If we look at the second global currency, the euro, with the Eurozone facing increasing uncertainty over bailouts for European Union Member States, as we saw particularly with Greece in 2012, and the recent potential resurgence of right-wing parties in Europe who seek to unravel the 'European Project', especially after 'Brexit', this has definitely played into the hands of US fortunes with the US dollar increasingly looking like remaining the currency of choice for the foreseeable future. In fact, between the Brexit referendum result and the triggering of Article 50 of the Lisbon Treaty by the United Kingdom, the British pound reportedly fell 17% against the US dollar, further consolidating the strength of the dollar.

MYANMAR: GENOCIDE WITH IMPUNITY

No doubt the currency of global trade will continue to dominate world finance and United States global influence. Indeed, the United States may also be seeking to counter-balance increasing Chinese clout by fostering trade and cooperation with Southeast Asian countries which benefit from cheap skilled labour. This was illustrated by the choice of countries President Obama first visited after his re-election in November 2012. They included Myanmar, Thailand and Cambodia.

With the West facing economic uncertainty and the increasingly unstable situation in the Middle East, with its possible impact on global oil prices in addition to the slowdown in the Chinese economy, sanctions on Russia and Brexit, trade will invariably take precedence over human rights issues. We continue to see this with the West in their dealings with Saudi Arabia, China and until relatively recently with Myanmar.

Since a state of emergency was declared on 10 June 2012, Myanmar has witnessed serious sectarian violence in its northern Rakhine State between Buddhist Rakhinis and minority Muslim Rohingyas, with UK-based NGOs reporting that both the Burmese army and police were targeting Muslim Rohingyas through mass arrests, violence, rape and systematic discrimination. Serious questions need to be answered by the then Myanmar authorities as to whether the massacre of Muslim minorities was indeed state sponsored. The loss of life, destruction of property, the displacement of families from their homesteads and the inaction of the government and the local administration in affected areas in terms of reparations and resettlement have been appalling. Anxious to flee the persecution, many had taken to desperate measures. This had resulted in the trafficking of Muslim Rohingyas by illegal gangs to countries like Indonesia and Malaysia, often resulting in the tragic deaths of women and children at sea while making the perilous journey in unseaworthy vessels. For an impoverished country that is only recently beginning to assert itself on the global stage as an up-and-coming democracy after decades of military oppression, it is unfortunate. It would appear that the state of Myanmar has abandoned the Rohingyas, whose primary purpose is the systematic uprooting and destruction of an entire ethnic group.

It was hoped that the landslide victory in November 2015 of pro-democracy leader Aung San Suu Kyi and her National League for Democracy (NLD) in the country's first democratic elections since 1990 would give the new government the authority to address the plight of Muslim Rohingyas in Myanmar and revise the contentious Citizenship Law (Muslim Rohingyas were not allowed to vote in the 2015 elections). Reports by different media streams, however, suggest that back in 2016 anti-Muslim sentiment was already on the rise, with mosques and Muslim prayer halls being razed to the ground by armed mobs. Upon being elected as 'State Counsellor', Aung San Suu Kyi surely had her task cut out in dealing with the Rohingya crises and the rise of Buddhist nationalism.

Following coordinated attacks, allegedly by a group of Muslim militants, on 9 October 2016 on three border posts between Myanmar and Bangladesh that left nine border policemen dead, a killing spree was unleashed by the Myanmar military as part of a military counter-insurgency campaign that had witnessed allegations of rape and torture against innocent Rohingya civilians, as well as burning of their homesteads, forcing thousands to flee to neighbouring Bangladesh. Surprisingly, reporting of these events at the time by mainstream Western media outlets were remarkably subdued. These gruesome events bear testimony to the sad reality that the Nobel Laureate Aung San Suu Kyi's grip on power is indeed still constrained by the military. Perplexingly, under Myanmar's constitution 25% of the seats in the legislature (Pyithu Hluttaw) are reserved for military representatives who also hold key ministries.

The government sought to whitewash the allegation of genocide by appointing a Commission led by a former military general, named Myint Swe, who was also the former head of military intelligence and is now Vice President. The Commission was widely criticized by human rights groups for lacking credibility because it was not independent and lacked outside experts. In fact, on 6 August, 2017 after a nine-month domestic inquiry, the National Investigation Commission on Rakhine State held a news conference on their findings into alleged abuses against ethnic Rohingyas, only to find that there was no evidence of crimes against humanity and ethnic cleansing, contradicting claims made by an earlier report (3 February 2017) issued by the Office of the High Commissioner for Human Rights which concluded that the attacks against the Rohingya 'very likely' amounted to crimes against humanity. Myint Swe further went on to deny charges that there had been gang rapes by the military as it swept through Rohingya villages in a security operation following the deadly attack against a border police post by insurgents in October 2016 in the Maungdaw area of Rakhine. Though the United Nations mandated its own fact-finding mission to travel to the Maungdaw area to conduct its own inquiry, the Myanmar government had denied access to any such mission. Disturbingly, the United Nations has gone on record to say the Rohingya are 'the most persecuted minority in the world'.

During the Syrian Refugee Crisis the washed-up body of a boy called Aylan Kurdi shocked the global conscience after pictures of his body was aired by all the major global news outlets. Another child's body was washed up on the bank of the river Naf on the Bangladesh-Myanmar border on 6 December 2016. It was a 16-month-old baby boy identified as Mohammed Shohayet. The image of the child lying dead in the mud was first posted on a web portal run by Rohingya Vision, later published by CNN and other leading media outlets. It then went viral on social media. Shohayet had drowned in the river Naf in Myanmar territory as the boat carrying his family sank mid-river following their desperate attempt to flee Myanmar to escape persecution of government forces on the night of 4 December. Most of the passengers on the ill-fated boat reportedly were from the village of Ye Dwin Chaung in northern Maungdaw. Prior to 2017, Western governments were falling head over heels over Nobel Laureate Aung San Suu Kyi, showing complete indifference to the genocide being perpetrated by Myanmar's security forces on Muslim Rohingyas which had begun while Myanmar was being run by a military dictatorship. It is apparent therefore that until recently the West had clearly lost its moral compass in failing to effectively address this tragedy.

Another deadly attack came on 25 August 2017, reportedly by insurgents, on police posts armed with knives and homemade bombs, killing 12 members of the security forces. After this a large exodus of Muslim Rohingyas began fleeing Rakhine State, escaping a renewed military crackdown. Reportedly more than 400,000 fled in the first four weeks after the crackdown. The Western media began to take notice of the barbarity of these attacks (as compared to previous ones), reporting them on an almost daily basis towards the end of August 2017, but on 6 September 2017 Aung San Suu Kyi denied outright that atrocities were being committed against the Rohingyas, claiming that it was 'fake news based on misinformation aimed at promoting the interests of terrorists'. But surely, shutting out foreign journalists from covering the troubled areas did not help in ascertaining the truth. Furthermore, the multitude of harrowing reports of murder, plunder, arson and rape by those fleeing the conflict arriving in Bangladesh seeking refuge from the military onslaught cannot simply be dismissed as fake news. Aung San Suu Kyi sought to divert media attention by stressing the country's commitment to fighting terrorists. *But then one must question whether the fight against so-called terrorists justifies ethnic cleansing and genocide. Most certainly not!*

The reaction of the major powers in the region was particularly interesting to observe. Despite concerns raised by the Indian Prime Minister while making an official visit to Myanmar on 5 September 2017, the Indian government itself had announced only days prior to the 25 August attack that it would be deporting its entire Rohingya population, thought to be around 40,000 and including some 16,000 refugees registered by the United Nations over concerns that terror networks may expand their links through hardline Rohingyas. In its submission to the Supreme Court of India the government claimed that the Rohingyas in India posed 'serious national security ramifications and threats' and should be deported. However the lawyers for the petitioners against deportation argued that the deportation of the Rohingyas, particularly children, being fully aware that they would be killed either in transit or on reaching Myanmar, was in violation of Fundamental Rights guaranteed under the United Nations Convention on the Rights of Children 1989, which India ratified in 1992.

In fact, after the 25 August attack, India's foreign ministry issued a strongly-worded statement promising to stand firmly with Myanmar in its 'fight against terrorism'. The intent behind India's position seems to represent India's desire to reach out and strike a chord with hard-lined Buddhist nationalist opinion. This is all part of India's strategy to counter Chinese influence among Southeast Asian countries by increasing its trade and investment links in the region. Myanmar's Sagaing area bordering India and its neighbouring Rakhine state is a crucial link for India's hydrocarbon and trade ambitions that seeks to connect north-east Indian states to the Sittwe port in Rakhine province through road and rail links and fuel pipelines.

It would appear that the well-orchestrated brutal strategy employed by the government of Myanmar, particularly following the attack by Rohingya insurgents on 25 August 2017, is nothing short of a 'final solution', expressed in its willingness to weather the international criticism over its handling of the Rohingya issue. A sizeable number of the Rohingya population have been forced to flee Rakhine by the brutal crackdown amid reports of murder, rape and arson being committed by the security forces and Buddhist nationalists. The United Nations High

Commissioner for Human Rights, Zeid Ra'ad Al Hussein, went on record on 11 September 2017 to state that with human rights investigators being denied access to fully assess the situation on the ground, the crisis would appear to be a 'textbook example of ethnic cleansing'. Curiously, Western governments are still yet to describe this mass exodus of a minority population through violence, involving murder, rape and plunder as genocide, but rather prefer to describe it as ethnic cleansing.

The potential flip side of this genocide is particularly worrying too. On 5 September 2017 the United Nations Secretary-General, Antonio Guterres, while condemning the attacks by the Arakan Rohingya Salvation Army, expressed concern that the security, humanitarian and human rights situation in Rakhine could also lead to increased radicalization. (It is pertinent to point out that when desperation gives rise to radicalization it then becomes entrenched.) On 29 September 2017 at a meeting of the United Nations Security Council, the UN Secretary-General further urged Myanmar to end with immediate effect the military operations that have caused more than half a million Rohingya Muslims to flee to Bangladesh, terming the crisis 'the world's fastest-developing refugee emergency and a humanitarian and human rights nightmare'. Mr Guterres went on to warn that the humanitarian crisis was acting as a breeding ground for radicalization, criminals and traffickers. He further stated that the broader crisis was 'generating multiple implications for neighbouring states and the larger region, including the risk of inter-communal strife' and demanded that Myanmar Authorities provide 'unfettered access' for humanitarian aid to get in as well as ensuring 'the safe, voluntary, dignified and sustainable return' of all those who had sought refuge across the border in neighbouring Bangladesh. At the same meeting the United States Ambassador to the United Nations, Nikki Haley, derided the Myanmar government for the bloodshed, calling the actions of the Myanmar authorities 'a brutal, sustained campaign to cleanse the country of an ethnic minority'.

Headed by its National Security Advisor, U Thaung Tun, the Myanmar delegation to the UN Security Council at the same meeting denied the accusation of genocide or ethnic cleansing, claiming that the Myanmar government would do everything to prevent it, rather than to adopt a policy to espouse it. Reiterating the point made by Aung San Suu Kyi in her televised speech on 19 September 2017, he too insisted that the Myanmar government needed to understand the real reasons behind the exodus. Such a blatant rebuff of the United Nations by Myanmar is only possible because it has the backing of China (a permanent member of the UN Security Council). China is a major investor in Myanmar with extensive trade and energy links and is pushing for preferential access to the deep sea port of Kyauk Pyu on the Bay of Bengal, an entry point for a Chinese oil and gas pipeline that would provide it with an alternative route for energy imports from the Middle East, enabling it to avoid using the Malacca Strait, which is a bottleneck for shipping.

Again this brings into sharp focus the increasing ineptitude of the United Nations and the necessity for reform to respond to these challenges, which if unaddressed will only get worse. The post–World War II political consensus is fast changing and the United Nations must adapt or risk jeopardizing its legitimacy and sustainability. The Myanmar situation should be taken as a 'wake-up call'. It is difficult to rationalize the fact that despite the horrors of the Holocaust, the United Nations is unable to stop genocide, even in 2017-18 when the country allegedly perpetrating it can continue to do so as long as it has the backing of a permanent member of the Security Council. In this context, the United Nations Security Council in its current format is 'unfit for purpose'.

On 23 November 2017, though Myanmar and Bangladesh signed a bilateral agreement on repatriating the Rohingyas back to Myanmar there appeared to be no significant progress on this front from Myanmar's side. Then on 6 June 2018, a Memorandum of Understanding was signed between the government of Myanmar, the Office of the UN High Commissioner for Refugees (UNHCR) and the UN Development Programme (UNDP) to create conditions that would be conducive to the voluntary, safe, dignified and sustainable return of refugees from Bangladesh and their reintegration in Myanmar. Unfortunately, in both cases the refugee community has had no input in the agreements and has neither been involved nor consulted.

In any case, it would be premature to repatriate the Rohingya Muslims on a voluntary basis without ensuring that their fundamental human rights are guaranteed, including their citizenship. Furthermore, there must be iron-clad assurances overseen by the international community that the Rohingyas will be allowed to return safely back to their lands and not squalid camps under military guard with enforceable agreements to ensure that they will be protected from further harm, discrimination and arbitrary punishment. Given the continued flow of refugees from Myanmar it can rightly be argued however, that it is still too dangerous for the Rohingyas to return voluntarily and with dignity. Shielded by the dominant powers in the region, China and India, it is difficult to see how much leverage the Bangladesh government will be able to exert on Myanmar.

Disturbingly, even today the Myanmar authorities are unwilling to accept the term 'Rohingya' as representing an indigenous ethnic group, although the Rohingyas have lived in Myanmar for generations. In 1982 they were stripped of their citizenship and rendered stateless. The Rohingya are now identified as illegal immigrants from Bangladesh and referred to as 'Bengali' and not Rohingya. Until the psyche of the Myanmar authorities and the people of Myanmar change course in this regard the Rohingyas will never be safe but subject to discrimination and potential future persecution should the refugees return.

In conclusion it can be said that the crucial issue for the Muslim Ummah is how the Western powers go about addressing their concerns now in preparation for the future, especially as it is being torn from within by conflict, authoritarian rule, the rise of extremist groups and the lack of economic empowerment of the masses, particularly the youth population. Interesting times lie ahead, particularly with the relationship between the world's only superpower, the United States and the Muslim Ummah, as President Trump positions the US on the international stage with a bullish foreign policy agenda as opposed to one of consensus. The emphasis should be on meaningful cooperation and effective dialogue, not confrontation. The unilateral withdrawal from the Iran nuclear deal, the shifting of the US Embassy to Jerusalem and the withdrawal from the Paris Climate Accord are only a few instances of non-consensus diplomacy. Critics argue that Mr Trump's contempt for Muslims is evidenced from the rhetoric that came out of his election campaign which suggested that Muslims as a whole are associated with terrorism and called for a total ban on all Muslims entering the United States.

Previously, the 'War on Terror' gave Western powers the leverage and ideological cover for a new wave of Western imperial policy to be projected upon Muslim countries. The horrific 9/11 attacks were by extension the platform for the invasion and subsequent occupation of Iraq in 2003 and the occupation of Afghanistan. In effect, they provided the template behind the rationale for Western imperialistic policy, ie perpetual strife in the Middle East, the control of strategic oil supplies and the fragmentation of nations into their ethnic and religious fractions such as the Shi'ites and Sunnis, not only in Iraq but across much of that region. Critics allege Osama bin Laden was a 'godsend' for hawkish elements within the US military establishment. With the end of the Cold War and the disintegration of the USSR, strategic military policy has changed for Western powers. The threat to Western liberal democracy and capitalism is no longer communism but 'radical Islam'. Painfully though, the pro-liberal Muslim world, which has nothing to do with violent radical Islam, is facing the brunt of Western imperial policy.

In keeping with Isaac Newton's third law, while one may argue that for every action, there is an equal and opposite reaction, in which case, the injustice suffered by the Muslim Ummah in the form of genocide, wars, occupations, perpetual strife and arbitrary governments should be met with by resorting to violence. I totally disagree. Rather, I firmly believe that this anguish should be translated into a rational response against persecution, ushering in democratic reforms and accountability in the Muslim Ummah and finding expression in a credible and effective political and economic alliance.

The failure of the United Nations to intervene in a timely way through its Security Council to either prevent all these conflicts from materializing or to provide a peaceful resolution to them by bringing the warring factions together under an effective, non-partisan leadership makes it arguably unfit for purpose. Recent failures to act decisively in Syria, Yemen and Myanmar in addition to the long-standing conflict between Israel and Palestinians, is illustrative of the UN Security Council's inept to provide meaningful conflict resolution in its current format, in which case, the United Nations is due for an overhaul of its composition, policies and procedures.

Sadly, today political dissent is being equated by repressive regimes in the Muslim Ummah to terrorism, and they authorise their security forces to clamp down with deadly force against democratic protest in the interests of so-called national security. It truly beggars belief that in the 21st century when the social fabric of the global population has changed so much with the explosion of mass communication through worldwide access to social media, advances in the sciences and increasing political awareness of the masses, that governments, democratic or otherwise, still continue to suppress legitimate peaceful protest with the use of overwhelming force. In reality, the safety and security of oppressive regimes in the Middle East has been conveniently translated into issues of national security. As human beings it is our innate nature to yearn to be free and to protest against oppression and injustice. Political and socio-economic movements that have sustained humanity over millennia have been inspired by our free will. All religions, including the three monotheist faiths, namely Judaism, Christianity and Islam, were essentially rebellions against persecution with Divine sanction and oversight. It will be worth reminding ourselves that apathy to injustice only breeds tyranny.

CHAPTER SEVEN

The Muslim Ummah – Out of the Abyss

If we use the concept of 'Shura' in a contemporary political setting it can be argued that it refers to democratic processes, to include democratic institutions and elections. Consequently, arbitrary governments and repressive political processes are contrary to political Islam. There is little conflict between (liberal) political Islam and political pluralism in its broad sense.

THE TITANS: THE EMERGING POWERS

Let us now turn our attention to Bangladesh, Pakistan and Indonesia. Not only do they together, in terms of population and manpower, today represent a third of the Muslim Ummah, any renewal of an Islamic Caliphate outside the Middle East in the form of a political and economic union akin to the European Union or as an effective regional and bilateral trading group is likely to be influenced by events past, present and future in these countries.

Bangladesh is not only an emerging economic power in South Asia but also happens to be the third largest Muslim majority country in the Muslim Ummah after Indonesia and Pakistan.

After achieving independence from West Pakistan following a nine-month bloody civil war that culminated in the surrender of 93,000 Pakistani troops of the Pakistan Eastern Command to the Allied Forces of India and Bangladesh (Mitro Bahini) represented by Lieutenant General Jagjit Singh Aurora in the capital city of Dacca on 16 December 1971, Bangladesh is continuing its trek on the road to a functional democracy.

Let us briefly examine some of the major turning points. With the 4th amendment to the Constitution being passed through the National Assembly in January 1975, President Sheikh Mujibur Rahman (the father of the nation) in the backdrop of the Cold War effectively sought to make Bangladesh a one-party state in the form of BAKSAL, sending shockwaves across the capitalist West. Though the BAKSAL system was officially due to come into force on 1 September 1975, it failed to materialise following the bloody massacre of the President and most of his family at their Dhanmondi residence in Dacca (later renamed Dhaka) on the fateful morning of 15 August 1975 by junior military officers disillusioned with the direction Bangladesh was heading towards. The persona of the father of the nation is encapsulated by the words of Fidel Castro. When attending the Summit of the Non-Aligned Movement (NAM) in Algiers in 1973, he remarked, 'I have not seen the Himalayas. But I have seen Sheikh Mujib. In personality and in courage, this man is the Himalayas. I have thus had the experience of witnessing the Himalayas'.

Then, following a series of coups and counter-coups after President Sheikh Mujibur Rahman's assassination, Major General Ziaur Rahman took over the reins of power as Chief Martial Law Administrator following the Sepoy Mutiny of 7 November 1975. With President Abusadat Mohammed Sayem subsequently relinquishing power in favour of Ziaur Rahman, the latter became a military President. Following Presidential Elections in June 1978, Ziaur Rahman sought to give his presidency and political ambition democratic legitimacy. The National Assembly of the Republic was brought back to life following General Elections in 1979. A heavy question mark though hangs over the integrity of these elections. Subsequently, on the morning of 30 May 1981,

President Ziaur Rahman was assassinated at the Circuit House in the port city of Chittagong in an abortive military coup.

Less than a year later, on 24 March 1982, Lieutenant General Hussain Muhammad Ershad took power in a bloodless coup from President Abdus Sattar (who was elected after Ziaur Rahman's assassination), suspending the constitution and imposing martial law. H.M. Ershad, like Ziaur Rahman, later became President of Bangladesh, forming his own political party, namely the Jatiya Party, as opposed to Ziaur Rahman's Bangladesh Nationalist Party (BNP). President Ershad, however, was forced to formally resign on 6 December 1990 following a mass upsurge protesting against farcical elections, widespread corruption and years of misrule. Since then Bangladesh has had both Sheikh Mujib's Awami League and Ziaur Rahman's BNP securing power through elections (conducted under caretaker governments till January 2014), the former being led by Sheikh Hasina Wajed, daughter of Sheikh Mujibur Rahman and the latter being led by Begum Khaleda Zia, widow of Ziaur Rahman. The acrimonious relationship between the two political rivals has done little to consolidate democratic tolerance in the political landscape of the country.

The Awami League and the BNP both accuse each other of tainting the judicial system by packing the courts with men of their own political persuasion. Regrettably, the Higher Courts have not escaped this controversy either. So much so that the Awami League refused to participate in Parliamentary elections under a caretaker government coming at the end of the BNP-led Government's term in office in October 2006, accusing the then Chief Justice of being pro-BNP. Nevertheless, both the Awami League and BNP-led Governments during their tenure in office have appointed an increasing number of judges to the Higher Courts. In the absence of due process of law in the selection process, critics have expressed concerns over the transparency and democratic accountability of higher judicial appointments.

The relationship between the higher judiciary and the executive branch of government has been brought into sharp focus following the unanimous judgement of the Appellate Division of the Supreme Court upholding the previous High Court decision of 5 May 2016 and declaring 'illegal and unconstitutional' the 16th Amendment to the Constitution, which empowered Parliament to remove Higher Court Judges for incapacity or misconduct and abolished the Chief Justice-led Supreme Judicial Council. The High Court in its judgement had categorically said the 16th amendment was against the principles of separation of powers and the independence of the judiciary. It was perhaps the observations made by the Appellate Division in the full text of the 799-page verdict, published on 1 August 2017, that unsurprisingly pushed the Government's tolerance beyond breaking point. Following public outbursts by government ministers against the verdict and the observations, the Chief Justice, human rights observers allege, was forced to relinquish his position amid allegations of graft, moral lapses and accusations of corruption. The irony is that Chief Justice Surendra Kumar Sinha, who presided over the Supreme Court hearing, was appointed during the tenure of the Awami League-led Government.

The military establishment has always kept a keen eye on political developments. The last time it directly interfered in the country's political affairs was between January 2007 and December 2008 following the widespread violence that gripped the country after the opposition alliance, led by the Awami League, refused to contest the January 2007 General Elections under the caretaker government of President Iajuddin Ahmed. Sheikh Hasina was subsequently sworn in as Prime Minister in January 2009 following the Awami League's landslide victory in the December 2008 General Elections.

Freedom of the Press in Bangladesh is not without its dangers. Journalists have gone missing and have even been killed in broad daylight, not to mention manhandling by the police. Also of concern is the closing down of different media streams that are viewed as particularly hostile and party-politically motivated against the government. For example, the BNP-led Government of Khaleda Zia went all guns blazing against Ekushey TV when it was elected to power in October 2001, dragging the TV channel through the courts. Again, after the Awami League-led

Government assumed power in January 2009 it is alleged to have forced the closure of the private television channels Channel-1, Diganta and Islam TV, as well as newspaper publications, such as Amar Desh, with its editor, Mahmadur Rahman, being arrested and jailed as recently as April 2013 on charges of sedition and the breach of the Information Communications and Technology (ICT) Act 2006 as well as inciting violence and religious tension.

According to the 2017 Press Freedom Index published by a Paris-based international organisation, 'Reporters without Borders', Bangladesh is ranked 146 among 180 countries around the world. To give this some context, Myanmar came in at 131, South Sudan at 145 and Russia at 148. A report published by Amnesty International titled 'Caught between fears and repression: Attacks on freedom of expression in Bangladesh' published in May 2017 claimed that since its re-election in 2014 the Awami League Government has intensified its crackdown on public debate and criticism, an allegation vehemently denied by the government of Prime Minister Sheikh Hasina. The report however, focuses on three main areas, namely the failure by the authorities to protect secular bloggers and activists from armed attack by armed groups, increasing restrictions on the media sector for criticising alleged government corruption and thirdly, Bangladesh's archaic legal and regulatory framework. The report highlights that politically motivated criminal charges have been brought against several editors and other high-profile media professionals from across the political spectrum, sending a clear message across the media landscape that news/media organisations that do not stay within their limits (by imposing self-censorship) will not be tolerated.

A major bone of contention is the Digital Security Act 2018, which was approved in its draft form by the Cabinet, presided over by the Prime Minister, on 29 January 2018. Different media organisations have expressed their concern that the Act when passed by Parliament (where the government maintains a strong majority) will stifle press freedom and freedom of expression as subjective interpretation of the various provisions of the Act will give rise to their potential misuse through their arbitrary and abusive application. The government has, however, argued that the Act is required to combat growing cyber-crime which was affecting both private and public organisations, including Bangladesh Bank.

Though the draft Act was approved, keeping a provision for revoking controversial sections of the ICT Act (namely, sections 54, 55, 56, 57 and 66), a government spokesman said that cases already filed under section 57 would nevertheless continue. According to this section of the ICT Act, if a person deliberately publishes any material in electronic format that 'causes to deteriorate law and order, prejudice the image of the state or person or hurt religious beliefs' he/she will be committing a non-bailable offence and an offender can be awarded a minimum of seven years in prison or up to a maximum of 14 years and a maximum fine of 10 crore taka. A statement published by the International Federation of Journalists (IFJ) on 30 January 2018, stated that while section 57 of the ICT Act was used arbitrarily to target journalists and curtail freedom of speech, it believed the proposed Digital Security Act provided more grounds to grossly misuse its provisions to harass journalists and restrict freedom of expression. It also expressed serious concern that the proposed Act, if implemented, would not only curb freedom of speech and expression but impede independent journalism – an allegation refuted by the Law Minister, Anisul Huq. The proposed Act has provisions for life sentences for spreading negative propaganda against the Liberation War of 1971 or the Father of the Nation using digital devices; up to five-year jail terms for deliberately publishing defamatory or false or distorted contents; up to 10 years for hurting religious sentiments (allegedly targeting so-called secular bloggers) or hate speech or causing deterioration of law and order, and up to 14 years on charges of spying, including entering government offices to gather information or recording secretly using electronic devices. Of concern, section 43 of the proposed Act empowers security agencies, including the police, 'if they believe' that an offence under the Act has been committed or is being committed, or the possibility thereof to search or arrest anyone 'without a warrant' issued by a court. Furthermore, members of the Editors' Council in a press statement stated that while it was promised that controversial sections such as 54, 55, 56, 57 and 66 of the ICT Act would be scrapped, their provisions have in effect been tacitly included in sections 25, 28, 29 and 31 of the proposed Digital Security Act. They were particularly critical of section 32 of the proposed Act, which treats the unauthorised collection of information from government organisations as espionage. Following consternation from various media outlets the draft Bill was reportedly sent to the law ministry for vetting to be subsequently submitted to the Cabinet for final approval.

On 9 April 2018 the Digital Security Bill was produced before the Parliament. The Parliamentary Standing Committee on Post, Telecom and ICT was given four weeks to report back to the Parliament following scrutiny of the Bill. In light of meetings held between representatives of the Editor's Council, the Association of Television Channel Owners and the Bangladesh Federal Union of Journalists and the Parliamentary Standing Committee on 22 May 2018, the Law Minister, who also attended, reportedly assured them that he would be making recommendations to the Committee to bring necessary amendments to the proposed Act. They include making those provisions that were vague in the proposed law, including those defining the spirit of the 1971 Liberation War, and actions to be considered offences of hurting religious sentiment and causing deterioration in law and order to be made more transparent. The Law Minister also reiterated that no law would be introduced which contradicts the constitution regarding freedom of press and freedom of speech while the Minister for Post, Telecoms and ICT, Mustafa Jabbar, who also participated in the meeting, stated that concerns raised would be considered.

However, to the dismay of journalists and rights defenders, the Parliament on 19 September 2018 passed the Digital Security Bill 2018 which was subsequently signed into law by the President on 8 October 2018. Many of the controversial provisions have been retained in the Act, most worryingly the power of the police to arrest without warrant anyone they suspect of committing an offence under the Act. It remains to be seen how this Act will be 'weaponised' to suppress political dissent especially in the run up to the Parliamentary election scheduled for December 2018. With the single stroke of a pen arguably Bangladesh has become a 'police state'. However at a press conference, the Prime Minister reassured journalists that those without any criminal mind-set needn't worry.

A citizen's right and ability to constructively criticize the government of the day, promoting transparency on the part of the authorities and thereby ensuring its accountability, is the very backbone of a fully functional democracy. Whether the government is interested in and sincere about providing a true level playing field for all political parties and transparency in the upcoming elections to Parliament in December 2018, the true test of this will be borne out by how free the media will be to report on events leading up to the national elections and give unfettered coverage to the election itself.

Democracy in Bangladesh faced its biggest challenge at the end of 2013, when the Awami League-led government came to the end of its term in office. The main opposition party at the time, the BNP, had insisted that Parliamentary elections should be held under a neutral caretaker government. The ruling Awami League, however, had continually reiterated that the General Election would be held under the incumbent cabinet, albeit a smaller cabinet (through supervision of the Election Commission) and not under a caretaker government. Previously, in June 2011, the 15th amendment to the Constitution scrapped the provision for a neutral caretaker government to oversee General Elections.

Following weeks of violent strikes and demonstrations, the BNP boycotted the Parliamentary elections, but the Awami League led-Government nevertheless went ahead with the General Election on 5 January 2014 without entering into any sort of meaningful dialogue with the opposition, which tested the democratic will of the people to its core. Bangladesh experienced political fallout, with the Awami League-led Government reportedly being accused of orchestrating the suppression of opposition party political activity through, for example, the mass arrest of political activists, media censorship, alleged extra-judicial killings and abductions immediately prior to the General Elections. What transpired was a return to power of the Awami League, securing an overwhelming majority of 234 seats out of 300, of which it gained 127 seats of the 154 that were uncontested by default. The official opposition, the Jatiya Party, secured a total of 34 seats but ironically has parliamentary members in the Cabinet. Consequently, the ruling party not only has an overwhelming majority in the National Parliament but at the same time the official opposition is part of that government.

Despite BNP's mass grassroots support, the government appears least interested in entering into any sort of dialogue with the BNP, while widespread allegations of heavy-handed tactics unleashed by the security forces against BNP supporters are extremely worrying in the context of furthering democratic tolerance between the main political parties. Should the BNP split into fractions as a response to government tactics, the Awami League will certainly have secured its political future, though it is difficult to predict how the political void will be filled.

In the interests of furthering and consolidating democratic norms and processes, political parties, particularly mainstream parties that command overwhelming support among the general population, should not refuse to participate in national elections. It was therefore unwise for the BNP not to contest the General Elections of January 2014. As a consequence, reportedly every effort has been unleashed by the ruling party establishment to consign the BNP to the political wilderness. In a democracy the final arbiter is the people, and political parties must have trust in the masses. In the event of a low turnout it would be extremely difficult for a political party to claim true democratic credence should they later form the government. There was widespread reporting by both media outlets in Bangladesh and overseas of a low turnout in the 2014 General Elections. In fact, according to the 'IFES Election Guide' the voter turnout was only 50%, of which the Awami League secured 79.14% of the votes cast but only 39.3% of the total electorate/registered voters. The BNP could cunningly have claimed that the majority of the remaining 61.7% had boycotted the election for their lack of faith in the Election Commission's ability to orchestrate a transparent, free and fair election having failed to facilitate a level playing field, thereby raising a counter-narrative to the Awami League political spin-doctors. Arguably that would have been stretching the truth a bit. Nevertheless, by comparison in 2008 the voter turnout was 87.13% while in 2001 it was 74.9%.

What Bangladesh crucially needs is a widely perceived impartial and strong Election Commission with the necessary legal powers to conduct free, fair and transparent Parliamentary elections. The main political parties in Bangladesh must develop a culture of political tolerance. If this cannot be expected from the current generation of leaders, then hopefully the next generation of political leaders will exhibit such democratic credentials.

The intervention by the President, Mr Abdul Hamid, to reconstitute the then Election Commission to give it a broader appeal by setting up a search committee in January 2017 was a step in the right direction. This followed months of talks with multiple political parties on the formation of a new Election Commission, including the Awami League, BNP, Jatiya Party (Ershad) as well as, Jamaat-e-Islam amongst others. Despite the appointment of a new Chief Election Commissioner and four Election Commissioners in February 2017, the BNP has on subsequent occasions aired its doubts on the integrity of the newly-appointed Election Commission.

The upcoming General Elections scheduled in December 2018 will be a defining turning point for Bangladesh, setting the stage for the future of national politics in the country. Not only will it test the two political adversaries' mettle, it will determine the sustainability of dynastic politics in the country. Should the BNP decide to contest the December 2018 Parliamentary elections, it is extremely unlikely that the Awami League will be able to hold on to its two thirds majority in Parliament after 10 years in power amid allegations of overbearing police repression of political dissent and corruption in the financial sector including the stock market. The voters need to see a credible alternative to the Awami League in the BNP; only then will the public put its confidence in them. Every parliamentary seat will have to be fought over.

If the BNP top brass feel inclined to sustain dynastic succession in their party leadership, then given the precarious situation that has arisen following the conviction of its Chairperson, Khaleda Zia, and subsequent incarceration on 08 February 2018, as well as the conviction of her heir apparent, Tarique Rahman, being sentenced to life imprisonment for his role in the 21 August 2014 grenade attack on Sheikh Hasina, the party's only recourse would be to recall the wife of Tarique Rahman, Dr. Zubaida Rahman, to take over the reign of the BNP in preparation for the Parliamentary elections scheduled to take place in December 2018, as she is not tainted by allegations of corruption. In fact, she may well turn out to be Bangladesh's reply to India's Sonia Gandhi. Furthermore, Tarique Rahman (who along with his family now lives in exile in the United Kingdom) has failed to galvanise public opinion in favour of the BNP against the alleged excesses of the Awami League-led Government and fails to command the same charisma of his late father, Ziaur Rahman. Accordingly, critics claim he lacks the leadership qualities required to govern a country like Bangladesh.

In the run up to the National Assembly elections, critics of the Awami League-led Government have alleged the absence of a level playing field, claiming that the country has been effectively transformed into a 'police state' with political opponents being harassed through abductions, extortion and the filing of multiple criminal cases against them. They also cite onerous legislation that curtails freedom of expression, such as the Digital Security Act.

The Awami League-led Government has placed the trial of collaborators of the Pakistan Army during Bangladesh's war of independence from West Pakistan high on its political agenda. Mass demonstrations began in earnest in February 2013, at Shahbag, in the capital, Dhaka, and then spread to the rest of the country, participators demanding the death penalty for those convicted. This demand then went a step further, demanding the abolition from the political arena of the Jamaat-e-Islam and accusing them of being opposed to the Liberation War, as well as being violent religious fundamentalists. There were also calls to banish religious-based politics in Bangladesh altogether. It seemed that a deliberate ploy was being hatched orchestrating a showdown between secularist and Islamist forces. As a consequence, Dhaka and other cities witnessed strikes and violent clashes with the police.

The government and its spin doctors blamed the violence on anti-liberation forces and violent religious extremists. The then main opposition party, BNP, however insisted that the events in Shahbag were nothing but a political ploy by the government to divert public opinion from allegations of government corruption and misrule. The brutal crackdown by the security forces on supporters of 'Hefazote Islam' in the early hours of 6 May 2013 in Dhaka, which resulted in numerous deaths, raises grave concerns over lack of civil liberties and political tolerance. The crackdown was a hasty reaction by the authorities over concerns that the demonstrations that were attended by tens of thousands of Hefazote Islam supporters could turn into a formidable challenge to the government if BNP activists joined in. (Hefazote Islam's appearance on the political platform was a spin-off to the Shahbag demonstrations.)

Many claim that given the notoriety associated with Jamaat-e-Islam in Bangladesh, restricting it would help a new generation of progressive Muslim leaders to enter the political spectrum, the only caveat being that this new wave of political leaders does not transpire to be reactionary. If the Jamaat-e-Islam is to endure then it needs to re-brand itself with a new Charter which, among other things, explicitly recognises the independence and sovereignty of Bangladesh and condemns in no uncertain terms the genocide of 1971. Following a ban by the High Court in 2013 on contesting the 2014 General Elections, having cancelled its registration with the Election Commission, Jamaat-e-Islam has been somewhat inactive in mainstream politics.

To shake off any semblance of being anti-independence, arguably the BNP will be wise to disentangle itself from Jamaat-e-Islam in its current form. An alliance with a revamped Jamaat-e-Islam may possibly prove to be politically expedient, depending on the shape, form and political ideology it adopts. Meanwhile, on 13 October 2018 the BNP, Jatiya Oikya Prokriya, and a fraction of the Jukta Front launched a new opposition alliance, the 'Jatiya Oikya Front', to contest the 11th Parliamentary elections. It remains to be seen how long this alliance will endure.

An upsurge against the political 'Old Guard' will indeed provide the platform for much-needed cross-party political reform. It will be interesting to see how things pan out, as it may very well provide a blueprint for what will happen in the rest of the Muslim Ummah as the new generation of middle classes, particularly in the Arab World, wrestle with their religious, political and cultural traditions in coming to terms with the 21st century.

A study of the political narrative of Bangladesh both past and present is perhaps reflective of the following quote by James Madison, founding father and fourth President of the United States of America, namely 'the accumulation of all powers, legislative, executive and judiciary, in the same hands, whether of one, a few, or many, and whether hereditary, self-appointed, or elective, may justly be pronounced the very definition of tyranny'.

Not only is Bangladesh my ancestral home, but I have had the unique opportunity to observe first-hand her transition from a dictatorship to a fledgling democracy and its aftermath. The turbulent history of Bangladesh is reminiscent of many Muslim majority countries which have been marred by corruption, farce elections, misrule and an overbearing military. The Arab Spring of 2011 that swept North Africa and parts of the Middle East was a reaction to similar circumstances.

Pakistan, as the only internationally recognised Muslim country to have a nuclear arsenal and currently the second largest Muslim majority state in the Muslim Ummah, has also had a chequered history of military intervention in state politics. Both General Zia-ul-Haq and General Parvez Musharraf seized political power from elected governments. In July 1977, General Zia-ul-Haq had Prime Minister Zulfikar Ali Bhutto arrested, dissolving the National Assembly together with all provincial assemblies and suspending the constitution. In October 1999, senior army officers loyal to General Parvez Musharaf arrested Prime Minister Nawaz Sharif in a coup d'état. Interestingly, both generals have proved useful to the West, in particular the United States. General Zia-ul-Haq proved instrumental in assisting the US-supported Mujahedeen in its war with Soviet Forces in Afghanistan. Later General Parvez Musharraf proved to be a useful ally in the United States-led 'War on Terror', particularly against the Taliban in Afghanistan.

Mr Asif Ali Zardari (widower of former Prime Minister Benazir Bhutto and son-in-law of former Prime Minister Zulfikar Ali Bhutto) was elected President of Pakistan in September 2008. It was widely reported in the Pakistan media that Mr Zardari was tainted with allegations of corruption. Following the 18th Amendment to the Constitution the office of President was stripped of key political powers previously invoked by former Presidents, including the power to dissolve Parliament and to dismiss the Prime Minister. While the 19th and 20th Amendments to the Constitution have strengthened the position of the office of the Prime Minister, in June 2012, Mr Yousuf Raza Gillani was nevertheless ousted and disqualified retrospectively from the office of Prime Minister by the Supreme Court of Pakistan, having found Mr Gillani guilty of contempt of court for failing to implement its earlier ruling directing the government to re-open the graft cases against President Zardari. Mr Gillani was succeeded by Mr Raja Parvez Ashraf. Subsequently, in January 2013, in what analysts suggest was the result of a power struggle between the judiciary and the PPP-led Government, the Supreme Court ordered the arrest of Prime Minister Raja Parvez Ashraf over corruption allegations relating to the time when he was Minister for Water and Power in 2010. While this did not necessarily lead to his resignation, the timing was somewhat precarious as Pakistan was due for elections later on in the year. Pakistan is a country blighted with sectarian violence between different Muslim sects, often with mosques being bombed. This in addition to the US drone strikes on the Pakistan-Afghan border; Pakistan is gradually descending into deeper political and financial crisis.

With Nawaz Sharif again becoming the Prime Minister following General Elections held in May 2013, he faced testing times in tackling a Taliban resurgence following the withdrawal of the bulk of the United States combat forces from Afghanistan in 2014. Mr Sharif's tact in dealing with the Pakistan military establishment proved capricious following the horrific Taliban attack on an army-run school in Pakistan's northern city of Peshawar on 16 December 2014 which resulted in the deaths of 130 pupils. In the meantime, in July 2016, Mr Sharif re-affirmed his commitment to seeing Kashmir becoming part of Pakistan, much to the annoyance of Mr Modi's government and stoking the one issue that acts as a constant thorn in the relationship between Pakistan and India.

Following the allegations of corruption that surfaced against Nawaz Sharif's children resulting from the leaked Panama papers in 2016, the Supreme Court disqualified Mr Sharif from office, despite his consistent denial of any wrongdoing. The Panama papers revealed that three of Mr Sharif's children owned offshore companies and assets not shown on his family's wealth statement. The insinuation that the offshore companies were meant to hide or launder wealth to avoid taxes called Mr Sharif's credentials into question. In its ruling, the Supreme Court further stated that Mr Sharif had been dishonest in not disclosing his earning from a Dubai-based company in his nomination papers during the 2013 General Elections. It went on to state that Mr Sharif was no longer 'eligible to be an honest member of Parliament'. The Supreme Court further recommended anti-corruption cases to be filed against several individuals including Mr Sharif, his daughter Maryam and her husband among others. Pakistan's Supreme Court has again shown that it has the power to challenge the leadership of the Prime Minister in what many see to be an enduring struggle between the higher judiciary and the executive, manipulated by the Pakistan's powerful military establishment. Interestingly, the Supreme Court had reportedly taken the unusual step of instituting its own investigation into the case with a dominant role for the military intelligence services. It is important to note that following its independence in 1947, Pakistan is yet to produce a civilian head of government or Prime Minister who has completed his or her full term in office.

On 6 July 2018 the National Accountability Bureau (NAB),

Pakistan's anti-graft court, sentenced Nawaz Sharif to ten years' imprisonment and his daughter and political heir Maryam to seven years after finding them guilty of corruption-related charges. The court ruled that Nawaz Sharif and his family laundered money in the 1990s to pay for four luxury apartments in central London, drawing on allegations that surfaced in the leaked Panama Papers published in 2016. On return from the United Kingdom on 13 July 2018, both were arrested and are now serving time in jail. The NAB also fined the family £10 million and ordered seizure of assets. The arrest was sure to influence the impending Pakistan's Parliamentary elections. Nawaz Sharif will no doubt seek to appeal the sentence, which he has put down to a military-backed conspiracy to prevent his party from securing a second term in the elections, allegedly in revenge for his attempts to assert civilian control on foreign policy and for putting General Musharraf on trial for treason.

Curiously, however, following Mr Nawaz Sharif's ousting from office he had nominated his brother Shehbaz, who was the Chief Minster for the Punjab province, to succeed him. Arguably it is time to do away with nepotism in Pakistani politics to bring greater accountability and transparency to the political process. Inevitably, it comes as no surprise therefore, that in the National Assembly Elections held on 25 July 2018 Pakistan Tehreek-e-Insaf (PTI) emerged as the single largest party, winning 116 seats out of 270 seats, but shy of the 20 seats required to command a simple majority. Pakistan will now be ruled by a coalition government headed by the leader of the PTI, Imran Khan, who in the run up to the elections struck a chord with the large youth population by promising a 'Naya Pakistan' (New Pakistan), fighting corruption and challenging the old political establishment. Coalition politics is tricky for even the most matured democracies and seasoned politicians. Critical for Imran Khan will be handling the economy and normalising relations with India while keeping Pakistan's military in tow. With 64% of the population below 30 years of age and 29% between the ages of 15–29, the new government must also take steps to invest in its youth to provide them with access to quality education, credible employment and meaningful empowerment opportunities. If it ignores their desire to materialise their hopes and aspirations, the PTI will do so at its own peril.

A former military General also ruled Indonesia, the largest Muslim majority state in the Muslim Ummah, for more than 30 years. Major General Suharto came to power in the aftermath of an abortive coup in 1965 accredited to communist elements. He became President in March 1967 and ruled with an iron hand until his resignation in May 1998. Under pressure from the United States and the International Monetary Fund (IMF) to introduce radical reforms following the economic collapse in 1997, coupled with defections of his Party faithful and mass student protests, President Suharto's fate was sealed. For the younger generation, alongside newfound political freedom, economic emancipation is equally important. The same can be said for Bangladesh and Pakistan.

These military dictators turned Presidents all believed that civilian rule was weak and that their countries were not ready for democratic rule. Regrettably, however, despite the fall of these despots, the average citizen is still yet to substantially benefit from these new fledgling democracies. These countries have a long trek and many hurdles to overcome before they can become mature democracies. Decades of corruption have embedded themselves in all spheres of administration, making it endemic, while all three countries today are facing an increasing influence of radical Islam, with the military in Bangladesh reportedly claiming that it foiled a coup planned by fanatical officers in January 2012. It will be interesting to observe what direction these titans of the Muslim Ummah take. Of the three, Indonesia is poised to be a 'top ten economy', while Bangladesh is making sound economic progress, driven particularly by private sector engagement with substantial exports of ready-made garments to European markets as well as the large foreign remittance it receives from its expats. Sandwiched between the emerging economic superpowers India and China, in the not-too-distant future Bangladesh is conveniently placed to achieve considerable economic prosperity, provided the political leadership in Dhaka can set aside their acrimonious relationship and work together for the prosperity of the country. Both Bangladesh and Pakistan must develop cultures of political tolerance within their own political landscapes, upholding the rule of law in society. Acrimonious and divisive politics is not conducive to a healthy democracy. Furthermore, governments of both countries must take its youth population seriously, as they form the majority of the population, providing them with the means to realise their full potential.

Initially, a renewed Caliphate could take the form of an economic forum between the titans. In that case, it is only rational that Pakistan should accept the reality of Bangladesh. It is with great despair that one sees the scorn the political elite and some elements of the Pakistani population harbour towards Bangladesh 46 years after it secured its independence from Pakistan following a genocide committed by Pakistani armed forces against fellow Muslims. Successive Pakistani governments have failed to make any meaningful explicit apology for the massacres perpetrated by its military. In the interests of forging a united Ummah that will provide economic emancipation to its peoples, Pakistan must learn to own up and move on.

MUSLIMS IN INDIA: THE LARGEST IN THE MUSLIM UMMAH

According to a report titled 'By 2050, India to have the world's largest populations of Hindus and Muslims' published by the Pew Research centre on 21 April 2015, India will host the largest population of Muslims in the world, estimated to be about 311 million (11% of the total number of global Muslims) given their young median age and high fertility rates among major religious groups in India. This despite the fact that Muslims in India are a religious minority. Nevertheless, Hinduism will still be the predominant religious faith in India and by the middle of the 21st century India is projected to have 1.3 billion Hindus. This will be the largest concentration of Hindus in the world, estimated to be about 90% of the global total. Still, a quarter of India's population will be predominantly Muslims. Given the demographics of

Muslims in India, the country has been seeking observer status in the Organisation of Islamic Countries (OIC) for the clout and influence it could exert at multilateral institutions and negotiations. The OIC accounts for around a third of the total membership of the UN, almost half of the membership of the African Union and full membership of the Arab League and the Gulf Cooperation Council (GCC). Furthermore, many Muslim countries share geographical proximity to India in Asia.

However, Pakistan has in the past always resented such a move, citing Article 3(e) of the Conditions for Accession to Observer Status at the OIC, which prevents a country from applying for observer status if it is in conflict with any existing member state. Pakistan has cited the appalling human rights situation in Indian-occupied Jammu and Kashmir as the source of conflict between itself and India. In previous OIC-CFM meetings, resolutions have been adopted criticising India's human rights record as recently as last year, in the Abidjan Declaration which urged India to stop forthwith its brutalities and crimes against humanity in Indian-occupied Jammu and Kashmir and to allow international groups access. However, at this year's OIC-CFM meeting held in Dhaka in May 2018, it proposed reforming and restructuring the Charter of the OIC to accommodate non-OIC countries with large Muslim populations as citizens to be inducted as observer states, which analysts have concluded as referring to India.

According to a report published by Bank of America Merrill Lynch in November 2017, India is set to emerge as the third largest economy by 2028, overtaking Japan in nominal GDP. The report mentioned that falling dependency ratios, financial maturity and increasing incomes and affordability would be key drivers behind India's growth, assuming that the Indian economy grows at 10 per cent (in nominal US GDP). The report highlighted that India has already superseded Brazil and Russia to emerge as the second largest BRICS economy after China, and is well on track to overtake the United Kingdom and France to emerge as the fifth largest economy after Germany by 2019.

It is only natural therefore that India's Muslim population will share in this prosperity too. However, with the rise and consolidation of Hindu nationalism and the country's history of religious strife between Hindus and Muslims, one must exercise a certain degree of caution and scepticism. If we examine the representation of Muslims in India's legislature for instance, as a barometer of Muslim participation and involvement in the highest echelons of power, an unsatisfactory picture emerges. In the 2014 elections to the 16th Lok Shoba (Lower House of Parliament), India elected only 23 Muslim MPs to the 545-member Lok Shoba, one of the lowest figures in its history. The most populous state, Uttar Pradesh, did not even elect a single Muslim MP, hardly surprising given that the now ruling BJP (Bharatiya Janata Party) did not field a single Muslim candidate despite the fact that Muslims constitute around 20% of the population of that state. To give some context, the state of Uttar Pradesh has 80 parliamentary seats, the largest in India. Furthermore, in total the BJP only fielded five Muslim candidates in the 16th Lok Shoba Elections, three from Jammu and Kashmir and two from the rest of India. By the way, none of them won.

In the Lower House of Parliament the largest number of Muslim MPs comes from West Bengal with four from Trinamool Congress and two each from Congress and CPI. Disturbingly, while Muslims constitute 10.5% of India's population today, its percentage representation in the 16th Lok Shoba is only 4.2%. Whether there will be an increase in such representation in par with the predicted increase in the population of Muslims in the future remains to be seen.

Some will argue that the rise of reactionary Hindu nationalism is of growing concern not only to Muslims but to secularist forces in the country. A recent manifestation of this came about in March 2017 with the appointment of a controversial Hindu priest, Yogi Adityanath, as Chief Minister of Uttar Pradesh by the BJP following its landslide victory in elections to the 17th Uttar Pradesh legislative Assembly. Given his firebrand Hindu supremacist vision, which also guides the religious activist group Hindu Yuva Vahini (HYV), which he founded, this is quite unsettling in a state where about a fifth of the 220 million inhabitants are Muslims. He has reportedly praised Donald

Trump's ban on refugees and immigrants from predominantly majority Muslim nations, arguing that similar action is needed to contain terror activities in India. Stoking racial tensions, he had in the past said that if a Muslim kills one Hindu man then they would kill 100 Muslim men. He has also spoken against mixed faith marriages, warning that Muslim men were involved in what he termed 'love Jihad' and alleging that they were deliberately wooing Hindu women for marriage and conversion to Islam.

Not even the Taj Mahal has escaped controversy from this toxic cocktail of nationalism and reactionary Hinduism. Some Hindu right-wing elements have always resented the fact that the Taj Mahal, an icon symbolising India to the world, was built by a Muslim Emperor (the Mughal Emperor Shahjahan). Reportedly, fringe elements on the Hindu right have even argued that the Taj Mahal is a Shiva temple and built on land dedicated to the worship of Shiva. Mainstream historians however, strongly refute this claim. At the heart of the controversy though is a larger debate to re-evaluate India's history. Many in the BJP, including Prime Minister Modi, believe India has endured '1200 years of slave mentality' which would include the time India was ruled by Muslim emperors (the Moghuls), a period of slavery no different from the British Raj. Embedded with the belief that Hindus were persecuted first by the Muslim emperors and then by the British Raj, many in the BJP political establishment believe they can only overcome this victimhood by repudiating everything that is Muslim and British in their past. According to various media streams, Sangeet Som, who is a member of the ruling BJP, claimed that the 'Taj Mahal should have no place in Indian history' labelling the 17th-century monument a 'blot on Indian culture', which had been 'built by traitors'. In June 2017, Yogi Adityanath kicked up a furore when he also said that the Taj Mahal did not 'reflect Indian culture'. He did however, later issue assurances on a visit to Agra that the Taj Mahal was a unique gem that his government was committed to protect and issues of why, when and how it was built should not be delved deeper into. He certainly realised in hindsight that the Taj Mahal, as an international tourist attraction, brings in a lot of foreign currency, as well as attracting domestic tourism, so any unrest over the site will have negative implications for the local economy.

The recent situation in the Indian state of Assam is stoking fear among the predominantly Bengali-speaking Muslim population there. Since India's partition in 1947, Assam has been shaken by protests, sometimes violent, over illegal immigration from across the border with Bangladesh, increasing sectarian tensions and riots between Assam's indigenous population and Bengali-speaking Muslim migrants. On 1 January 2018 India published the first draft of a list of citizens for the north-eastern state of Assam which will be incorporated into the National Register of Citizens (NRC). To make the list, applicants must provide documents proving that they or their family lived in the country before 24 March 1971 and it excludes those who arrived during and after the 1971 war leading to the independence of Bangladesh from Pakistan.

The concerns of the Bengali-speaking Muslims have reached fever pitch due to the proposed amendment to the Citizenship Act, 1955. The amendment would allow 'illegal migrants' who are Hindus, Sikhs, Buddhists, Jains, Parsis and Christians (but not Muslims) from Afghanistan, Bangladesh and Pakistan to be eligible for citizenship, providing they have been residing in India for at least six years. In the rest of India, the Citizenship (Amendment) Bill 2016 has been seen as a violation of Article 14 of India's Constitution, which embodies the 'Right to Equality'. It remains to be seen what happens to those Bengali-speaking Muslims who fail to make it on the NRC and the effect the proposed amendment to the Citizenship Act 1955 will have. Will these so-called 'illegal migrants' endure similar treatment from militant nationalists fired up by religion as the Rohingyas did in Myanmar? In which case, it would seem Bangladesh will be converted into a dumping ground for illegal migrants in South Asia putting enormous stress on its economy and infrastructure.

Disturbingly, armed mobs have been marauding the streets, attacking and lynching predominantly Muslim butchers who sell meat (the cow being sacred to Hindus). While condemned by

Prime Minister Modi, the attacks show a strong wave of politically-motivated intolerance towards Muslims in Hindustan. On 17 July 2018 the Supreme Court of India condemned the epidemic of mob lynching in India, and asked the Indian Parliament to draft legislation that would stop people from taking the law into their own hands. In India, the slaughter of cows and the consumption of beef is banned in most states. However, reportedly since Modi and his party the BJP assumed power in 2014, this beef ban has allegedly been used by Hindu ultra-nationalists (self-styed 'cow vigilantes') to justify their attacks on innocent Muslims. What shocks the rational consciousness is the garlanding of eight men by a Minister in Mr Modi's cabinet, Jayant Sinha, who were convicted of lynching a meat trader named Alimuddin Ansari in Jharkhand's Ramgarh district. Though the eight men were convicted by a lower (fast-track) court, their life sentences were subsequently suspended by the Jharkhand High Court and they were released on bail. The case will be heard again. Cellphone footage gleefully shot by the culprits show themselves hitting the victim, yet a lawyer representing some of the convicts claimed that it was the police who had led Mr Ansari away from the mob that beat him to death. This argument was rejected by the original trial court. Arguably it was premature of the Minister to facilitate these men until and unless they get a full acquittal following a re-trial given the sensitivities surrounding mob lynching in India.

With upcoming national elections the ruling BJP, which itself runs on a religious nationalist platform, will seek to galvanise Hindus into a larger voting bloc under the banner of nationalism. It will be interesting to observe whether 'identity politics' alone will be the determining factor in the 2019 national elections. Analysts argue that this is unlikely, as the country's economic projection and the Modi government's past record will no doubt play on the minds of the electorate.

Nevertheless, the reality is that elements of Hindu ultra-nationalists have manifested themselves in mainstream politics following the demolition of the 16th-century Babri Mosque on 6 December 1992 and they have since gained increasing popularity, culminating in the election of some of them to political office as well as the marginalisation of Muslims in many aspects of mainstream society. This is in contrast to the relatively liberal policies of the Congress Party which has governed India for much of the 70 years since its independence from the British Raj, but due to lack of effective leadership and internal in-fighting it has now been left on the fringes of the political process with its worst-ever electoral performance in the 16ᵗʰ Lok Shoba Elections.

THE TRADITIONAL HEARTLANDS: SAUDI ARABIA AND IRAN AND THEIR ENDURING STUGGLE FOR FREEDOM

SAUDI ARABIA: A regime in decline, and the internal contradiction of Wahabi Islam

Today the Kingdom of Saudi Arabia ('al-Mamlakah al-Arabiyah as-Su'udiyah') is an 'absolute monarchy' in every sense of the term, as opposed, for example, to a constitutional monarchy such as can be seen in the United Kingdom and much of Europe where constitutions and democratically-elected Parliaments constrain the power of the King or Queen. The Saudi kingdom is ruled by King Salman bin Abd al-Aziz Al Saud (since 23 January 2015) who is both the head of state and head of government. There are no national elections or political parties (as is understood in the West) to represent the views and aspirations of the people. Rather politics in Saudi Arabia has centred on policy decisions made on the basis of consultations between influential members of the Royal Family and the religious establishment. In December 2016, elections for two-thirds of the seats to 284 municipal councils were held around the country, and for the first time women were allowed to vote and stand as candidates. However these elections were held on a non-party basis. Furthermore, these municipal councils have limited decision-making powers on local issues anyway.

As the Prime Minister too, the King appoints his Council of Ministers every four years. The 150 members of the Majlis Ash-Shura (the de facto legislative branch of the government) are also appointed by the King to serve a four-year term. The 'Basic Law of Government' issued by Royal Decree in March 1992 serves as the constitutional framework based on the Qur'an and Sunnah and is subject to interpretation (it sets out the system of governance, rights of citizens, and powers and duties of the government). Under the laws of succession only male descendants (including grandsons) of the founder of Saudi Arabia, the late King Abd al-Aziz ibn Abd al-Rahman Al Saud, are entitled to rule the country.

Consequently, in what can only be described as a subtle coup on the political power structures of the royal household, on 21 June 2017, King Salman bin Abd al-Aziz Al Saud, in a move to rout any potential rival to the succession of his son Prince Mohammed bin Salman, appointed him as Crown Prince, removing his nephew, Prince Mohammed bin Nayef. The new heir to the throne is perceived as representing a new younger generation of Saudis, as well as being closely aligned to the United States. When the Crown Prince, Mohammed bin Salman, who is also the Defence Minister, succeeds his father, given his relative youth, he will likely set the tone for Saudi Arabia's internal and foreign policy for much of this century. If events of the past years are anything to go by Saudi Arabia risks increasing economic stresses from perusing an aggressive foreign policy to counter Iranian influence in the region as well as any internal dissent. The Crown Prince has been the driving force behind Saudi Arabia's war in Yemen and diplomatic tiff with Qatar. With relative low wholesale oil prices over the past few years, Saudi Arabia was and is still bearing a massive financial burden in pursing conflicts in the region which invariably affect its ordinary citizens. Signs of protest are already playing out, albeit on a subtle level for fear of arrest. Despite Mohammed bin Salman's intention to reform the economy and society as part of the 'Vision 2030 Project' it must nevertheless, be on his own terms, with no scope for dissent. This is very much the nature of the actions and thought processes of a 'benevolent dictator' (if such a terminology is valid) who is essentially a self-opinionated autocrat or despot.

Political repression is rife in Saudi Arabia and is exercised through denial of human rights. There are restrictions on universal rights such as freedom of expression (including via the internet on social media platforms), freedom of assembly, and freedom of association, freedom of movement and religion, not to mention gender discrimination. Saudi Arabia has always imprisoned its political dissidents. Amnesty International has accused the judicial system of carrying out unfair trials alongside arbitrary sentencing guidelines, with the Royal Family exerting their power through the courts. Numerous human rights organisations have repeatedly reported that 'political prisoners' are often held for months without charge or trial. Chillingly, sending a clear message that any internal dissent to its rule will not be tolerated, Saudi authorities on 2 January 2016 executed 46 'alleged terrorists' including prominent Shi'ite cleric Sheikh Nimr al-Nimr, following which Shi'ite demonstrations broke out across the region with the Saudi Embassy in Tehran being ransacked by an angry mob. As a result, Saudi Arabia broke off diplomatic ties with Iran, which threatened to escalate sectarian strife in the region and destabilise peace initiatives to end the conflict in Syria. However, it was the killing of the *Washington Post* columnist and Saudi national Jamal Khashoggi, a well-known critic of Saudi Arabia, in the Saudi consulate in Istanbul on 2 October 2018, allegedly by 'rouge agents' within the Saudi intelligence service, that sent shockwaves across the globe with some US lawmakers calling on the government to invoke the Global Magnitsky Act to punish those involved.

Harassment of women, particularly those belonging to religious and ethnic minority groups, had until recently been a predominant feature of Saudi society, as evidenced through the excesses carried out by the Committee for the Promotion of Virtue and Prevention of Vice (CPVPV). It is well documented and reported that women had been publicly scolded for their appearance or association. Back in 2008, the United Nations Special Rapporteur on Violence Against Women reported that the CPVPV was 'responsible for serious human rights abuses in harassing, threatening and arresting women who deviate from accepted norms'. However, with reforms being introduced in

April 2016 the CPVPV were instructed to report those suspected of moral infraction to the security forces and could only make an arrest themselves if the police were present. (Among the most common types of violations for which the CPVPV could report were lack of gender segregation, improper dress and public expression.) While the 2016 reforms were something of a welcome development in protecting the dignity of women in Saudi Arabia, the immense social pressures to conform to an all-male interpretation of moral policy and religious codes made the implementation of any reforms extremely difficult. In any case, critics claimed that this fell short of any meaningful reforms to effectively rein in the CPVPV. With hundreds of CPVPV members being unregulated volunteers they were until recently in a position to exceed their authority with impunity. Therefore, despite the 2016 announcement, the lack of accountability across the board and unclear codification of the rules allowed the CPVPV to continue with its excesses. Relatively more recently in 2017, as the Crown Prince has gone about consolidating his political position and driving his social reform agenda as part of the 2030 Vision project, the government has sought to change the role of the religious police into an agency primarily charged with offering religious advice and guidance instead of direct confrontation. Steadily, the younger generation of Saudis is now beginning to enjoy freedoms that we in the West take for granted.

Significantly, on 27 September 2017 by a Royal Decree signed by King Salman bin Abd al-Aziz Al Saud, women in Saudi Arabia have from June 2018 been allowed to get driving licences allowing them to drive 'in accordance with Islamic Laws', ending a longstanding ban that has come to symbolise the oppression of women in this ultra-conservative kingdom. On 18 April 2018, after a 35-year ban, Saudi Arabia opened its first cinema to be open to both men and women. In September 2017 women were allowed entry to the National Stadium for the first time, though they were assigned to their own section in the normally male-only venue to watch celebrations marking the anniversary of the founding of Saudi Arabia. The kingdom has some of the world's tightest curbs on women's rights, despite government reforms aimed at boosting female employment as part of the 'Vision 2030' reform plan. While reforms currently under way are no doubt a positive step in empowering women to contribute to the country's economy, more can be done. The Ummah, particularly Saudi Arabia, must realise that with half of all Muslims being female they must be given the opportunity to aspire, albeit within a rational understanding of Shar'iah law that will allow the Ummah to compete on the global stage. Under Saudi Arabia's current guardianship system a male family member, usually the father, husband or brother, must grant permission for a woman's education, travel and other public activities, although changes do appear to be on the horizon.

The increasing disparity of wealth, marked by high unemployment among the youth population and increasing number of Saudis living on limited financial resources, may very well result in a violent shift to the political power structure of the country or even the fall of the monarchy. Behind the ostentatious façade of wealth that Saudi Arabia portrays to the world, a large proportion of its population are impoverished, enjoying little infrastructural development. Given the demographics of the Saudi state, the political hierarchy must come to realise that the younger generation is unmistakably a force to be reckoned with. According to the CIA World Factbook, the percentage of the population under 25 is 44.67% with the total fertility rate being 2.09 (children born/women) with an estimated population as of July 2017 of 28,571,770 (though immigrants make up 30 percent of the total population as per United Nation's Data in 2015). Also according to the Factbook, between 10-15% of the population are Shi'ite, with most forms of public religious expression that are inconsistent with the government-sanctioned interpretation of Sunni Islam being restricted.

The easing of sanctions against Iran by the P5 +1 in 2015 had the practical effect of keeping the wholesale price of oil down, with Saudi Arabia increasing its output to counter Iran's influence on the global oil production platform.

In December 2015 Saudi Arabia announced the formation of a military alliance of 34 Islamic countries to combat 'terrorism', and this has now spread to 41 countries. Notable omissions however, include Shi'ite-dominated Iran and Iraq. Dubbed the 'Muslim NATO', Saudi Arabia is in effect spearheading a project to be used as a politicized weapon against nations as well as movements that Saudi Arabia regards as hostile to itself. In fact, it is alleged that the alliance is a direct response to the Shi'ite-Sunni schism that shapes much of Middle Eastern politics, especially in the wake of the fallout of the failed Arab Spring, but more importantly to provide an effective counter-measure to the easing of sanctions by the West against Shi'ite Iran, which has enabled it to finance its proxy wars with Saudi Arabia in a struggle for regional dominance. This was brought into sharp focus when it was reported that the Saudi defence forces spokesman, Major-General Ahmed al-Asiri, told the Wall Street Journal in April 2017 that the military alliance was not restricted to confronting terrorist organisations like ISIL and Al Qaeda but that the coalition could, at the request of a member, move against rebel groups and militias posing a threat to that member country. This so-called military alliance will no doubt serve as a striking force against any second Arab uprising, which Saudi Arabia or other despotic regimes within the coalition will no doubt deem to be the work of 'terrorists' according to their definition of the term.

In February 2016 Saudi Arabia carried out a massive military exercise dubbed 'Northern Thunder' involving troops from 20 Arab and other Sunni Muslim countries. Participants included NATO-member Turkey, the region's most populous and militarily powerful state, Egypt and nuclear-armed Pakistan. While some political analysts at the time viewed it as a precursor to an invasion of Syria, soon after, however, Russian President Vladimir Putin dramatically announced a scaling down of the bombing campaign in Syria by the Russian Air Force.

The Stockholm International Peace Research Institute (Sipri) reported in February 2017 that the Middle East nearly doubled its arms imports between 2012 and 2016, the highest in any five-year period since the end of the Cold War, with Saudi Arabia being the world's second largest importer of arms, increasing its intake by 212%, mainly from the United States and the United Kingdom.

Many of the weapons sold to Saudi Arabia by UK weapons manufacturing companies under government licences are allegedly being used against targets in Yemen in attacks that have resulted in the deaths of thousands of civilians. Yet the United Kingdom still finds it ethical to sell ammunition to the Saudi war effort, as the government believes there is no clear risk of these weapons being used in serious violation of international humanitarian law. Moreover, the British Government considers Saudi Arabia to have the right to intervene militarily so as to stop Yemen from falling to forces avowedly hostile to Saudi Arabia, which shares an 800-mile border with Yemen. In fact, on 26 October 2016 in a vote taken in the House of Commons a Labour motion to suspend support for the Saudi-led coalition's military action in Yemen pending a United Nations probe into alleged breaches of international law was defeated overwhelmingly by 283 votes to 193, a vote that involved both Tory and dissident Labour MPs. The shadow Foreign Secretary, Emily Thornberry, who proposed the Labour motion, expressed her scepticism, during the course of the debate, towards the UK government's faith in the Saudi Joint Incidents Assessment Team (JIAT), stating that its output to date gave no confidence that it could carry out a comprehensive investigation of this sort, let alone an independent one.

On a state visit to Saudi Arabia in May 2017, President Trump signed a 110-billion dollar arms deal that included a 15 billion dollar purchase of the highly advanced Terminal High Altitude Area Defence (THAAD) missile system. According to the State Department the deal also included the purchase of tanks and helicopters for border security, ships for coastal security, intelligence-gathering aircraft and cybersecurity tools. It must be emphasised that Congressional approval is required for such arms deals. A number of factors should no doubt weigh on the minds of Congress, namely the Saudi-led war in Yemen and the unfolding humanitarian crises, the continuing GCC crises, Saudi Arabia's alleged support for extremism and terrorism, its record on human rights abuses as well as seeking to maintain Israel's qualitative military edge over its Arab neighbours. Be under no illusion that for the United States and Europe, Israel's security is paramount. Therefore, no Arab country will be permitted to turn the tables militarily in their favour at Israel's expense. It better suits Western strategic military interest to have Arab countries engage in armed conflict or military rivalry amongst themselves rather than have them direct their firepower against Israel. No Western power wishes to see a repeat of the Arab military alliance that culminated in the 1967 war with Israel.

It would not be out of place to argue that the Saudi military intervention in the Middle East following the Arab Spring, such as in Bahrain and more heavily in Yemen, is a desperate response by the Saudi regime to ensure its own survival, hence the spending spree on military hardware. This increased demand for military arsenals and capabilities in the Middle East by Saudi Arabia has proved to be a crucial tool in dealing with regional conflicts and internal tensions. So what we have ended up with more recently is Saudi Arabia going on a spending spree to increase its military strength to reap mayhem in neighbouring Yemen (a Muslim country) as a means to counter the rise of Iranian influence there. The irony of this geopolitics is extremely perplexing and worrying, to say the least. Saudi Arabia views Iran as its main regional rival as it seeks to assert its own hegemony in the Middle East, blaming Iran for destabilising the region by supporting the Assad regime in Syria, backing terrorist organisations like Hezbollah in Lebanon, as well as supporting violent militias that seek to undermine the now defunct government of Abd Rabbuh Mansoor al-Hadi in Yemen.

In 2016 the Saudi leadership had announced plans to establish a 'sovereign wealth fund' by selling off shares in Saudi Aramco (putting the value of the company at 2 trillion dollars) in a move to diversify its economy, partly as a reaction to previous falling oil prices, but more importantly to make the Saudi regime a major global investor purchasing strategic financial and industrial assets abroad. While the Crown Prince, Mohammad bin Salman, is personally spearheading this much publicised drive for diversification, the King is reportedly taking a more cautious approach with respect to the IPO which could see the sale postponed to at least 2019. While the 'Vision 2030' reforms focus for the main part on the Saudi economy, seeking to reduce its dependency on oil revenues as well as providing a more relaxed environment for young Saudis, investors and tourists, the proposed reforms are also set to affect many of the social systems of this ultra-conservative kingdom, and this is likely to be met with by resistance from the powerful religious establishment. In view of this concern, in January 2017, Crown Prince Mohammad bin Salman warned that he would consider punitive measures against any religious clerics who incited violence against his reform plans.

In an interview with the *Guardian* newspaper on 24 October 2017, the Crown Prince vowed to return the country to 'moderate Islam', seeking global support to transform the hard-line kingdom into an open society that empowers citizens and attracts investors. He stated that Saudi Arabia in its response to the Iranian revolution in 1979 became increasingly orthodox, which did not reflect Saudi Arabia. Rather he envisions Saudi Arabia reverting to a moderate Islamic state open to the world and all religions, and instead of wasting 30 years combating extremist thoughts these beliefs would be discarded with immediate effect. But a closer study of historical events will demonstrate that Saudi Arabia's insular narrative was not solely an adverse response to the Islamic Revolution in Iran. In fact, it was a response to a combination of factors that played out in 1979. They included the siege of the Grand Mosque in Mecca on the first day of the new Islamic Century (1400 AH) by Sunni fundamentalists seeking to inspire an apocalyptic narrative challenging the House of Saud. Furthermore, it also included a reaction to the December 1979 Soviet invasion of Afghanistan, which had sent thousands of communist troops into the country to immediately assume complete military and political control of the capital Kabul and large swathes of the country, which essentially sent a subtle message that the Muslim Ummah was vulnerable to communist invasion.

The Crown Prince's statements come in the light of cultural reforms and economic incentives that were unimaginable over the last few decades during which the Kingdom was accused of promoting an extremist brand of Islam. The Crown Prince's remarks come against a backdrop of moves to further consolidate his authority in an effort to sideline clerics who have failed to provide him with unreserved support, as they perceive that the reforms may very well break the alliance between the religious establishment and the House of Saud. Reportedly many prominent clerics have been arrested for making subtle critical remarks against Crown Prince Mohammed bin Salman's social reforms. The Crown Prince has also demanded unquestioning loyalty from the senior officials he has entrusted to drive the 'Vision 2030' Project aimed at overhauling many aspects of Saudi life.

The 4 November 2017 purge of high-ranking princes and officials dubbed by the media the Saudi 'Night of the Long Knives' was a pre-emptive strike by Crown Prince Mohammed bin Salman to effectively cull any potential power struggle over his rule, both in the long term following his father's death and in the short term should King Salman abdicate in favour of the Crown Prince. This well-thought-out and premeditated purge started with the sacking of Prince Mutaib bin Abdullah, son of the deceased King Abdullah and head of the Saudi National Guard (a tribal force created to protect the Royal Family and key oil installations and in fact the last security force that could potentially undermine Mohammed bin Salman's rule). Then, within hours of a Royal Decree establishing an anti-corruption committee headed by Mohammed bin Salman, eleven princes, together with several ministers and heads of TV stations, were rounded up and detained. The purge resulted in the seizing of the financial assets of these princes, which included those of Prince Walid bin Talal, the richest man in the Arab world. The obvious concern is that wealthy princes could use their wealth to challenge Mohammed bin Salman's rule by sponsoring dissent abroad and promoting adverse media coverage of the Crown Prince's economic and social policy.

There are naturally concerns over whether the Kingdom indeed has the political tenacity to follow through on its economic ambitions, and whether the Crown Prince (presuming he is sincere in his rhetoric) can overcome opposition to social reforms from the nation's ultra-conservative base, which if implemented will amount to nothing short of a cultural revolution for Saudi Arabia. In the worst-case scenario a power struggle may ensue between reactionary members of the royal household in connivance with hard-lined clerics and reformers seeking a more moderate nation. The political survival of the Crown Prince will depend very much upon his dealings with the Saudi youth, who constitute a sizeable percentage of the population, in living up to their expectations of political transparency and economic expediency.

IRAN: Islamic Theocracy verses modernisation – The potential superpower of the Middle East and the scourge of Saudi Arabia

The Islamic Republic of Iran (*Jomhuri-yr Eslami-ye Iran*) is a theocratic republic with its Supreme Leader, Ali Hoseini-Khamenei (since 4 June 1989) being the Head of State. Iran claims itself to be a multi-party democracy with President Hassan Fereidun Rouhani being the Head of Government following his recent election by popular vote in May 2017 for another four-year term. While citizens elect their President as well as members of the legislature, the whole process is overseen by undemocratic institutions run by Shi'ite clerics and jurists. In this context, the Guardian Council (Shura-ye Negahban) approves and vets the list of candidates to stand for Parliamentary elections, thereby effectively restricting the electoral process, while the Revolutionary Guards wield tremendous political power. The vetting process was originally intended to ensure that prospective candidates meet the minimum criteria for office, but this has over time become a way to eliminate those who are not politically favourable to the political establishment. The Guardian Council is a 12-member body selected by the Supreme Leader and approved by the Parliament (the Majlis). Five of the 12 Guardian Council members are also members of the Assembly of Experts. The Supreme Leader, who is elected by the Assembly of Experts, is a position held for life (theoretically subject to dismissal) and provides oversight upholding the values of the Islamic Republic while exercising control over the powerful Revolutionary Guards.

Although the constitution assigns the Assembly of Experts the task of monitoring the Supreme Leader, there is no constitutionally-sanctioned formal mechanism through which the Assembly of Experts can effectively challenge the Supreme Leader.

According to the CIA World Factbook the percentage of population under 25 is 38.88%, the total fertility rate being 1.97 (children born/women) with an estimated population as of July 2017 of 82,021,56, ranking it the most populous country in the Middle East. Shi'ites are between 90-95 percent of the population with 5-10% being Sunni. According to the 2018 Global Firepower (GFP) ranking based on its PowerIndex ('PwrIndx') score, Iran is 13th in the world and third in the Middle East ahead of Israel and Saudi Arabia, which occupy fourth and fifth position respectively. According to data from the Organization of Petroleum Exporting Countries (OPEC), as of 2017, Iran had 155,000 million barrels of proven crude oils reserves (falling slightly behind Saudi Arabia as the third largest) and 33,810 billion cubic metres of proven natural gas reserves, making it the second largest in the world.

After Saudi Arabia, Iran is the second-largest country in the Middle East and the 17th largest in the world by landmass. It is bordered to the northwest by Armenia, the Republic of Azerbaijan and the Azerbaijani enclave of Nakhchivan; to the north by the Caspian Sea; to the northeast by Turkmenistan; to the east by Afghanistan and Pakistan; to the south by the Persian Gulf and the Gulf of Oman; and to the West by Turkey and Iraq. Iran's central location in Eurasia and Western Asia, and its proximity to the Strait of Hormuz, gives its geostrategic importance.

Iran is at a critical crossroads. On the one hand, unpredictable wholesale oil prices, the precarious state of the nuclear deal following the US withdrawal (discussed below) and the slow rate of economic growth as Iran tries to balance its public debt against public assets, compounded by year-on-year increasing unemployment, and the demand by a youth population to see more transparency and cooperation with the West, has given a voice for moderates seeking further reform, as opposed to hard-liners who fear that Iran's increasing links with the West will destroy the Islamic Revolution from within. This increasing tension between the moderates and the hard-liners is being played out as tensions escalate between Iran's Supreme Leader, Ayatollah Ali Hoseini-Khamenei, and President Hassan Fereidun Rouhani after his re-election, which witnessed him increasing his mandate by 5 million votes. Back in June 2017 the Supreme Leader reportedly humiliated the President, saying that he should not polarise society in the same way as did, in his opinion, Iran's first post 1979 President, Abolhassan Bani-Sadr, who was impeached and later exiled after falling foul of the clerical establishment. This underlines how important it is that the nuclear deal is not ripped up by the West, for this will surely consolidate the position of hardliners in the Iranian political establishment who would restrict further transparency in Iran's political process.

Despite the European Union's commitment to the continued full and effective implementation of the Joint Comprehensive Plan of Action (JCPOA) to ensure that Iran's nuclear programme remains exclusively for peaceful purposes and not to build a nuclear bomb, President Trump appeared hell bent on ripping up the agreement by threatening in a national address to the nation on 13 October 2017 that he would not certify Iran's compliance to the agreement unless Congress and the United States' allies made tough and significant amendments to the agreement. He claimed that the deal was too lenient and that Iran had in any case broken parts of the agreement by not complying with heavy-water limits and not allowing access to international inspectors, as well as continued development of its ballistic capabilities.

In November, 2017, however, Yukiya Amano, Director-General of the International Atomic Agency, said that its inspectors were able to access all locations, including military sites, if needed. In seeking to undermine the agreement, not only was Donald Trump seeking to undermine the Obama administration's signature foreign policy achievement, he was also seeking to appease Israel and Iran's regional rival, Saudi Arabia. Evidently, since the 1979 Islamic Revolution in Iran, it has always been US foreign policy in the Middle East to instigate rivalry between these two regional powers, stirring up tension in the region in a bid to secure control of the price of oil and to sell its military hardware.

The Iranian population, particularly its youth, have shown that they have the resilience and capacity to organise themselves and stand up to defend their right of franchise, as evidenced when protestors went out on to the streets in major cities nationwide protesting at the re-election of Mahmoud Ahmadinejad in 2009 to a second term as President, amid allegations of election fraud. The 'Iranian Green Movement' as it has come to be known was the first credible step by the Iranian people to undermine the power and authority of the clerics, given that Mr Ahmadinejad was a pro-establishment figure. Despite the relatively peaceful nature of the protests and demonstrations, heavy-handed tactics were employed against the protestors by the police and paramilitary forces (Basij militia), who suppressed the protests with batons, pepper spray and in some instances live ammunition. Opposition groups reported thousands being arrested and tortured in prisons around the country, with former inmates alleging widespread rape of women prisoners or the threat of rape. The opposition also claimed that the relatives of those who died in prison were forced to sign documents stating that the inmates had died from heart attacks or meningitis. During the protests the Iranian authorities closed universities in Tehran, blocked websites and banned rallies.

Recognising that gradual institutional reform will be insufficient to effect real change, the government of President Hassan Rouhani must take expeditious steps to bring about much-needed transparency to the electoral system by ushering in electoral reform that will allow ordinary Iranians to aspire to the highest offices of the land. Equally importantly, the government must promote economic empowerment and redefine the role of restrictive orthodox religious bias in political institutions and civic society. In this context, reformists argue that the office of the Supreme Leader should either be abolished or subject to public vote, with the power of the Revolutionary Guard subject to more democratic control.

Interestingly, towards the end of December 2017 demonstrators began chanting anti-government slogans in several cities across Iran, protesting against alleged corruption and rising prices. The outbreak of unrest reflected increasing discontent over Iran's costly involvement in regional conflicts as part of its strategy to counter Saudi Arabia's dominance in the region. The Iranian regime currently backs Syria's President, Bashar al-Assad, in his country's civil war, Shi'ite militias in Iraq, Houthi rebels in Yemen and Hezbollah in Lebanon. All this while unemployment stands at 12.4%, according to the Statistical Centre of Iran, with inflation running at 10%. Youth unemployment is reportedly at 27%. The scale and ferocity of the protests had the government and religious establishment struggling to respond to the crisis, which it blamed on 'external enemies' stirring up trouble (analysts believe this to mean the United States, Israel and Saudi Arabia), a claim vehemently denied by the US. More than 20 protestors were reportedly killed during the demonstrations. The majority of protestors arrested were under 25, which shows that the demonstrations were largely spearheaded by an exasperated youth population. They are frustrated that social freedoms and political openness are being suppressed by the political elite as well as slow economic growth, despite the lifting of sanctions under the nuclear deal.

Following rallies in support of the government on 3 January 2018, the Head of the Revolutionary Guards, Major General Mohammad Ali Jafari, played down the anti-government protests, claiming that the number of protestors did not exceed 15,000 nationwide with a maximum of 1,500 people in any one demonstration. He went on to claim that security preparedness and people's vigilance had led to the defeat of the 'enemies' and that the Revolutionary Guards only had to intervene in a 'limited' way in three provinces. He also blamed anti-revolutionary agents and pro-Monarchists for anarchy and insecurity. Nevertheless, the reality is that the government and religious establishment in Iran must start to introduce credible reforms that will bring social freedoms, political openness and economic empowerment to a generation of Iranians which is growing up in a world of social media where ideas and values are readily disseminated.

Unfortunately, but not unexpectedly, on 8 May 2018 President Trump announced that the United States would be withdrawing from the JCPOA and re-imposing sanctions against Iran, going against the advice of its European allies, particularly France, Germany and the United Kingdom. In response, the President of Iran, Hassan Rouhani, reaffirmed Iran's commitment to the nuclear deal provided the remaining signatories to the JCPOA were willing to remain committed themselves. Initial indications were that the other signatories would honour the agreement, including China and Russia. In the background frantic diplomatic moves can be anticipated to renegotiate the deal to alleviate the concerns of the United States, since the Trump administration made it clear that secondary sanctions would apply on foreign companies (including European Union companies) that trade with Iran. From a practical context the European Union is unlikely to jeopardise its trading relationship with the United States. The question remains though how far the Iranian leadership will be willing to go to make further concessions when the United States has shown that it is not willing to honour its commitments. Iran must find a way to overcome this crisis without compromising its sovereignty. Though Iran's trade with the European Union has increased significantly following the lifting of sanctions, China, South Korea and Turkey remain Iran's top three trading partners and Iran will surely be seeking trade assurances with them too. Unsurprisingly, Israel and Saudi Arabia publicly supported Mr Trump's withdrawal. Hardliners in the Iranian military and political establishment emboldened by the withdrawal by the United States will be hawkishly following developments as they unfold and seeking to undermine the authority of President Hassan Rouhani, who is viewed as a moderate.

Commencing at 12:01am on 07 August 2018, sanctions were re-imposed on Iran that included restrictions on the Iranian government's access to US bank notes, its freedom to trade in gold and precious metals and the sale or transfer to or from Iran of graphite and metals, as well as unspecified sanctions relating to the Iranian currency. According to US officials, tariffs were also being placed on Iran's automotive sector and the country was prohibited from purchasing US passenger aircraft, while the US would no longer purchase certain Iranian commodities. In his address to the 73rd session of the United Nations General Assembly on 25

September 2018, Donald Trump confirmed that further sanctions would be imposed in November 2018 taking direct aim at Iran's oil and energy sector, financial institutions connected with Iran's Central Bank, port operators and shipbuilding sectors. The key agenda behind these sanctions is to cripple the Iranian economy, forcing the Iranian government to renegotiate the JCPOA, which President Trump has always been against, as well as forcing Iran's military and political elite to end its support for so-called terrorism in the region. Iran's currency, the Rial, has continued its downward spiral, with its value plummeting by 80% against the US dollar in the last year alone. The Iranian public will no doubt suffer the brunt of these sanctions, particularly its middle class. All this plays into the fortunes of Iran's regional adversary, Saudi Arabia. The danger lies, however, in the fact that if the people bring down the government of President Hassan Rouhani and not the political establishment a hard line government may take over the reins of power. At about the same time President Trump raised tariffs on Turkey's steel and aluminium from 20 percent to 50 percent, causing the Turkish Lira to fall in value against the dollar. If a US President can cripple the currency of Muslim countries, those countries need to rethink their economic strategies.

In conclusion, a mutual security arrangement between Saudi Arabia and Iran as part of a renewed Caliphate will no doubt save both countries hundreds of billions of dollars that can be invested in infrastructural projects to benefit both its peoples rather than purchasing military hardware from the West to inflict maximum damage in proxy wars being fought in the region to devastating effect. A ratcheting down of the hostile polarisation between these two ideologically-opposed regimes has the real potential to transform the political and economic landscape of the Middle East. As the next generation of Saudis and Iranians yearn for more political openness, transparency and participation in their countries' political and economic future, which appears to be an absurdity now, will be inevitable tomorrow. If the Middle East is to prosper with a global presence in trade, commerce and political leadership, then both Saudi Arabia and Iran must go through nothing short of revolution by instituting transparent representative democracies and decisive and swift institutional reform, as well as rethinking their commitment to the rigid and orthodox role of religion in political and public life by resorting to a rational discourse. Furthermore, as with Saudi Arabia, Iran has a morality police which has no democratic oversight. Given the notoriety with which they operate they should be done away with, especially under a renewed Caliphate.

CHAPTER EIGHT

One Ummah: Renewal of the Islamic Caliphate

It is the radical interpretation of Islam as a violent political response to perceived victimisation of the Muslim Ummah that is at odds with Western foreign policy. Political analysts and strategists argue that there is substance in such a perception. Fifteen years after the United States military machine went into Afghanistan it still has troops there, 8400 at the time of President Obama's departure from office, with the Trump Administration in July 2017 promising to send an additional 4000 troops. On 21 August 2017, President Trump, while addressing troops at Fort Myer in Virginia emphasised that, without announcing troop levels or arbitrary timetables or placing restrictions on how the US military choose to exercise its military power, he would be extending his country's role in Afghanistan but will not be committed to nation building. Meanwhile, the US continues to have a military presence in Iraq fifteen years after launching 'shock and awe'. With the US continuing to retain a strong naval presence in Bahrain and Qatar some will therefore, seek to contend that the Muslim Ummah is under siege from US imperial policy. Whether that is the case or not, surely the Muslim Ummah has been substantially weakened in terms of the political unrest in Iraq, the failure of the Arab Spring of 2011, the ongoing crises in Syria and Libya compounded by the mayhem that was perpetrated by ISIL, the suppression of democratic protests in Bahrain, the humanitarian catastrophe in Yemen and the continued reign of despots in the Middle East with the tacit acquiescence of Western governments.

What the Muslim Ummah faces today is an urgent need for a rational political stratagem through non-cooperation and non-violence, as opposed to a violent radical response, directed at undemocratic governments and despotic rule, not only in the Middle East but the wider Muslim world also, that will bring about political pluralism and economic emancipation, dismantling decades of dynastic rule and mismanagement of economic resources. Should the populations of the Middle East rise up again against their authoritarian rulers it is absolutely imperative that a second Arab Revolution is not hijacked like the first Arab Spring (where authoritarian rule has come back to power in Egypt, Libya and Yemen have effectively become failed states, while Bahrain continues to repress democratic opposition and Syria has disintegrated into catastrophic meltdown). Should a second Arab Spring fail, it will take at least another generation before any attempt to introduce democratic reforms in the Middle East will become viable. Should existing Middle Eastern/Arab regimes voluntarily embrace both transparent and functional democratic reforms, pre-empting mass upheaval, then transitional criteria such as those discussed at the end of this chapter could serve as a platform for further rational research and debate.

ISLAM AND DEMOCRACY

In the context of re-establishing an Islamic Caliphate, there is much debate about Islam and its compatibility with democracy. Importantly, it is imperative to determine what form of democracy should be adopted or exercised in a renewed Caliphate. If we look at Western democracy we will observe that it comes in different shades of grey. In the West, democracy is essentially a vehicle of government that represents a political superstructure requiring support from an economic substructure, namely free market economics and free enterprise. At the heart of this financial machine are predominantly the banks. Consequently when the banks began to collapse both in the United States and Europe in 2008, Western democracy was under threat. In an attempt to retain confidence in the markets and prevent civil unrest, governments desperately pumped billions to bail them out. As a result increasing austerity measures were introduced by governments across Europe to overcome their respective deficits. Coupled with fragile currency markets, falls in major banking shares and a slowdown in economic growth in China and their own respective economies, the US and Europe are far from overcoming this financial crisis. Though Europe appears to have avoided for now another recession, there is no place for complacency, especially in the face of the uncertainties surrounding Brexit, the rise of right-wing populism and the potential unravelling of the European Union in the future.

Unless the vast majority of working-class people feel the benefit of any economic recovery, there will be a natural inclination to pin the blame for their economic woes on scapegoats. All this is a recipe for increased social tension. The successes of some far-right and anti-establishment political parties across the EU in the May 2014 European Parliamentary Elections, for example, illustrated an undercurrent of tension not only on immigration but also on the political union of Europe as a whole. This played out more starkly in the EU Referendum held in the United Kingdom on 23 June 2016 which witnessed 52% voting in favour of Brexit. Consequently, the UK is poised to the leave the EU after Prime Minister Theresa May triggered Article 50 of the Lisbon Treaty on 29 March 2017, formally starting Brexit negotiations.

The protests that took place against government austerity measures in many European cities following the 2008 financial crisis, including those in Greece, Spain and the United Kingdom, were examples of frustration and disillusionment against governments. Though this was often denied and downplayed by respective governments, it is important to realise that when a government deploys state security forces to suppress wide legitimate protest with heavy-handed tactics, the democratic legitimacy of that government is seriously called into question. This can only undermine democratic values.

Central to the concept of liberal democracy, which is often used interchangeably with pluralist democracy, is that governments are elected on the basis of competition between political parties, a tolerance of wide-ranging political beliefs and electoral choice. A key feature of liberal democracy is the absence of a concentration of power. Instead there is a wide dispersal of political power among competing interests (including pressure groups), with a number of access points available to them. This ability for interest or pressure groups to press their demands and lobby government to influence policy establishes a channel of communication between them, creating a reliable link between the government and the governed. However, with austerity measures being rolled out by governments across Europe, trade unions as pressure groups are being prevented from carrying out their role effectively under a liberal democracy. In the United Kingdom for example, major Trade Unions, including the Public Commercial Services Union (PCS), are increasingly finding it difficult to defend working conditions, pay and pension rights for their members and prevent job losses, despite resorting to lobbying members of parliament, organising substantial marches in London and holding lawful strikes after successfully balloting their members for industrial action. The Trade Union Act 2016 increased the threshold of union members required to vote in favour of taking industrial action. The Conservative Government, however, has claimed that this would ensure unions had a democratic mandate before they called their members out to take part in industrial action.

The basis of representative democracy involves holding regular, free and fair elections that are not only transparent but also provide a level playing field for prospective candidates. The notion of 'one person one vote' gives the electorate a sense of purpose and belonging in determining the shape and direction of their future government. In real terms, however, the electorate only ever gets to effectively exercise its democratic credentials by voting on Election Day every few years. In a parliamentary democracy when the party in power has a comfortable majority in the legislature, it becomes next to impossible to reverse subsequent policy if the government is determined to implement it no matter how unpopular it may prove to be (even if it was not included in its election manifesto pledge). This ties in with the concept of 'strong and effective government' and the 'tyranny of the majority'. With respect to the United Kingdom, Lord Hailsham termed it an 'elective dictatorship'. Examples include Tony Blair's decision to take the United Kingdom to war over Iraq in 2003, which was widely opposed, with more than a million people marching in London and other major cities on 15 February 2003. For Blair, his spin-doctors, much of his government and some media streams, the decision to go to war amounted to the 'price of leadership and the cost of conviction'.

In terms of how representative governments are of the electorate, let us translate the percentages in the context of the United Kingdom. In the 2005 General Election, for instance, Tony Blair's Government secured 35.2% share of the votes but 55% of the seats in the House of Commons, while the Conservative party secured 32.4% share of the votes but only 30% of the seats. Again in 2010, the coalition government secured 59.1% share of the votes but secured 56% of the seats in the House of Commons, while in 2015 the Conservative Party won 36.9% share of the votes but 51% of the seats, with Labour winning 30.4% of the votes but only 36% of the seats. And in the snap General Election held in June 2017, the Conservative party won 42.4% share of the vote but 48.9% of the seats while Labour secured 40% of the vote but only 40.3% of the seats. Much of this discrepancy comes down to the 'First Past the Post' electoral system employed at General Elections. Nevertheless, this must be examined against the backdrop that only 61.4%, 65.1%, 66.1% and 68.7% of the electorate turned out to vote in the 2005, 2010, 2015 and 2017 General Elections respectively. What that means is that in 2005 the Labour Government came to power with a mandate of 21.5% of the total electorate, while in 2010 the Coalition Government came to power with a mandate of 38.5% of the total electorate. In 2015 the Conservative Government came to power with a mandate of 24.3% of the total electorate, whereas in 2017 the Conservatives came to power with the DUP with a mandate of 29.8% of the total electorate. Consequently, under the First Past the Post electoral system, while returning a political party commanding an overall majority in the House of Commons in 2005 and 2015, neither party was able to command a mandate of more than a quarter of the total electorate.

Electoral success in the United States has as much to do with campaign funding as with party policies. In the run-up to the 2012 US Presidential Elections, Republican candidate Mitt Romney and incumbent President Barack Obama received billions of dollars in campaign funding. As a consequence of the US Supreme Court decision in Citizens United v Federal Election Commission Unions, for-profit corporations and other associations are no longer restricted from providing unlimited amounts of money from their general treasury funds for independent 'electioneering communications' (such as political advertising). In fact, the Justices ruled that such political spending was protected under the First Amendment to the United States Constitution. As a result, special interest groups can now spend without limit, calling for the election or defeat of individual candidates. Speaking at the Carter Center prior to the 2012 Election, former US President Jimmy Carter criticised the US electoral process, describing it as riddled with 'financial corruption' which dramatically favoured the elite. This begs the question how truly independent is the office of the United States President, whose occupant is so heavily dependent on corporate financial support. Furthermore, in terms of representation, in the November 2016 Presidential Election, Donald Trump secured the Presidency by winning more than the required 270 Electoral College votes, despite the fact the Hilary Clinton secured two million more of the popular vote.

In contrast to a wide and democratic dispersal of power required by a liberal democracy, C. Wright Mills, in The Power Elite, provides an illuminating account of power structures in the

US, explaining that political power is concentrated in the hands of a nexus of powerful groups including big corporate businesses, the US military and political stakeholders surrounding the Presidency. Consequently, this consortium of power elites shapes key policy decisions, including strategic, economic, defence and foreign policy. Unions, small businesses and consumer lobbyists, on the other hand, are only ever able to exert any sort of real influence from the fringes of the political process. He goes on to say that liberal democracy in the US is a sham.

In his critique of liberal democracy, Gaetano Mosca in his work *The Ruling Class* claims that with liberal democracies the resources or attributes that are necessary for political rule are always unequally distributed, and that a cohesive minority will always be in control of the levers of power, manipulating and controlling the masses, even in a parliamentary democracy. Robert Dahl in his work *A Preface to Economic Democracy* had argued that the unequal ownership of economic resources tends to concentrate political power in the hands of a few, which runs parallel to the Marxist critique of pluralist democracy. As Robert Michels puts it, this 'Iron Law of Oligarchy' permeates all democratic systems across Western Europe and the US. In terms of manipulating public perception, it is particularly dangerous when the different media streams are controlled by vested interests. Then again, the media's ability to manipulate a story is dependent upon the naivety and complacency of the readership. In real terms politicians use the media to sell strategic policy issues to the public. Yet the media are only as powerful as their readers and followers.

Despite its many shortcomings, democracy should nevertheless be the preferred norm. It need not necessarily have to be based on the Western model and certainly not enforced upon Muslim countries by the Western military machine. Though the notion of living in a democracy gives the populace a sense of engagement in the political process, in reality, in countries exhibiting democratic credentials supported by capitalist infrastructures, the establishment and ruling elite will invariably pull the levers of power. This is evidenced by the socio-economic make-up of the majority of those elected to their national legislatures. This is true of all democratic countries, but more so in countries riddled with corruption.

Given the negative connotations in the West surrounding Islam and democracy, let us be bold enough to explore the term 'Islamic democracy'. It essentially comes down to the degree to which Islamic laws and ethics are incorporated into the affairs of state and their compatibility with preconceived notions of Western democracy. The critical question is whether Shari'ah should be the bedrock of government policy or co-exist with non-Shari'ah compliant legislation. While Malaysia has adopted or retained Islam as its state religion, Islamic law is not the only source of law. In Shi'ite-dominated Iran, Shari'ah is substantially integrated into the affairs of state, including legislation. Also linked with the term 'Islamic democracy' is the degree of democratic participation in the policy-making process in the form of elected representation. Most Muslim majority countries in South and South-East Asia, including Bangladesh, Pakistan, Indonesia, Malaysia etc, have elected legislative chambers. As a consequence of the Arab Spring, many Muslim majority states in the Middle East and North Africa sought to opt for greater elected representation in the legislative process. A renewed Caliphate must therefore be able to reconcile key democratic values with competing interests within the spirit of Islamic jurisprudence. There is little conflict between (liberal) political Islam and political pluralism in its broad sense. If we use the concept of 'Shura' in a contemporary political setting, it can be argued that it refers to democratic processes to include democratic institutions and elections.

THE ISIL PHENOMENON: THE TRANSGRESSOR

In capturing major Iraqi cities, including the second largest city, Mosul, in June 2014 with territorial gains spreading from Syria into Iraq, insurgents in the shape of the Islamic State in Iraq and the Levant (ISIL), also referred to as Da'esh, managed to achieve the horrifying reality of setting up a viable political entity in the form of a transnational Islamic Caliphate based on an extremist interpretation of Shari'ah. ISIL had indeed taken maximum advantage of the civil war in Syria and the Sunni resentment in Iraq against the authoritarian rule of former Shi'ite Prime Minister Nouri al-Maliki. It would not be out of place to argue that while ISIL represented a credible threat to Shi'ite influence in the Middle East it was also being cautiously tolerated by Sunni despots in the region. The reason was that ISIL was proving to be a double-edged sword, being associated with multiple terrorist acts in the West as well as attracting thousands of foreign citizens both from the West and from the Middle East to its ranks with the potential in the long run of threatening Sunni rule in the Middle East. Therefore, the longer the regional powers delayed in taking effective military action against the insurgency, the more formidable an antagonist ISIL would have become. In the worst case scenario, Iraq and Syria could have splintered (although that risk is still there), with sectarian wars in the region becoming more prevalent, leaving a deeply-divided Muslim Ummah in its wake. It must be stressed that any attempt to re-establish an Islamic Caliphate through violence and destruction will have serious consequences in terms of its sustainability. This is particularly so if a narrow narrative of Shari'ah is enforced on the populace with an iron hand. The absence of democratic norms and practices will give rise to despotic leaders who are unaccountable to any legitimate democratic process.

While world leaders were 'sitting in committee' discussing how to deal with the threat of ISIL, tens of thousands of innocent civilians in Syria and Iraq were suffering violent death, displacement from their homes and appalling living conditions in bombed-out buildings and overcrowded refugee camps. More credible steps could have been taken by the international community earlier on to strike out at ISIL on multiple platforms, politically, financially and militarily. While this terrorist manifestation has been subdued for now, particularly in much of Iraq and Syria, it must not be allowed to mutate into something more cataclysmic that could threaten to open up a 'Pandora's Box'. Having lost considerable territory, die-hard members of ISIL will seek to regroup in failed states such as Libya or worse still return to Europe, manifesting themselves in sleeper cells.

The recent Refugee Crisis of 2015 witnessed the largest

movement of people across European borders since World War II, with hundreds of thousands of refugees originating mostly from Syria and Iraq escaping conflict there, but also from Eritrea and Afghanistan. Many of them have made the perilous crossing across the Mediterranean Sea in overcrowded and unseaworthy vessels, having entrusted themselves and their families to unscrupulous human traffickers. Tragically, thousands have died from drowning. The global conscience was shocked when images of the body of Aylan Kurdi, aged three, lying face down in the surf washed up on a beach near the Turkish resort of Bodrum was beamed across the globe. His family had been trying to make the crossing to the Greek island of Kos.

With European governmental policies constantly changing in response to the crisis, for those refugees who have made the crossings to Europe, whether by land or sea, their plight is by no means over. Undermining the Schengen Agreement, some European countries, such as Hungary, have erected razor wire fences. In 2016 an agreement was reached between Turkey and the EU on the condition that those refugees who made the crossing to the Greek islands would be returned to Turkey.

In the West, it is notably France that has faced the wrath of ISIL. The tragic events in Paris on Friday 13 November 2015 that witnessed coordinated attacks being perpetrated simultaneously, resulting in the death of 130 innocent civilians, is of grave concern. The sites included the Bataclan Theatre and the Stade de France, as well as a number of cafés and restaurants. Prior to that on 7 January 2015 members of ISIL attacked the offices of the satirical magazine Charlie Hebdo.

The sophistication with which these attacks were carried out, not only in terms of planning and effective execution but also in terms of funding, arms procurement and recruitment of suicide bombers and gunmen, is indicative of some degree of foreign involvement, as well as a serious failure of European security agencies in carrying out effective surveillance in preventing these terrorist attacks.

The fear is the threat of a serious backlash against Muslim

communities across Europe, which is the principle driver of ISIL behind these attacks. Their extremist ideological narrative feeds on promoting suspicion, anger and hatred. Their purpose in Europe and the United States is to divide communities. The number of hate crimes against Muslims has been on the rise in the United Kingdom, particularly following the Westminster Bridge attack, suicide bombing in the Manchester Arena and the London Bridge attack in 2017, and in France and other European countries since the Paris attacks and in light of the Refugee Crisis in 2015. Right-wing political parties and interests, including some anti-immigration media streams, have done well to exploit this and instigate an undercurrent of tension against immigrant communities in Europe, which is in line with the ISIL narrative of creating an 'us and them' mentality in the West.

It must be stressed that there is nothing Islamic about ISIL. Not only does it represent a global terror network threatening regional and global stability, but potentially, if allowed to fester, it will serve as a catalyst for the Muslim Ummah to implode upon itself, resulting in the Ummah becoming more fractious and impeding any possibility of a unified platform. ISIL is comparable to a rabid dog. Every effort must be taken by the Muslim Ummah to eradicate this scourge of humanity. ISIL claimed responsibility for a spate of terrorist attacks in the Holy month of Ramadan in 2016, killing not only innocent westerners as in Dhaka, Bangladesh, following an armed attack at the Holy Artisan Bakery café, but by butchering Muslims in a suicide attack in Baghdad which killed almost 300 innocent civilians and wiped out entire families who had gone out shopping in preparation for the Eid celebrations. Numerous women and children lost their lives. There can be no justification in Islam for such heinous crimes. ISIL has indeed turned into a deranged and reactionary force. Their warped ideology, based on their extremist interpretation of Shari'ah, underlines the absolute need that the destructive actions of ISIL must be challenged effectively with a counter-narrative.

THE CALIPHATE: A BRIEF HISTORICAL PERSPECTIVE

The last widely-acknowledged Caliphate was associated with the Ottoman Empire, which used the symbolic power of its Caliph to rule across vast swathes of the Arab world. The Caliphate under Ottoman rule was effectively ended with the establishment of the Turkish Republic in 1923 (though it was officially abolished by its first President, Kamal Ataturk, on 3 March 1924). Since then, for secularists and Arab nationalists the Caliphate has been linked with reactionary forces and ideologies and the history of Ottoman rule. While the Ahmadiyya Muslim Community has defined its leader as the 'Caliph' since the early 20th century, this has been rejected by mainstream Muslims.

It is generally accepted that the word 'Caliph' comes from the Arabic word 'Khalifa', meaning 'successor', a Caliphate being an Islamic state (under a single command structure headed by the Caliph). This general notion has over time lent itself to manipulation by different political and religious leaders to justify their rule and influence. The starkest example of such a misrepresentation was the declaration of a Caliphate by Abu Bakr al-Baghdadi, naming himself the Caliph in the Iraqi city of Mosul on 29 June 2014. There is common consensus among Islamic scholars and theologians that this latest manifestation is an abhorrent distortion of what a Caliphate should truly represent. Unfortunately, Western media outlets are increasingly associating the term Caliphate with a terrorist institution synonymous with murder, rape, plunder and mayhem. Abu Bakr al-Baghdadi's declaration of a Caliphate (in the form of ISIL) and its war against the West is reminiscent of the declaration made by the Ottoman Sultan and Caliph, Mehmet IV when he declared war and jihad against Great Britain, France and Russia on November 11, 1914, announcing that it had become obligatory for all Muslims, young or old, to support the struggle against the 'infidels'. The proclamation's effect was minimal. The Arabs in particular, spearheaded by nationalist fever, preferred freedom rather than so-called Islamic rule under the Ottomans. The Ottoman Sultan had sided with the 'Central Powers' during World War I, an alliance consisting of Austria, Hungary and Germany. The collapse of the Ottoman armies in 1917-1918 ultimately led to the destruction of the last widely-recognised Caliphate in 1924.

It is unfortunate that the term 'Caliphate' has different connotations for Muslims across the globe. This is probably because a study of historical texts evidences a myriad of inferences that give rise to complexities in reaching a definitive meaning.

The starting point of any rational discourse should, without a doubt, be the succession following the death of the Prophet Muhammad. Of significance, at the time of the Prophet's death He did not specifically name anyone, not even one of His closest companions, as His political successor. Nor did He form a committee to nominate a successor from amongst themselves or from the Ummah. This left open the door for elective representation rather than selection or patronage, which was nothing short of revolutionary in the context of tribal Arabia. The first Caliphate was that of the 'Khulafa' Ur Rashidin' (the rightly-guided Caliphs who ruled between 632 till 661). Not only did neither of them inherit the role but they had all heard the revelations from the Prophet Himself and been guided by His example. Unfortunately, it was during the formative years of the early Islamic community which also experienced the first wave of Fitnas (civil wars) to engulf the then Muslim Ummah (discussed in Chapter Four), that the terms Caliph and ultimately Caliphate would become distorted. It took the form of dynastic rule, with all the trappings of an absolute monarch. Critics, particularly the Shi'ites, claim that the Umayyad Caliphs (the first succession of Caliphs to govern the Islamic Ummah imposing dynastic succession ruling as kings between 661 till 750) failed to govern in accordance with the Holy Qur'an and the Prophetic traditions. For the Shi'ites, however, the Caliph whom they term the Imam is not only the political head of the Ummah but also the spiritual representative of the Prophet on earth with the capacity to interpret Divine Law.

It would be worth noting that with the exception of Imam Ali (the first Shi'ite Imam) and Imam Mahdi (the twelfth and last Shi'ite Imam who Shi'ites believe to be in occultation) the remaining Shi'ite Imams were either brutally murdered or poisoned at the orders of the Umayyad and Abbasid Caliphs. Tragically, Imam Husayn (the Prophet's grandson), along with his family and a small band of followers, were brutally murdered at the command of the Umayyad Caliph, Yazid I, son of Mu'awiyah. So brutal was Husayn's martyrdom that he was decapitated and sent to Yazid I, not only to satisfy his lust for power but to ensure that his armed militia had actually killed Husayn, in case they should have backed down, given the magnanimous persona of Husayn, who reportedly resembled his grandfather, the Prophet Muhammad. (It was Ali's rival Mu'waiyah who effectively established the Umayyad Caliphate, wrestling it away from the Hashemite Clan to which Ali belonged).

Of the Umayyad Caliphs, the most notable was Abd al-Malik. Not only did he succeed in bringing an end to tribal and sectarian strife and re-establishing the authority of the Umayyad capital in Damascus, but significantly he is credited for building the Dome of the Rock in Jerusalem which stands today on Haram al-Sharif mountain, or as the Jews call it Temple Mount. Expansion under the Umayyad Caliphate saw Arab territories spread through North Africa as far as Spain, while in the east, their control extended beyond Samarkand and Kabul.

Growing discontent among non-Arab Muslims over the discriminatory policies adopted against them by the Umayyad Caliphs, and the crippling expense of financing military expansion with the siege of Constantinople, which ended in disaster, provoked a revolution that initially expressed itself in supporting the followers of Ali and his descendants. In 747 a serious rebellion broke out in the Shi'ite strongholds of Kufa and Khurasan against the Umayyads, and in 750 the last Umayyad Caliph, Marwan II, was defeated in the Battle of the River Zab by the combined Arab and Persian forces of the revolt's military leader, Abu Muslim, whose support for the Abbasids was steadfast. A key theme behind the rebellion was Islamic unity rather than Arab supremacy aimed at assimilating the different peoples and races of the empire.

Unlike the Umayyad Caliphs, the Abbasids claimed direct descent from the family of the Prophet Muhammad through His uncle, Abbas ibn Abd al-Muttalib. The first Abbasid Caliph was Abu al-Abbas, who gained the title of 'al-Saffah' (the Slaughterer), for in securing his accession he killed all potential rivals, including the surviving members of the Umayyad family and members of his own Abbasid family, who were seen as a threat. He did not even spare Abu Muslim, the military leader with whose help the Umayyads were defeated. The capital of the Abbasid Caliphate was shifted to what is now Baghdad. (An interesting observation must be made at this point. Violence begets violence! For the Abbasid Caliphate was effectively brought to an end by the sacking of Baghdad by the Mongol hordes, when the city was razed to the ground with heaps of slaughtered bodies piled in the streets.)

Despite the undemocratic nature of the Abbasid Caliphate, under its successive Caliphs the Islamic world experienced what many historians have come to claim was the 'golden age' of Islamic culture. The Abbasid dynasty ruled the Islamic Caliphate from 750 to 1258, making it one of the longest and most influential Islamic dynasties. For most of its early history it was the largest empire in the world, and through its trading routes it had contact with Chinese and Indians cultures in the East and the Byzantines in the West, allowing it to adopt and synthesize ideas from them. Notably, it was during the rule of the fifth Caliph of the Abbasid dynasty, Harun al-Rashid, that the arts and sciences really flourished under his patronage, so much so that under his rule, Baghdad became the world's most important centre for science, philosophy, medicine and education (this is a far cry from present-day Baghdad). The vast size of the Caliphate meant that it not only shared borders but interacted with many distant empires, so scholars at Baghdad could collect, translate, and expand upon the knowledge of other civilizations, namely the Egyptians, Persians, Indians, Chinese, Greeks, Romans and Byzantines. The successors of Harun al-Rashid, especially his son al-Ma'mun, continued his policies of supporting artists, scientists and scholars. Al-Ma'mun founded the 'Bayt al-Hikma' (the House of Wisdom) in Baghdad.

A library, an institute for translators, and in many ways an early form of university, the House of Wisdom hosted Muslim and non-Muslim scholars who sought to translate and gather the cumulative knowledge of human history in one place and in one language, namely Arabic. At the House of Wisdom, important ideas from around the world came together.

The introduction of Indian numerals, which have become standard in the Islamic and Western worlds, greatly aided mathematics and scientific discovery. Scholars such as al-Kindi revolutionized mathematics and synthesized Greek philosophy with Islamic thought. Al-Biruni and Abu Nasr Mansur—among many other scholars—made important contributions to geometry and astronomy. Al-Khwarizmi, expanding upon Greek mathematical concepts, developed Algebra. Ibn al-Haytham made important contributions to the field of optics and is generally held to have developed the concept of the scientific method. Abu Musa Jabir ibn Hayyan is credited as the father of chemistry for introducing a scientific and experimental approach to alchemy. A number of very practical innovations took place, especially in the field of agriculture. Improved methods of irrigation allowed more land to be cultivated, and new types of mills and turbines were used to reduce the need for labour (though slavery was still very common both in the countryside and in cities). Crops and farming techniques were adopted from far-flung neighbouring cultures. Rice, cotton and sugar were taken from India, citrus fruits from China, and sorghum from Africa. Thanks to Islamic farmers, these crops eventually made their way to the West. Such Islamic innovation would continue, even as the Abbasid dynasty fell into chaos.

The Abbasid Caliphate was also an extensive and formidable trading empire, generating unprecedented wealth. Trading ships brought in silks, spices, aromatics, fine crockery, exotic animals and animal skins, and precious stones and other sought-after goods from India and China, both for the internal market and for export to Europe. Trade with the Byzantines also brought in gold, fine clothes, marble, furs and armour. Ancient overland routes to the east of the empire snaked their way through Central Asia to India and China.

Slowly but steadily, Abbasid power weakened in the face of independent governors, called emirs, and an overbearing military that had substantial influence over the Caliphs. In real terms subsequently the Abbasid Caliphs' power and influence extended no further than the cities and areas immediately around them, while the regional governors (emirs) wielded increasing power of their own. Furthermore, by the 11th century, the Abbasid Caliphate faced a wave of attacks from different fronts. In Europe, Christian forces were beginning their military advance into Muslim Spain, while by the end of the century the Christian Crusaders were threatening the very heartland of the Caliphate in their quest to conquer the Holy Land.

The Seljuks, on the other hand, who had broken out from Central Asia, ruled over Persia, Syria and parts of Asia Minor, taking Baghdad in 1055 after driving out the Buyids, releasing the Abbasid Caliph in the process. Though the Seljuks had embraced Islam in the mid-tenth century, by the time the crusading army arrived in the Middle East their rule had fragmented among a number of semi-independent Seljuk chiefs or Sultans. This disunity allowed the Crusaders to take Jerusalem in 1099, butchering the Muslim and Jewish inhabitants and establishing a chain of coastal fortresses, including those at Antioch, Edessa and Tripoli. However, the Abbasid Empire was effectively destroyed by the Mongol horde led by Hulegu Khan when they sacked Baghdad in 1258, burning the city and slaughtering its inhabitants. Chroniclers estimate that tens of thousands, if not hundreds of thousands, of civilians were massacred, while the House of Wisdom, which housed priceless texts and ancient manuscripts preserved and translated by Arab scholars, was plundered.

Salah al-Din Yusuf ibn Ayyub, commonly referred to as Saladin (1137-1193), dismantled the Fatimid Caliphate (mentioned below), when in 1171 he proclaimed a return to Sunni Islam in Egypt. More notably Saladin etched his name in history by taking the city of Jerusalem in October 1187, ending nine decades of occupation by the Franks in what is remembered as the Crusades. Founder of the Ayyubid dynasty, Saladin is revered by Western chroniclers not only for his chivalry in battle but also by the fact that he did not avenge the Christians living in Jerusalem by slaughtering them when he conquered the Holy City. This despite the fact that the first crusading army butchered the Muslim and Jewish inhabitants there in 1099. Saladin is revered by Muslim chroniclers for impeding the third Crusade (1189-1192), although it was led by the greatest military champions Christendom could throw at him in the form of Richard the Lionheart, by effectively foiling the Crusades in general and by preventing Jerusalem from being recaptured during his reign.

The Fatimid Caliphate, which took its name from Fatimah, the daughter of the Prophet Muhammad, wife of Ali and mother of Imams Hasan and Husayn from whom they claimed descent, was essentially a rival religious movement to mainstream Sunni Islam, and was dedicated to its dismantling, representing as it did the Isma'ili sect of Shi'ite Islam. It refused to recognise the Abbasid Caliphs, whom it deemed usurpers. The Fatimid Caliphs saw themselves not only as emperors but additionally as Imams, who, according to their religious doctrine, were also the spiritual heads of the Caliphate, an embodiment of ALLAH's infallible guidance. The Fatimids established Cairo as the capital of their empire, which at its peak stretched across parts of North Africa, Palestine, southern Syria, Yemen and the Hijaz, and were dedicated to their aim of establishing an Isma'ili Imamate. The Fatimid dynasty ruled its empire from 909 to 1171.

The Fatimid Caliphs were both a religious and political dynasty, and their decline is attributed to an internal strife rising from growing dissent over religious doctrine and from internal power struggles. The Isma'ili theology was at odds with the central consensus among the Sunni majority and became increasingly marginalised and discarded. With the Caliphs dedicating their full time and energy to ruling as an essentially civilian government, the military's importance increased, but fractional infighting among the different ethnicities not only weakened the military but also damaged and undermined the personal authority of the Caliphs. So much so that the later Caliphs were pawns in the hands of their viziers and generals, a situation made worse by recurring famines and plagues.

Following the sacking of Baghdad by the Mongol hordes in 1258, the Muslim Ummah faced the threat of annihilation. However the new Sultans of Egypt, the Mamelukes, having supplanted the Ayyubid dynasty of Saladin in September 1260, met the Mongols in battle and won a decisive victory, thereby preventing the Mongol horde from consigning Islam and the Caliphate into obscurity. The Mamelukes are also remembered for capturing the last vestige of the Crusades by taking the coastal city of Acre following a siege in 1291.

The concept of the Caliphate took on a new significance with the Ottoman Empire. This became more prominent when the empire was in decline with the erosion of its military and political power and territorial losses inflicted in a series of wars with European rivals from the 18th century, with nationalist uprisings in its various territories chipping away at Ottoman power. It was during this period that the Ottoman Sultans styled themselves more as Caliphs, claiming leadership of the Muslim world in an attempt to restore their legitimacy. However, their Caliphate was effectively brought to an end in 1924 by President Kamal Ataturk following the establishment of the Turkish Republic in 1923 after the Ottoman Empire had been defeated in World War I. This would bring to a conclusion the system of rule styled under an Islamic Caliphate that had existed in one form or another for 1300 years. Consequently, it would be the forces of nationalism and secularism that would bring to an end the last Islamic Caliphate, which, historians argue, was weak and lacking authority in its last years and bore no resemblance to what a true Caliphate should represent, i.e., a unifying force and not a divisive one.

It may be worth noting that the Ottoman Empire spanned more than 600 years, from 1301 till 1922, and at its peak in the 15th and 16th century it threatened for a time to overpower European civilization. It encompassed most of south-western Europe to the gates of Vienna, including present-day Hungary, the Balkans, Greece and parts of Ukraine, as well as, parts of the Middle East now occupied by Iraq, Syria, Israel and Egypt, North Africa as far west as Algeria and large parts of the Arabian Peninsula. It was the undisputed global superpower at the height of its power. The seizure of Constantinople (now Istanbul) in 1453 and the siege of Vienna in 1529, which would have fallen had it not been for the difficulty of supplying such a large Ottoman army away from its major centres of power, sent shock waves down the collective spine of Europe.

Perhaps the most revered of the Ottoman Sultans was Suleyman 'the Magnificent', (who ruled from 1520 to 1566). Following the defeat of the Ottoman Empire at the end of World War I, much of what remained of the Empire was carved up between the British and the French. For the Ottoman Caliphate, control of the holy sites of Mecca and Medina gave them legitimacy over the Muslim Ummah. No wonder recent Saudi rulers have bestowed upon themselves the title of 'Custodian of the Holy Sites'.

A common theme is evidently clear for the reason behind the decline of previous Caliphates: it involved an internal and external contradiction. For instance, there was internal dissent over a lack of central control by the Caliphs over their regional rulers. Furthermore, a powerful military would very often have threatened and rivalled the authority and power of the Caliphs, coupled with the threat of external military invasion. When empires start to crumble from within, their fall is inevitable.

A RENEWED CALIPHATE

Any notion of re-establishing an Islamic Caliphate based upon the concept of a unitary state will more than likely prove self-defeating and can only breed extremism. Today the Muslim Ummah is divided among 50-plus nation states forged in large part as a struggle against colonial rule and exploitation. It cannot be stressed enough that the advocates of a renewed Islamic Caliphate need to respond effectively to the contemporary global political situation. Given this, it could initially take the form of a forum fostering economic cooperation between founding participating Muslim countries, subsequently taking on a more political role accommodating other countries wishing to join. Core characteristics could include a common citizenship; a single currency; a Federal Reserve Bank but operating on the principles of Islamic Shari'ah; a single customs union; a representative central political authority respecting the national, political and in parts the legal sovereignty of individual member states much like the EU; an independent legal entity sitting as the highest appellate body on the interpretation of (Federal) legislation; and a common foreign and defence policy similar to the US federal system. The West and particularly Israel have nothing to lose from the establishment of a new Islamic Caliphate and everything to gain from it in terms of regional security and economic cooperation. The bedrock upon which the Caliphate should be re-established, however, to give it any chance of success, can only be the practice of political pluralism among the member states.

As a consequence of the military's involvement in state affairs both past and present, not only in South Asia but also in the Middle East and North Africa, it is imperative for the proponents of a renewed Islamic Caliphate to first assess and evaluate what role the armed forces should play. It would be a wasted effort for a renewed Caliphate to be hijacked by the military 'Old Guard' sitting on the fringes of political power shadowing elected governments. In the interests of securing a viable Islamic Caliphate the military's involvement in the democratic make-up of participating member states must be evaluated. Much like the North Atlantic Treaty Organisation (NATO), it would also be important to consider whether there should be a standing military force brought under a (democratic) central command structure to face external aggression and to keep the peace among participating states. The Islamic Military Alliance to Fight Terrorism (IMAFT) led by Saudi Arabia, dubbed the Muslim NATO, is not representative of such a theme, as it is more divisive than it is inclusive. Not only is IMAFT essentially a political stratagem by Saudi Arabia to contain its geopolitical rival Shi'ite Iran, it is also a scheme to thwart democratic upheavals against despotic governments that are members of the military coalition. Importantly, it is imperative to determine what form of democracy will be exercised in a renewed caliphate, given that democracy comes in different shades as highlighted above.

It goes without saying that a renewed Islamic Caliphate must operate under a binding legal framework. This could take the form of enabling treaties similar to the EU model and/or a constitution based on the US federal system. The proponents of a renewed Caliphate should have a realistic blueprint or roadmap against which to form strategic policy objectives, otherwise all efforts will be self-defeating. We notice organisations working actively in many Muslim countries advocating the revival of an Islamic Caliphate but often resorting to unpragmatic and sometimes radical methods. This is both counter-productive and unfortunate. At the very heart of a renewed Caliphate is the mind-set of global Muslims. They must believe in its implementation and appreciate its financial benefits in terms of economic empowerment and security. At the same time, policy-makers within Muslim states must aspire to such a renewal. In this context, the Arab Spring that started in 2011 as a rebellion against despotic rule was a step in the right direction, only subsequently to become unfortunately hijacked. The new political framework and constitution must reflect a desire to uphold the core values of a united Caliphate. While many regard the capitulation of the Ottoman Empire on 30 October 1918 (in signing the Treaty of Mudros) as the demise of the Islamic Caliphate and seek its revival, it would be counter-productive if advocates in favour of a renewed Caliphate strive for a return to an Ottoman-style Caliphate based on its last days. It is important to make the point that an Islamic renascence is not synonymous with an Islamic revival but rather a renewal.

Among other things, an Islamic Caliphate should ensure that all citizens of the Caliphate are equal under the law, irrespective of their religious beliefs, ethnicity or gender. They must be protected by their respective national constitutions, supplementing a Charter of Civil Liberties adopted as Federal Law or Treaty Articles enforceable in domestic courts with the final appeal to the highest appellate or federal court. A renewed Islamic Caliphate, in the interests of promoting economic stability in the Middle East and the wider Muslim world, should aggressively pursue a peace treaty with Israel by mutually-agreed land swaps, reaching a consensus on the right of return and the status of the holy city of Jerusalem, among other things. With respect to Jerusalem, a possible way forward could be establishing a principality within Jerusalem encompassing Islam's holy sites as the capital of a viable independent state of Palestine. This goal to seek peace with Israel resulting in a viable two-state solution may form part of the preamble to a federal constitution or enabling Treaty Articles if the Islamic Caliphate is based on the EU model. Like Europe and the US, Israel is facing economic hardship, with a relatively substantial percentage of its GDP going on defence spending that could otherwise have been spent on social justice, a lower cost of living and a clear government response to concerns of an increasingly squeezed middle class. The recent discovery of major gas fields off Israel's north Mediterranean coast is likely to reduce its dependency on gas imports primarily from Egypt. It is reported that it may even turn Israel into a natural gas exporting country. This may increase its political leverage with neighbouring countries, hopefully turning into a working partnership for economic emancipation. It is hoped that if the present generation of Israeli politicians and the establishment fail to work towards an effective resolution to the Palestinian conflict, then the next generations of Israelis will transform the landscape of Israeli politics, working to achieve economic emancipation of all Israeli citizens by proactively pursuing peace, not war.

The nature of warfare is set to change in the foreseeable future. Conventional war, as we know it, is now being recognised by Western governments as no longer financially sustainable or logistically viable, with Western governments reining in their conventional military expenditure. Unmanned warfare is likely to be the emphasis placed by Western military strategists, in the form of cyber warfare such as the 'Stuxnet virus' attack on Iran's nuclear programme in 2010, as well as drone attacks like the ones currently being used on suspected ISIL targets in Syria and Iraq. The increased use of readily-deployable armed strike forces similar to those involved in the assassination of Osama bin Laden appears to be a preferred tactical initiative.

Financial warfare in the form of crippling economic sanctions is presumably set to stay high on the agenda. We saw this in the form of Western sanctions on Iran that included an EU ban on all oil imports from Iran imposed in July 2012, coupled with US measures against Iran's Central Bank in response to Iran's alleged uranium enrichment programme. Despite the JCPOA between Iran and the P5+1, the US under Donald Trump has effectively withdrawn from the agreement and reimposed sanctions. Another stark example is the increased Western sanctions imposed in 2012 on Syria in response to atrocities carried out by the Syrian regime against its citizens. The financing and arming of rebellions by Western powers against 'rogue governments', as we saw in Libya in 2011 and subsequently in Syria, evidently appear to be a new military strategy.

The nuclear option is always there as a last resort for the West, which is why it is so important for Western governments that developing countries, particularly Muslim countries, do not attain nuclear weapons. Pakistan is the only Muslim country to be internationally recognised as possessing a nuclear arsenal, predictably to be used in case of a nuclear conflict with its age-old adversary, India. It is very unlikely Pakistan has reason to ever deploy its nuclear arsenal against any other country. Conflict between the two neighbours is also likely to draw China into the fray. Consequently, any nuclear exchanges in South Asia will be catastrophic for the emerging economic superpowers. Whatever progress India and Pakistan have achieved since their independence from British colonial rule would be thrown away.

A renewed Islamic Caliphate of independent nations should be in a position to effectively respond to this change in military stratagem by Western powers to defend itself against hawkish military interests and vested stakeholders. In which case, it too must be in a position to exercise 'collective defence' similar to the provisions contained in Article 5 of the Washington Treaty that lies at the heart of NATO. It essentially enshrines the principle that an armed attack against one ally in the Alliance is considered to be an attack against all allies, which calls for taking such action as it deems necessary, including the use of armed force, to restore and maintain the security of the Alliance and its territories as supplemented by Article 6.

Many governments in Muslim majority countries, for instance in South Asia and the Middle East, are enacting and enforcing so-called anti-terror laws with the principal aim of silencing party political opposition, and in the process, as an added benefit to vested stakeholders, undermining the chances of any Islamic renascence. The consequence of this is disillusionment among the young who resort to lapses in moral judgement, fostering acts of criminality. Many of these countries are infested with rampant corruption in all spheres of socio-economic life ruled by elected political dynasties or hereditary despots. Either way, they are backed by an opportunist class of elites and an overzealous military.

Unsurprisingly, in these countries even peaceful political dissent is regarded as synonymous to terrorism where such opposition is seen to actually or potentially challenge the existing political leadership. A stark example is Saudi Arabia. In 2014, following the Arab Spring of 2011, which rocked the political establishment in the Middle East to its core, the Kingdom introduced new counter-terrorism legislation and a series of related Royal decrees which, that owing to their vague and overly broad nature, effectively extended the definition of terrorism to encompass peaceful protest, political speech, and organized action where such actions were aimed at 'harming public order, or disturbing the security of society or the continuity of the state... or insulting the reputation and standing of the state' without providing definitive guidance as to what would constitute such actions. On 31 January 2014, Saudi authorities promulgated the Penal Law for Crimes of Terrorism and its Financing (the 'terrorism law'); then on 3 February 2014, three days later, the late King Abdullah issued Royal Decree 44, followed by further Regulations issued by the Saudi Interior Ministry on 7 March 2014. In the case of the latter, Articles 2, 4, 6, 8 and 9 of the Regulations are particularly worrying in the context of suppressing political dissent. The Saudi state now, in real terms, has full power to crush any protest or criticism, no matter how peaceful or constructive it may be. Poignant then that it was Abu Bakr, the first Caliph of the Muslim Ummah, who on assuming power gave the Ummah the power to remove him should he fail to rule according to the Holy Qur'an and Sunnah of the Prophet (the two main sources of the Shar'iah). Consistently, the Saudi monarchy, backed by the religious establishment, spare no expense in highlighting that they are indeed ruling in the light of the Qur'an and Sunnah. But then critics will contend that they are doing so according to their interpretation of Shar'iah based on a narrow Wahabi narrative.

The ascension to power of King Salman in early 2015 does not bode well for the future of Saudi politics, which seems bleaker than ever. While the 'Saudi Vision 2030' Project he introduced in 2016 addresses austerity, economic diversification and privatization of public services as well as, promising more jobs and more entertainment, King Salman has remained silent about any meaningful or credible political reforms. In the absence of democratic restructuring, like all authoritarian regimes, police repression is likely to remain part and parcel of the Saudi political system. The Saudi political and religious establishment (whether rightly or wrongly) fears that if the people were given the right to vote they could potentially elect 'Islamists' backed by Iran. Should such a phobia translate itself into reality it would invariably result in a catastrophic backlash against the Salafi Wahabi narrative, not to mention the Saudi royal establishment. Interestingly therefore, an intimate relationship exists between the two, evidenced by the fact that both the Saudi royal and 'core' Wahabi establishment have their hands in each other's pockets, for they share a symbiotic relationship.

The declaration of a Caliphate has enormous ideological and theological importance for Muslims. As a precursor to a renewed Islamic Caliphate it would be fitting to have a day of remembrance and prayer for Muslims killed since the end of the Second World War, whether that be as a result of persecution by tyrannical rulers of political dissidents such as those by rulers in the Middle East, ethnic cleansing of Muslim minorities such as the genocide committed against Muslim Bosniaks and more recently of Muslim Rohingyas, as well as the countless external invasions and occupations of Muslim countries which have resulted in the violent deaths of tens of thousands non-combatants. A highlight of the day can be a two-minute silence observed by Muslims across the globe, marked by a simple prayer for those who have lost their lives as a consequence of persecution. The day can aptly be called 'Martyrs' Remembrance Day' and commemorated once a year, preferably on the 'Day of Ashura', on the 10th of Muharram in the Islamic Calendar between the time of Asr and Maghrib, whose significance in Islam can hardly be overestimated. This Remembrance Day will signify to the world that Muslims across the globe stand united as one Ummah in their remembrance of those Muslims who have died from persecution as well as, resisting their own transgressions.

A SECOND ARAB SPRING: PRESCRIPTIVE CRITERIA

As mentioned earlier, prescriptive criteria must be developed and adopted to provide an effective strategy to fill in the vacuum following a successful revolution that will ensure a peaceful transition to democratic processes. A more regulatory approach is required to sustain any future Arab uprising. The consequence of failing to do so with the first Arab uprising has only led to a more volatile Middle East.

A possible way forward, particularly with the Middle East and North Africa, could begin with the appointment of a 'caretaker/transitional' executive body to fill in the political void following the fall of an authoritarian ruler or government. Its composition must be from the members of the civil society whose primary mandate will be to initiate the holding of a General Election, maintain law and order, in addition to running the day to day affairs of government. A separate 'constitutional committee' (consisting of the nation's eminent jurists and constitutional experts) must be put in motion to draft a constitution that will reflect the spirit of revolution as well as the will and aspirations of the people enshrining democratic processes and institutions and promoting an independent judiciary and civil liberties. This committee must report back to the caretaker/transitional body within six months. A referendum will then be held to adopt the draft constitution. Once adopted, an independent Election Commission will set a date for holding a General Election. Ideally, this should be held within 12 months of the formation of the caretaker/transitional executive body.

Political parties will have the opportunity to register themselves with the Election Commission as soon as the referendum approving the draft constitution is held, as the political parties contesting the elections must operate within the parameters of the newly-adopted constitution. Following the General Election, Parliament must also pass a vote of confidence in the new constitution. Those states having monarchs will either become constitutional monarchies or give way to republics to be enshrined in the new constitution.

It is imperative that the military provide allegiance to the caretaker body and thereafter the elected government. The military's role in affairs of the state must be set out in the constitution, in which case, the military must step back from harbouring political ambitions. The caretaker administration must resign as soon as the newly-formed parliamentary government is sworn in. The constitutional committee in the meantime would have resigned as soon as the draft constitution was approved in the referendum. The draft constitution must give the voting public the option to opt for a republic much like the US federal system, or a constitutional monarchy similar to the United Kingdom model. Members of the caretaker executive body and the constitutional committee should not be entitled to stand as candidates for the General Election, in the interests of ensuring non-party political bias.

To ensure independence of the higher judiciary, higher court judges must be appointed by a 'Judicial Appointments Board' consisting of appellate Supreme Court judges on the basis of merit and seniority and not dependent upon political patronage. Removal on grounds of 'conduct unbefitting of the office' of a higher court judge should also be in the hands of such a board. While Parliament will have the power to reject such a dismissal with a two-thirds majority, it should not be allowed to be in a position to instigate dismissal of higher court judges. With the newly-adopted constitution being the supreme law of the state, the Supreme Court must also act within the powers bestowed upon it by the constitution. While advocating a separation of powers between the three branches of government it is only appropriate that checks and balances be put in place also. Therefore, while higher court judges will be appointed by the Judicial Appointments Board, Parliament will also have the opportunity to veto such appointments with a two-thirds majority, advising the Appointments Board to reconsider the appointment.

In the interests of eliminating dynastic rule, the same Prime Minister, as the head of the government who exercises executive power, must not be allowed to run for that office for more than two terms, whether consecutive or concurrent. At the same time, Members of Parliament must not be allowed to run for re-election after three terms, whether consecutively or concurrently. North Africa in particular had despots ruling their respective countries for decades at a time prior to the first Arab Spring. Hosni Mubarak had ruled Egypt for almost 30 years, while Muammar Gaddafi had ruled Libya for 42 years and Zine al-Abidine Ben Ali ruled Tunisia for 24 years before fleeing the country or being disposed of in face of mass protests to their rule. The President, as head of state, in the case of a republic (where the Prime Minister as head of government exercise executive power with his Cabinet in Parliament), should only be allowed to serve one term, whether appointed by Parliament or subject to direct elections. In the case of a constitutional monarchy any state patronage must not extend beyond the immediate family of the royal household.

All citizens of the state, whatever their gender, religious persuasion or ethnicity must be equal under the law, to be guaranteed by the constitution. While there will be one central government, so as to ensure broad national social cohesion, regions will have devolved powers defined and enshrined in the constitution. The preamble to the constitution must, however, make it clear that while the state remains independent and sovereign it is committed nevertheless to an economic and political alliance based for instance on the EU model or US federal system in the form of a renewed Caliphate

CONCLUSION

Thoughts to Ponder Upon

Today the Muslim Ummah is at a critical crossroads. To prosper and sustain itself the Ummah must be able to rationalize its religious identity and heritage with the challenges of modernity and globalization. Since the end of the Cold War, hundreds of thousands of Muslim civilians or non-combatants have died either through genocide as in Chechnya, Bosnia and more recently in Myanmar or as a consequence of occupation and wars in the Middle East and Afghanistan. Entire generations have grown up knowing nothing but conflict which has resulted in the loss of loved ones, dire poverty and lack of basic needs through colossal damage to infrastructure. Tragically, countless thousands are spending their childhood suffering from psychological trauma, which feeds into an extremist narrative. Exploiting their grievances, reactionary forces in the shape of Al-Qaeda and ISIL threaten to undermine the spirit of true Islam with their warped ideologies.

A study by the US-based Pew Research Center published in April 2015 titled 'Projected Global Muslim Population, 2010-2050', estimates that by 2050 the number of Muslims worldwide will grow to 2.76 billion, or 29.7% of the world's population (a third of mankind). The proportion of the world's Muslims who live in sub-Saharan Africa will increase from 15.5% in 2010 to

24.3% by 2050, while Asia, which is currently home to most of the world's Muslims (61.7%), will have a smaller share of 52.8%. As for the Middle East and North Africa, the region will roughly maintain its current share, rising only slightly from 19.8% to 20.0% in 2050. Consequently, given the likely political and economic demographics of the Muslim Ummah in the foreseeable future, the Muslim Ummah does not need either a Sunni revival or a Shi'ite revival but a renewal of Islam's political and religious narrative that will act as a catalyst for the dissemination of rational thought, ensuring political empowerment to the masses in the form of effective democratic institutions and processes as well as economic emancipation through liberal economic and social policies. Furthermore, to compete on a global platform, governments in the Muslim Ummah must subsidize the education and healthcare of their people.

The rise of the 'Trump doctrine' which challenges the established neo-liberal establishment in the United States will have far-reaching consequences for the Middle East, while Brexit can be seen as the beginning of a populous movement to break away from the post-World War II neo-liberal political consensus. A new global political narrative is taking shape not only in the United States and Europe but also in South and Southeast Asia and the Middle East. It involves a toxic mix of nationalism, populism and protectionism with religious undertones. It thrives on economic disparity and cultural profiling, making scapegoats of minorities and immigrant communities. It is insular in outlook, giving rise to increasing protectionism and aggressive foreign policy objectives. Individual freedoms are increasingly being eroded in the name of national security, with political power being concentrated either in the hands of elected politicians or ruling dynasties. A matter of grave concern is the rise of populist 'strong men' shaping the political and economic destiny of tens of millions of people both now and for the foreseeable future too. They include Donald Trump and Vladimir Putin. Then there is Mohammed Bin Salman, Crown Prince of Saudi Arabia; Benjamin Netanyahu, Prime Minister of Israel; Recep Tayyip Erdogan, President of Turkey; and Xi Jinping, who is President for life in China. All are ready to exercise military might to settle their disputes, sidelining the United Nations if need be. Critically, the unparalleled position the United States occupies in the world today as the only true super power requires it to exercise its military might responsibly and ethically. Failure to do so will only fester resentment, division and polarization.

The refugee crisis of 2015 should serve as a dire warning of the consequences of the fallout from strife and famine as witnessed in North Africa and the Middle East. As the European Union responds to the refugee crisis, this is likely to threaten its future sustainability. One of the key motivators behind Brexit was concerns relating to immigration (particularly Turkey's potential membership of the EU), and the pressure on services and social cohesion. Furthermore, the growing popularity of the French National Front headed by Marine Le Pen and the Alternative fur Deutschland (AfD) in Germany can be seen as a backlash against the established order. Immigrants, particularly Muslims, will increasingly find themselves on the receiving end of the scorn of the new political elite. Add to this the increasing incidence of terrorist attacks in Europe, and it will surely give rise to an ugly mix causing irreparable social division.

While mainstream political parties and religious leaders of different faith groups across Europe speak of unity and social cohesion, there is no denying that a serious undercurrent of disquiet prevails against many migrant communities. Across Europe nationalist and far-right parties are making significant electoral gains, basing their campaigning strategy on an anti-immigration manifesto. This was brought into stark view in the German General Elections held on 24 September 2017, when the AfD secured 12.6% of the vote, making it the third largest party in the Deutscher Bundestag and securing 94 seats out of 630. For the first time not only did the AfD secure seats in the Parliament but since the end of the second world war Germany now has a far-right nationalist party sitting in the legislature. The AfD's surge to power comes in the wake of its anti-immigration stance and hostility towards Islam and by extension to Muslims. As Europe's main power broker, this development in German politics is particularly worrying.

After anti-immigration sentiment became the focus of the main political contenders in General Elections in Italy in March 2018, two eurosceptic populist anti-establishment parties, namely the 5 Star Movement (5SM) and the far-right League Party, gained the maximum seats in Parliament. In June 2018 the recently-elected Austrian government comprising a coalition of the centre-right Austrian Peoples' Party and the far-right, nationalist Freedom Party, both of whom campaigned on anti-immigration platforms, announced it would close seven mosques and expel 60 Imams because of suspected 'extremism'. (For the first time far-right parties have become part of a coalition government in Western Europe). Critics of the move, however, claim that this was an example of nationalistic Islamophobia characterizing the Austrian political climate, fuelled by a fear and resentment of the 600,000 Muslims out of a population of 8.8 million. In September 2018 the nationalist Swedish Democrats party secured about 18% of the vote, up from 12.9% in the previous election, making it the third largest party.

Africa, India and China, which will represent a third of mankind by 2030, will be a force to be reckoned with, in terms of their political, military and economic clout on the world stage. The latter two in particular will seek to increase their influence in South and South-East Asia, where a substantial percentage of global trade and infrastructure is likely to be in the near future. Interestingly, China is becoming increasingly assertive, which is indicative over its stance over the islands and maritime boundary in the South China Sea backed by its extensive naval patrols and building of military infrastructure on many of these islands. As BRICS (Brazil, Russia, India, China and South Africa) economies continue to grow, China is predicted by 2030 to surpass the United States as the largest economy, with India predicted to be a top three economy. Economists claim that notwithstanding a recent slowdown in growth, which is normal after intensive industrialization, China still has strong growth potential, with growth in the United States potentially decelerating in the future due to a maturing economy and ageing demographics. If current trends continue, the United States, Europe and the Middle East will end up playing catch-up. Consequently, uncertain times lie ahead for the global economy and political stability as the United States and Europe will seek to re-adjust their economic strategies to a new world order complicated by a rogue nation like North Korea threatening Western allies in the region. This is the reason behind recent initiatives to de-escalate tension with North Korea and her Western allies. Furthermore, leading global currencies like the US dollar and the Euro may potentially lose their clout against the Chinese yuan and the Indian rupee.

According to a 2016 United Nations report titled 'Sustainable Development Goals', the world population is expected to reach 8.5 billion by 2030 while in 2050 the global population is predicted to be 9.7 billion and by 2100 it is projected to reach an astounding 11 billion. With major concentrations of population growth occurring in the poorest countries (many of them in Muslim majority countries) it is only natural to envisage an inevitable struggle for over-stretched resources, resulting in conflict and social upheavals. Today if we look at South Sudan, north-east Nigeria, Somalia and Yemen for example, famine spurred on by conflict and changing climatic conditions is resulting in catastrophic humanitarian crises, reportedly the worst since 1945 according to Stephen O'Brien, UN Under-Secretary General for humanitarian affairs and emergency relief, speaking to the United Nations Security Council in March 2017. This will only get worse looking into the future as regional conflicts in Africa and the Middle East are likely to increase, with climatic conditions predicted to get worse. Consequently, to stop the Muslim Ummah from collapsing under its own weight of corruption, increasing disparity of economic wealth and political repression it is imperative that reform re-adjusts the political and socio-economic narrative. Meanwhile, the long-term impact of the United States withdrawal from the Paris Climate Change Accord announced by President Donald Trump on 2 June 2017 remains to be seen.

The very real risk of lethal pandemics unleashing themselves on the global population requires immediate investment and cooperation by world governments. Lack of resources and infrastructure among poorer countries (especially Muslim countries with a very high population density) in facing such deadly outbreaks will result not only in the death of tens, if not hundreds of thousands, but have a profound impact on society that will result in a breakdown of social order. Furthermore, given that the global economy is interlinked by trade, death in catastrophic numbers in any one country will have implications worldwide. Moreover, with easy access to global travel it will be too late for world governments to respond should a deadly virus like Ebola or a drug-resistant mutated form of it for instance, take the form of a pandemic. According to the Centers for Disease Control and Prevention (CDC), in 2014-2016, out of a total of 28,616 cases, the Ebola virus disease (EVD) reportedly killed 11,310 in Guinea, Liberia and Sierra Leone. The impact of the 'Black Death' in Europe in the 14th century (1346-53) which killed more than a third of Europe's population and caused social upheaval as well as, the relatively recent 'H1N1 influenza A virus' pandemic of 1918-19, otherwise known as the 'Spanish Flu', which killed 20–50 million people and affected 500 million worldwide (a third of the global human population) should be a wake-up call. No country today has the desired infrastructure in the form of required hospitals, medical professionals and health services to cope alone with a fast-paced lethal pandemic.

Furthermore, the real potential for antibiotic resistant bacteria engulfing entire communities from the unregulated use of antibiotics, particularly in South-east Asian countries, poses a serious risk of an epidemic of antibiotic-resistant infections. In fact, researchers from the National Institute of Allergy and Infectious Diseases (NIAID) reported back in August 2008 that the majority of deaths caused by the influenza pandemic of 1918-1919 were not caused by the influenza virus alone but by bacterial pneumonia following the influenza infection, and a future influenza pandemic may replicate itself in a similar manner.

A sixth of all children in the world today are living in areas affected by conflict, according to a report titled 'War on Children: Time to End Violations Against Children in Armed Conflict', published by Save the Children in 2018. Children living in high intensity conflicts very often lack access to education and health facilities and are more prone to be exposed to serious violence. According to the report, the Middle East is where children are most likely to live in a conflict zone. In 2016, about 2 in 5 children in this region were living within 50km of a conflict event in their country, while children in Syria, Iraq, Yemen and other warzones in the region are at a high risk of being killed and maimed, forced into military recruitment, subject to sexual violence, abductions, attacks on schools and hospitals and denied humanitarian access. Africa rates second after the Middle East. The Democratic Republic of Congo and South Sudan are countries where children too have been subject to sexual exploitation, violence and military recruitment.

The numbers are staggering and their suffering is incomprehensible to many in the Western world, for it is difficult for us to fathom the inhuman suffering these children are having to endure due to conflict. It is important to stress that most of these children will bear psychological trauma that will scar their lives well into their adulthood and potentially affect their adult development. It is only through careful intervention by state authorities that they may integrate themselves back into society, realising their full potential. While UN Peacekeeping operations have helped release thousands of child soldiers through deployment of Child Protection Advisors they are restricted to conflict-ridden countries where United Nations Peacekeepers are on the ground and have access to conflict zones. Children trapped in countries such as Syria, Yemen and other active conflict-ridden countries will find it increasingly difficult to escape the horrors of violence. But then those children that have escaped conflict zones have not been spared either. Many children during the refugee crises in 2015 got separated from their parents, often being trafficked and abducted. A new global initiative to tackle child trafficking, abduction and exploitation has become imperative as more children are at risk now than at any time in the last 20 years.

The Muslim Ummah cannot afford to be locked in the past, immersing itself in nostalgia and fantasizing about re-enacting the 'Golden Age' when it was the centre of innovation and rational discourse, by adopting irrational actions. Rather it must be pragmatic and forward looking, re-asserting its faith in its true potential, promoting and adopting democratic reforms and processes and promoting economic empowerment for its peoples. The most credible means to achieve this is through an effective economic and political alliance. The Muslim Ummah must begin to reassert itself on a rational and united platform. A failure do so, and indeed it may find itself a lonesome wanderer on a dark and sinister path.

APPENDICES

APPENDIX 1

THE 99 DESCRIPTIONS/ATTRIBUTES
OF ALLAH

'ALLAH's are the fairest names. Invoke Him by them. And leave the company of those who blaspheme His name. They will be requited for what they do.' (**Chapter 7, Al-Araf, Verse 180**)

Ar-Rahman	The Most Beneficent
Ar-Rahim	The Most Merciful
Al-Malik	The King, The Sovereign
Al-Quddus	The Holy, The Divine, The Pure, The Purifier
As-Salam	The Source of Peace and Safety
Al-Mumin	The Remover of Fear, The Granter of Security, The inspiration of Faith
Al-Muhaimin	The Controller
Al-Aziz	The Almighty, The invulnerable, The Honourable, The Victorious
Al-Jabbar	The Compeller
Al-Mutakabbir	The Majestic, The Supreme
Al-Khaliq	The Creator
Al-Bari	The Evolver, The Maker of order

Al-Musawwir	The Grand Designer
Al-Gaffar	The Forgiver
Al-Qahhar	The Subduer
Al-Wahhab	The Bestower
Ar-Razzaq	The Provider, The Sustainer
Al-Fattah	The Opener, The Giver of Victory
Al-Aleem	The All-Knowing, The Omniscent
Al-Qabid	The Restrainer
Al-Basit	The Expander
Al-Kafid	The Abaser
Ar-Rafi	The Exalter
Al-Muizz	The Bestower of Honour
Al-Muthill	The Humiliator
As-Samee	The All-Hearing
Al-Baseer	The All-Seeing
Al-Hakam	The Judge, The Dispenser of Justice, The Arbitrator
Al-Adl	The Just
Al-Lateef	The Most Affectionate, The Knower of Subtleties
Al-Khabir	The All-Aware
Al-Haleem	The Forbearing, The Indulgent
Al-Azeem	The Great, The Magnificent
Al-Ghafoor	The Most-Forgiving
Ash-Shakoor	The Grateful
Al-Aliyy	The Sublime
Al-Kabir	The Most Great

Al-Haseeb	The Preserver
Al-Muqeet	The Sustainer
Al-Jaleel	The Majestic, The Exalted
Al-Kareem	The Most Generous, The Bountiful
Ar-Raqeeb	The Watchful
Al-Mujeeb	The Responsive
Al-Wasi	The Vast, The All-Embracing, The Omnipresent, The Boundless
Al-Hakeem	The All-Wise
Al-Wadood	The Most Loving
Al-Majeed	The All-Glorious, The Majestic
Al-Baith	The Resurrector
Ash-Shaheed	The Witness
Al-Haqq	The Truth
Al-Wakeel	The Trustee
Al-Qawiyy	The Most Strong
Al-Mateen	The Most Firm, The Most Steadfast
Al-Waliyy	The Guardian
Al-Hameed	The Praised One
Al-Muhsi	The Appraiser
Al-Mubdi	The Originator
Al-Mueed	The Restorer
Al-Muhyi	The Granter of Life
Al-Mumeet	The bringer of Death
Al-Hayy	The Ever-living One
Al-Qayyum	The Subsisting, The independent
Al-Wajid	The Finder

Al-Majid	The illustrious, The Magnificent
Al-Wahid	The One and Only (Lord)
Al-Ahad	The One, The indivisible
As-Samad	The Eternal, The Absolute, The Self-Sustainer
Al-Qadir	The All-Powerful
Al-Muqtadir	The Mighty, The Powerful
Al-Muqaddim	The Promoter, The One who brings forth
Al-Muakhkhir	The Delayer
Al-Awwal	The First, One who is not preceded
Al-Akhir	The Endless, Eternally Perpetually
Az-Zahir	One Who Manifests
Al-Batin	The Unseen
Al-Wali	The One who Governs all Affairs
Al-Mutaali	Exalted in Greatness, in Honour
Al-Barr	The Benevolent
At-Tawwab	One who Accepts His servant's repentance
Al-Muntaqim	The Lord of Retribution
Al-Afuww	The Pardoner, The Forgiving
Ar-Raoof	The Most Kind and Compassionate
Malikul-Mulk	Master of the Dominion/Sovereignty
Thul-Jalali wal Ikram	The Lord of Majesty and Bounty Lord of Glory and Honour
Al-Muqst	The Equitable One
Al-Jami	The Gatherer of Men on the Day of Resurrection
Al-Ghaniyy	The Self-sufficient
Al-Mughni	The Enricher
Al-Mani	The Preventer of Harm

Ad-Darr	The Creator of Harm
An-Nafi	The Creator of Good
An-Noor	Light Upon Light
Al-Hadi	The Guide
Al-Badee	The Originator (of the Heavens and the Earth)
Al-Baqi	The Everlasting
Al-Warith	The Inheritor of All
Ar-Rasheed	The Teacher of Righteousness
As-Saboor	The Most Patient

APPENDIX 2

The Prophets mentioned in the Holy Qur'an.

The Holy Qur'an mentions 25 of the most prominent Prophets by name. Of ALLAH's Prophets, four were sent with Books of Guidance. They are the Tawrat (Torah) revealed to Prophet Musa (Moses); the Zabur (Psalms) revealed to Prophet Dawud (David); the Injil (the original Gospel) revealed to Prophet Isa (Jesus) and the Qur'an revealed to the final Prophet and Messenger Muhammad. The first Prophet was Adam and the last Prophet is Muhammad (Peace Be Upon Them). Muslims believe the Prophets mentioned in the Holy Qur'an are all Prophets of Islam for they all preached the worship of and submission to the one true God.

Qur'anic Names	Biblical Names
Adam	Adam
Idris	Enoch
Nuh	Noah
Hud	------
Salih	Salih
Ibrahim	Abraham
Isma'il	Ishmael
Ishaq	Isaac
Lut	Lot
Ya'qub	Jacob
Yusuf	Joseph
Shu'aib	-------
Ayyub	Job
Musa	Moses
Harun	Aaron
Dhu'l-Kifl	Ezekiel
Dawud	David
Sulaiman	Solomon
Ilias	Elias
Al Yasa	Elisha
Yunus	Jonah
Zakariyya	Zachariah
Yaha	John
Isa	Jesus
Muhammad	-----

APPENDIX 3
Timeline of Major Events Post-Cold War

If we consider the timeline of events following the end of the Cold War it gives rise to many questions, in particular whether the triumph of Western liberal democracy and capitalism over communism has ushered in a 'clash of civilisations' between the West and Islam, as well as, the emerging internal conflict within the Muslim Ummah itself. The list below has been selected in the light of pivotal events but is by no means exhaustive.

POST-COLD WAR: Following the fall of the Berlin Wall, unification of Germany and the breakup of the USSR

1991

■ Chechnya declares independence from Russia that subsequently ushers in a decade long war between an overbearing and heavily armed Russian Federal Army and so-called Chechen Insurgents. The Chechen capital, Grozny suffers catastrophic bombardment. Horrific human rights abuses by Russian Federal Forces results in a huge number of Chechen refugees.

1992

■ The start of the Bosnian civil war and ensuing 'ethnic cleansing' of Muslim Bosniaks by Serb Forces. Following the Jewish Holocaust under Nazi Germany, Europe experiences its first 'genocide' post World War II with the Srebrenica massacre, though Serbia continues to deny allegations of genocide.

■ Democratic local elections are hijacked by the military in Algeria in an attempt to stem the rise of perceived Islamic fundamentalism in Algeria by denying victory to the FIS.

1993

■ Oslo Accords signed in Washington, D.C. The PLO and Israel embark on a 'land for peace' deal. However, following the assassination of the Israeli Prime Minister Yitzhak Rabin in 1995 by an Israeli soldier, Israeli policy subsequently hardens and the Peace Process derails.

2001

■ 9/11 terrorist attacks on the Twin Towers in New York and the Pentagon in Washington, D.C.

■ US led forces invade Afghanistan after the Taliban fail to surrender Osama bin Laden who is believed to have been behind the 9/11 attacks.

2003

■ The US and Britain lead a 'Coalition of the Willing' invading Iraq on the pretext that it had developed weapons of mass destruction that could strike Western targets. What transpires, however, is regime change, i.e., the fall, capture and execution of Iraqi dictator, Saddam Hussein. A protracted armed conflict ensues in the political vacuum that follows resulting in the death of hundreds of thousands of Iraqi civilians.

2006

■ Israel invades Lebanon, launching the second Lebanon War.

■ Economic sanctions tighten their grip on Iran. Europe declares a ban on oil imports from Iran for its alleged uranium enrichment programme.

2011

- The Arab Spring – Tunisia's President Ben Ali flees to Saudi Arabia, President Mubarak of Egypt resigns in the face of countrywide protests and pressure from the United States; Gaddafi is overthrown and killed by a frenzied mob after being captured in his home town of Sirte.

- Osama bin Laden, leader of Al-Qaeda is killed by US Special Forces in a night-time raid on his residence in Abbottabad, Pakistan.

- Failed bid by the Palestinian National Authority to secure United Nations recognition of Palestinian statehood.

- A Norwegian ultra-far-right wing extremist, Anders Behring Breivik, massacres 77 civilians on Utoya Island to protest against what he views as the Islamization of Europe after setting a fertilizer bomb near government offices in Oslo.

- Oil rich Christian South Sudan gains independence from Sudan.

2012

- Airing of the amateur video, 'The Innocence of Muslims' on YouTube causes protests and outrage across the Muslim World.

- Days after Barack Obama's re-election as US President, Israeli Defence Forces carryout hundreds of airstrikes on Gaza in response to rockets fired by Hamas into Israeli cities, including Tel Aviv. Israel agrees to a ceasefire with Hamas brokered by the Egyptian government.

- The United Nations recognises Palestine as a 'non-member state'.

2013

- France sends troops into Mali to prevent Islamic extremists from taking the capital, Bamako.

- The Arab Spring is effectively handicapped by the removal of Egypt's first democratically elected government in a military coup. The military then clamp down on the Muslim Brotherhood with an iron hand.

- US sponsored peace talks that began in July under the stewardship of US Secretary of State John Kerry fails to materialise, with both Palestinians and Israeli negotiators pointing the finger at each other for sabotaging the talks.

2014

- Israeli airstrikes and naval bombardment of Gaza (including an Israeli ground invasion) result in more than 2100 Palestinians being killed, mostly civilians of whom 501 are children, when Israel launch Operation 'Protective Edge' to stop rocket fire from Gaza into Israel and to destroy Hamas' military capability.

- The so-called 'Islamic State of Iraq and the Levant' (ISIL) or Da'esh emerges on to the global scene after taking the major Iraqi city of Mosul with its leader Abu-Bakr Al-Baghdadi declaring a so-called Caliphate. ISIL wreaks mayhem across Syria and Iraq. Propagating an extremist Sunni narrative it poses a direct threat to any potential resurgence of Shi'ite Islam in the region as a consequence of the Arab Spring.

- General Abdul-Fattah al-Sisi, former head of the Egyptian military that effectively disposed the government of Mr Morsi, wins the Presidential elections held between 26 and 28 May 2014 with the Muslim Brotherhood being branded a terrorist organisation. Saudi Arabia is the first country to recognise the former General as Egypt's new 'legitimate' President.

2015

■ More than a million migrants cross into Europe, with many refugees fleeing the fighting in Syria representing the largest exodus/movement of people in Europe since World War II.

■ Paris is subject to multiple terror attacks carried out by ISIL operatives, killing scores of civilians. France declares war on Da'esh bombing ISIL targets in Syria. The UK Government follows suit.

■ Saudi Arabia launches military operations in Yemen by using airstrikes to stem the advance of Houthi Shi'ite forces allied to Iran and to restore disposed President, Abd-Rabbu Monsour Hadi.

■ Iran and the P5+1 reach a framework agreement on Iran's nuclear programme.

■ Saudi Arabia announces the formation of an Islamic military coalition of 34 (Sunni States) to combat so-called terrorism. Notable omissions include Shi'ite dominated Iran and Iraq.

2016

■ Saudi Arabia carries out a massive military exercise dubbed 'Northern Thunder' involving troops from 20 Arab and other Sunni Muslim Countries. Participants include NATO-member Turkey, the region's most populous and militarily powerful state – Egypt and nuclear-armed Pakistan. Some view it as a precursor to an invasion of Syria. Soon after, Russian President, Vladimir Putin dramatically announces a scaling down of the bombing campaign in Syria by the Russian Air Force.

■ The Saudi leadership announces plans to establish a 'sovereign wealth fund' by selling off state-owned assets in Saudi Aramco in a move to diversify its economy, partly as a reaction to falling oil prices but more importantly to make the Saudi regime a major global investor purchasing strategic financial and industrial assets abroad.

■ Sending a clear message that any internal dissent to its rule will not be tolerated, Saudi authorities execute 46 alleged terrorists, including prominent Shi'ite cleric Sheikh Nimr al-Nimr, following which Shi'ite demonstrations break out across the region with the Saudi Embassy in Tehran being ransacked by an angry mob. As a result, Saudi Arabia breaks off diplomatic ties with Iran, which threatens to escalate sectarian strife in the region and destabillise peace initiatives to end the conflict in Syria.

■ The EU and Turkey reach an agreement on the migrant crisis, adopting a restrictive asylum policy.

■ Turkey and Israel reconcile their differences, ending a six-year diplomatic standoff following a raid by Israeli naval commandos on an aid flotilla in 2010 resulting in the death of nine Turkish activists.

■ Disillusioned at the increasingly authoritative style of Turkey's President, Recep Tayyip Erdogan, as well as the erosion of Turkey's secular traditions by Mr Erdogan's Islamist-aligned government, an attempted coup is launched by elements within the Turkish Armed Forces, but it fails to materialise in the face of mass protests by supporters of the President. Following the abortive coup thousands of arrests and dismissals are made of alleged coup plotters including soldiers, senior military leaders, judges and academics thereby consolidating and increasing the President's grip on power. A state of emergency is declared, while the President pledges to bring back the death penalty.

■ The battle to retake the Iraqi city of Mosul from ISIL begins.

■ The Republican nominee, billionaire Donald Trump, unexpectedly wins the United States Presidential election, pledging to undermine NATO as well as drawing back the

United States from active involvement in the Middle East, including a reluctance to support democratic uprisings against the status quo.

- The United Nations Security Council passes resolution 2334 (2016) demanding that Israel 'immediately and completely cease all settlement activities in the occupied Palestinian territory, including East Jerusalem' stating that the establishment of settlements by Israel has 'no legal validity and constitutes a flagrant violation under international law'. Both Israel and US President-elect Donald Trump dismiss the vote.

- A short-lived ceasefire in the Syrian conflict is agreed between the government and weakened rebel groups, to be followed by peace talks, orchestrated by Russia and backed by Turkey. Importantly, 'Jihadist' groups are excluded, including ISIL, which controls territory in eastern Syria and across the border with Iraq, the Syrian affiliate of Al Qaeda, which is the strongest in the country's north west, and groups linked to them. The Kurdish YPG is also excluded. Russia pledges continued military action to destroy ISIL.

2017

- Donald Trump is sworn in as the 45th President of the United States of America and within the first few days of his presidency he signs an executive order on immigration control, putting a temporary ban on citizens of seven Muslim-majority countries (including dual nationals) from entering the United States until a much tighter visa system and 'extreme vetting' is put in place, and suspends the admission of all refuges for 120 days with an indefinite ban on Syrian refugees.

- Following a suspected chemical attack by Assad forces on the rebel-held town of Khan Sheikhoun in north-western Syria killing at least 89 people, including 33 children, with hundreds suffering symptoms consistent with a reaction to nerve agents, President Trump raises the stakes and orders a military strike involving United States Navy destroyers firing 59 Tomahawk cruise missiles at the Al-Shayrat airfield in the western Homs province, believed to be the military installation from where the Syrian aircraft responsible for the chemical attack took off. This was the first time since the beginning of the Syrian conflict that the United States had targeted Syrian government forces. This is followed by a meeting of G7 foreign ministers asking Russia to cut ties with the Assad regime. Russia and Iran threaten retaliation against further aggression by the United States against Syria.

- Russia vetoes (for the eighth time) a United Nations Security Council draft resolution on Syria aimed at condemning the Syrian government for the chemical weapons attack that killed dozens of civilians.

- In another U-turn to his pre-election rhetoric Donald Trump pledges the United States commitment to NATO.

- In a potent expression of military might, and firing a warning shot across the bows of Iran's and North Korea's political and military establishment, the United States drops its largest conventional (non-nuclear) bomb, the GBU-43/B Massive Ordinance Air Blast Bomb (MOAB) for the first time in combat, targeting a tunnel complex in the Nangarhar province of Afghanistan allegedly used by IS positions close to the Pakistan border.

- The Turkish President, Recep Tayyip Erdogan, wins a historic referendum on a package of constitutional amendments that will grant him sweeping new powers to further consolidate his power following the failed coup in July 2016.

- Hassan Rouhani is re-elected President of Iran in what is claimed to be a victory of moderates over hardliners. At about the same time, President Trump tours the Middle East and in what is evidently 'a significant expansion of the security relationship' between the two countries the United States and

Saudi Arabia sign an arms deal worth 350 billion dollars over ten years with 110 billion dollars to be spent immediately. As tensions continue to build up in the Middle East over Saudi's involvement in Yemen and countering Iran's political influence, the deal is intended to bolster Saudi Arabia's military capability and influence in the region as well as securing the Saudi ruling dynasty's grip on power in face of future internal and external threats.

- On the heels of Donald Trump's visit to the Gulf, Saudi Arabia, Bahrain, the United Arab Emirates and Egypt amongst others break diplomatic ties with the sovereign state of Qatar, alleging that it supports terrorism (in the form of the Muslim Brotherhood and Hamas) and Iran in destabilizing the region. Qatar rejects the allegations as 'unjustified and baseless'.

- The UK capital, London, is subject to multiple terror attacks for which ISIL claims responsibility. More than 30 civilians are killed in three separate incidents. The British Prime Minister, following the London Bridge terrorist incident declares 'enough is enough'. Meanwhile, the number of hate crimes against Muslims increase.

- The Syrian Democratic Forces (SDF) as well as, Kurdish and Arab militias supported by heavy coalition airstrikes led by the United States, begin their attack on the ISIL stronghold of Raqqa. Such a move is without a doubt a determined strategy by the coalition forces to finally break the backbone of ISIL. However, at the initial stages of this military action tens of thousands of civilians are displaced with reported 'staggering loss of civilian life'.

- The King of Saudi Arabia, Salman bin Abd al-Aziz Al Saud, in a move to rout out any potential rival to his son's (Prince Mohammed bin Salman, aged 31) succession, nominates him as Crown Prince, removing Prince Mohammed bin Nayef. The new heir to the throne is perceived as representing a new younger generation of Saudis, as well as being closely aligned to the United States. A fierce opponent to Iranian influence in the region, as defence minister he has been the driving force behind Saudi Arabia's war in Yemen and diplomatic tiff with Qatar.

- On the sidelines of the G20 Meeting in Hamburg, Germany and both the United States and Russia agree to a ceasefire deal (de-escalation zone) in south-western Syria in a renewed effort to phase down the fighting to allow more humanitarian aid to reach the war-torn nation.

- Iraqi forces supported by the United States forces retake the Iraqi city of Mosul.

- Following the killing of two Israeli soldiers near the Al-Aqsa Mosque, Israel installs metal detectors at the Haram al-Sharif in Jerusalem in what was viewed as a move by Israel to take control of the site.

- More than 400,000 Rohingya Muslims flee a brutal military crackdown by the military in Myanmar in the north Rakhine State following an attack by insurgents against military outposts.

- President Trump announces that he will not re-certify the 'Nuclear Deal' with Iran, much to the dismay of the remaining P5 +1 signatories.

- Defying global opposition, Donald Trump announces from the White House to the world that the United States is officially recognizing Jerusalem as the capital of Israel, directing the state department to start making arrangements to move the United States Embassy to Jerusalem. Following the announcement, widespread protests erupt in Gaza and the West Bank with the Organization of Islamic Countries (OIC) declaring the decision 'null and void'.

- Complicating an already desperate situation in Syria, Turkey launches a military offensive in northern Syria.

2018

- Israeli Prime Minister Benjamin Netanyahu praises Israeli troops following the death of at least 16 Palestinian protestors during a Hamas-led protest attended by thousands of demonstrators near Gaza's border with Israel in a day of violence on 30th March dubbed the 'Great March of Return' ahead of six weeks of planned protest to press for the right of Palestinians to return to areas controlled by Israel. A further 58 Palestinians protestors are killed in a single day at the same border when protesting against the opening of the United States Embassy in Jerusalem, the bloodiest since the 2014 Israel-Hamas war.

- In Syria, following a suspected chemical weapons attack on the rebel-held suburb of Douma by government forces killing at least 42 civilians and injuring hundreds, a new 'Cold War' is ushered in, with the United States, the United Kingdom and France taking military action against Russian-backed President Bashar al-Assad.

- Donald Trump doubles the tariff on steel and aluminium imports from Turkey, which only adds to its NATO ally's economic woes, causing the Turkish lira to drop to its lowest level against the US dollar.

- In a move supported by Israel, the US cuts off decades of funding to the UN Relief and Works Agency (UNRWA) which provides Palestinian Refugees with health care, education and social services in the West Bank, Gaza strip, Jordan, Syria and Lebanon, stating that the organisation is 'irredeemably flawed' and demanding that reforms are carried out. The US claims that it is shouldering a 'very disproportionate share of the burden of UNRWA's costs'. The US further alleges that UNRWA is 'simply unsustainable' by expanding the number of Palestinian people eligible for assistance.

- With a view to exert increasing pressure on the Palestinian leadership to acquiesce, the US administration announces the closure of the PLO office in Washington, D.C., on the pretext of its leaders' resistance to peace talks (on their terms) but more importantly on the grounds that the Palestinian authorities are seeking to prosecute Israel for alleged war crimes in the International Criminal Court (ICC). The US National Security Advisor, John Bolton, threatens the ICC with sanctions if it carries out investigations into Israel while at the United Nations General Assembly, US President Donald Trump challenges the legitimacy of ICC by announcing that it has no jurisdiction or authority.

■ After three weeks of denial, Saudi Arabia admits to the killing of the Washington Post columnist and Saudi national Jamal Khashoggi, a well-known critic of Saudi Arabia, in the Saudi consulate in Istanbul on 2 October 2018, allegedly by 'rouge agents' within the Saudi intelligence service. This sends shockwaves across the globe.

■ In November, President Donald Trump imposes the toughest sanctions to date against Iran, targeting its oil and energy sector, financial institutions connected with Iran's Central Bank, port operators and shipbuilding sectors.

APPENDIX 4
Recommended Further Reading and Useful Websites

For readers requiring further in-depth analysis of the topics covered here, the author recommends the following books (or their subsequent editions) and websites. For some book titles the date quoted are of the reprints.

Quranic References:

Abdel Haleem M.A.S., *The Qur'an* (OUP, 2010)

Al-Hilali Dr. M.T. & Khan Dr. M.M., *Interpretation of the Meanings of The Noble Qur'an* (Darussalam, 1999)

Pickthall M, *The Meaning of the Glorious Qur'an* (Taj, 1986)

Rodwell J.M., *The Koran* (Pheonix, 2009)

The Presidency of Islamic Researchers, IFTA, Call and Guidance, *The Holy Qur-an, English Translations of the Meanings and Commentary* (King Fahd Holy Qur'an Printing Complex, 1405 AH)

www.noblequran.com

Hadith References:

Khan Dr. M.M., *Summarized Sahih Al-Bukhari* (Darussalam, 1996)

Textbook References:

Armstrong K, *The Battle For God* (HarperCollins, 2000)

Armstrong K, *Islam, A Short History* (Pheonix, 2001)

Armstrong K, *Muhammad, A Biography of the Prophet* (Pheonix, 2004)

Aslan R, *No God But God* (Arrow Books, 2006)

Esack F, *The Qur'an, A User's Guide* (Oneworld, 2005)

Horrie C & Chippendale P, *What is Islam* (Virgin Books, 2003)

Kathir I, The Signs Before *The Day of Judgement* (Dar Al Taqwa, 2007)

Lewis B, *The Crisis of Islam* (Phoenix, 2004)

Lunde P, *Islam A Brief History* (DK, 2005)

Muhammad F.N., *Islamiat For Students* (Ferozsons, 2001)

Rogerson B, *The Prophet Muhammad*, A Biography (Abacus, 2004)

Ruthven M, *Islam, A Very Short Introduction* (OUP, 2000)

Sarwar G, *Islam, Beliefs And Teachings* (The Muslim Education Trust, 1982)

Taylor A, *The rise and fall of Great Empires* (Quercus, 2008)

Thomson A, *Dajjal, The King who has no clothes* (Ta-Ha, 1995)

Wilkinson P, *Religions* (DK, 2008)

Websites:

www.al–islam.org

www.aljazeera.com

www.amnesty.org

www.bbc.co.uk

www.cia.gov/library

www.dhakatribune.com

www.electionguide.org

www.euractiv.com

www.genocidewatch.com

www.globalfirepower.com

www.guardian.co.uk

www.hrw.org

www.independent.co.uk

www.indianexpress.com

www.irrawaddy.com
www.jewishvirtuallibrary.org
www.nytimes.com
www.middleeasteye.net
www.ochaopt.org
www.pewforum.org
www.reuters.com
www.rt.com
www.savethechildren.net
www.securitycouncilreport.org
www.telegraph.co.uk
www.thedailystar.net
www.timesofisrael.com
www.hindustantimes.com
www.un.org
www.washingtonpost.com

AUTHOR'S PROFILE

Sheikh Mohammed Jakir Ahmed Jabbar, is an avid reader. His interests include the study of Islam, comparative religions, international trade and commercial law, post-Cold War global politics, modern and contemporary European history and astronomy. From his early teens the author has endeavoured to understand the core message of Islam by studying numerous English translations and interpretations of the Holy Qur'an and numerous Ahadith collections, as well as works of Islamic scholars that were available at the time. When the author was only sixteen, his father presented him with his first English translation of The Glorious Qur'an by M. Pickthall. Since then the author has never looked back. This intellectual thirst to understand the central message of Islam reinforced and consolidated itself well into his adulthood. Today the author has an extensive private library of books and academic materials by acclaimed scholars in their respective fields.

The author graduated in Law with honours from the University of Wolverhampton in 1997. In October 2015, he successfully completed a Master's Degree in International Commercial Law with the University of Northumbria at Newcastle; under its Distance Learning Programme he secured a commendation for his dissertation titled, 'Has the WTO multilateral trading system benefited its developing-country members and is there scope for reform? A critical analysis'. To tickle the author's curiosity on a multitude of different bite-size areas of legal study, he successfully completed a Certificate of Higher Education in February 2017 with the Cardiff University Continuing and Professional Education Centre, securing distinctions in all modules taken.

The author started his working career as a Reporter for Hansard at the National Assembly for Wales. He subsequently served as Registrar and Archives Officer for the Legal Services Division at the Welsh Development Agency until April 2002. Taking a temporary break from his career in Wales, he returned to Dhaka, Bangladesh to take care of his late mother's business interests. During his time in Dhaka he also taught undergraduate students under the University of London LL.B external curriculum at a private law academy and wrote a revision aid for students studying A-Level Government and Politics under EDEXCEL, which was extremely successful. In 2004 the author founded Renascence Publications. He later returned to Wales to pursue higher academic interests in 2005.

Alongside his current employment, the author had also been actively involved in his trade union. In their annual elections, towards the end of 2011 he was elected the Public Commercial Services (PCS) Union Wales Regional Committee Representative on the PCS National Black Members' Committee. Following on, in March 2013, he was also elected the PCS South Wales Revenue and Customs Branch BME Representative. Presenting the Muslim perspective, back in 2008, he served on the Steering Committee for the 'Spiritual Capital' Cardiff research project to study the contribution different faith communities have made to the city of Cardiff and their relationship to the government in Cardiff. The project was a partnership between the Regeneration Institute at Cardiff University and the Public Trust Partnership. In November 2016, the author was elected parent school governor at a highly respectable primary school in Cardiff. In February 2018, he was appointed a Justice of the Peace (magistrate) for England and Wales.

The author is an amateur poet and has had his poetry published in newspapers in Bangladesh and in numerous anthologies published in the United Kingdom and the United States of America.

The author has also spoken on numerous occasions on 'Islamic tolerance and justice' at a number of annual Islamic Conventions held in Bangladesh, the largest according to organisers, being to an estimated gathering of 70,000 attendees.

Other published books by the same author:

ISLAM & THE WEST: A Rational Perspective

ISBN: 978-1-8651-298-7

Published by Mereo Books

Publication date: November 2014

Available to purchase at Amazon.com, Barnes & Noble,
Googlebooks, Waterstones and WH Smith

'When the global conscience is manipulated by mainstream media into xenophobia, hatred and ignorance then humanity will truly have lost its freedom of rational thought and therefore its liberty.'

The Author